There is an Alternative

There is an Alternative: Subsistence and Worldwide Resistance to Corporate Globalization

edited by Veronika Bennholdt-Thomsen,
Nicholas G. Faraclas and Claudia von Werlhof

Spinifex Press
VICTORIA

Zed Books
LONDON · NEW YORK

There is an Alternative: Subsistence and Worldwide Resistance to Corporate Globalization was first published by Zed Books Ltd, 7 Cynthia Street, London N1 9JF, UK and Room 400, 175 Fifth Avenue, New York, NY 10010, USA, and, in Australia and New Zealand, by Spinifex Press, 504 Queensbury Street, North Melbourne, Victoria 3003, Australia, in 2001.

Distributed in the USA exclusively by Palgrave, a division of St Martin's Press, LLC, 175 Fifth Avenue, New York, NY 10010, USA

Copyright © the contributors, 2001

Cover designed by Andrew Corbett
Set in Monotype Ehrhardt and Franklin Gothic by Ewan Smith
Printed and bound in Great Britain by Biddles Ltd, Guildford and King's Lynn

The National Library of Australia Cataloguing-in-Publication entry:

There is an alternative : subsistence and worldwide resistance to corporate globalization.

Bibliography.

Includes index.

ISBN 1 876756 17 9

1. Globalization 2. Subsistence economy. I. Bennholdt-Thomsen, Veronika. II. Werlhof, Claudia von, 1943– . III. Faraclas, Nick.

337

A catalogue record for this book is available from the British Library
Library of Congress Cataloging-in-Publication Data: available

ISBN 1 84277 005 5 cased
ISBN 1 84277 006 3 limp

Contents

About the Contributors

Farida Akhter (Bangladesh) is executive director of UBINIG (Policy Research for Alternative Development) Dhaka. As an economist, she has done research in the fields of women's development, health issues, agriculture, marine fisheries, hand-loom industries, garment industries, population and other related development issues, and has taken part in action programmes in the field of social development and feminist publishing in Bangladesh. She is currently co-operating with FINRRAGE (Feminist International Network for Resistance to Reproductive and Genetic Engineering), and with other networks on Food Ecology and on Resistance Against Trafficking in Women and Children.

Veronika Bennholdt-Thomsen (Germany) is Director of the Institute of the Theory and Practice of Subsistence (ITPS) at Bielefeld, Germany. She is a visiting professor at the University for Soil Culture in Vienna, Austria. She has undertaken research in Mexico and Germany, specifically on Sustainable Regional Economics in East Westphalia. Her publications include work on Women's Studies, Peasant Studies, Social Anthropology and the matriarchal community of Juchitan (Mexico).

Leigh S. Brownhill (Canada) studied at the University of Guelph and is a founding member of First Woman, the East and Southern African Women's Oral History and Indigenous Knowledge Network.

Gustavo Esteva (Mexico) is a grassroots activist and deprofessionalized intellectual, and an adviser to the Zapatista Army for National Liberation. Having been a public officer and university professor in Mexico, and having taught world-wide, he works in co-operation with the United Nations Research Institute for Social Development and indigeneous groups, peasants and urban marginals, contributing to the creation of social, economic, technological and ecological alternatives.

Nicholas G. Faraclas (Greece/USA) is Senior Lecturer in Linguistics at the University of Papua New Guinea. He has a PhD from the University of California at Berkeley. He teaches and does research in the areas of popular education and theoretical, descriptive and applied linguistics. He is involved in community-based literacy activities in Latin America, Africa and the South Pacific, and works with indigenous organizations in Papua New Guinea, the Solomon Islands, Vanuatu, West Papua, Bougainville and Kanaky (New Caledonia).

Silvia Federici (Italy) is Associate Professor of Political Philosophy and International Studies at New College of Hofstra University, USA. She is involved in teaching, research and political activism in the feminist movement and in campaigns against the death penalty and the World Bank's educational policies in Africa. She teaches in the United States and Nigeria.

Susan Hawthorne (Australia) is an activist, poet and circus performer. Her PhD on Feminism, Globalization and (Bio)diversity was awarded by the University of Melbourne. She has recently written about cyberfeminism and is co-founder of Spinifex Press.

Renate Klein (Switzerland) is Associate Professor of Women's Studies at Deakin University, Melbourne. She is the author and editor of books on reproductive medicine, women's studies theory, radical feminism and cyberfeminism. A feminist activist, she is co-founder of FINRRAGE (Feminist International Network for Resistance to Reproductive and Genetic Engineering).

Elisabeth Meyer-Renschhausen (Germany) is Visiting Professor at the Humboldt-Universität Berlin lecturing on women's studies in the agrarian sciences. Her PhD field was the women's movement in Bremen. Her research areas include social movements, gender studies, cultural anthropology, eating habits, women in rural 'development' and the 'new gardens' movement.

Christa Müller (Germany) is an Academic Researcher at *anstiftung*-foundation in Munich. She was awarded a PhD in economic sociology by the University of Bielefeld. She has undertaken fieldwork in Costa Rica, Mexico and Germany, and is co-founder of the Bielefeld Institute of the Theory and Practice of Subsistence (ITPS). She received the Schweisfurth Research Prize for Ecological Economics in 1998.

Helena Norberg-Hodge (United Kingdom) is founder and Director of the International Society for Ecology and Culture (ISEC) and the Ladakh Project. Her work includes researching on how to create and stimulate new thinking and international action in response to the political and economic process of globalization. She is a founding member of the International Forum on Globalization (IFG). In 1986 she was awarded the Right Livelihood Award (the Alternative Nobel Prize).

Ariel Salleh (Australia) from the University of Western Sidney, New South Wales, has a PhD in ethics (Griffith), and works in the fields of ecofeminism, environmental ethics, deep ecology and Green politics in Australia and the USA.

Saral Sarkar (India/Germany) studied and taught German language and literature at the Goethe Institute in Hyderabad. After moving to Germany, Sarkar began writing and doing research on the Green movement in Germany and became an activist in the movement against globalization and neoliberal politics.

Vandana Shiva (India) is Director of the Research Foundation for Science, Technology and Ecology (RFST), New Delhi, and has a PhD in Physics from the University of Western Ontario, Canada. She is the founder of Navdanya, a national movement to protect the diversity and integrity of living resources, especially native seeds, food security and food safety, and has published work on organic and sustainable agriculture. She has been involved in grassroot campaigns in the areas of intellectual property rights and biodiversity (the 'Neem', 'Basmati' and 'Monsanto' campaigns). Her areas of interest include biotechnology, genetic engineering, gender issues and indigenous knowledge. She is founder of Diverse Women for Diversity and is an adviser to various governments and institutions as well as lecturing at universities world-wide. Her many awards include the Right Livelihood Award 1993 (the Alternative Nobel Prize).

Terisa Turner (Canada) has a PhD from the London School of Economics and Political Science. She has undertaken research in Europe, the USA, West and East Africa, the Middle East, Latin America and the Caribbean on gender, the environment and resource conflicts.

Claudia von Werlhof (Germany/Austria) is Professor at the Institute of Political Sciences, University of Innsbruck, Austria. When lecturing at the University of Bielefeld she undertook field research in Central America and Venezuela on the international division of labour, women, under-development and agriculture. Theoretical work is concerned with feminist theory of society, patriarchy and technology; social movements; and eco-feminism. She is an activist against the MAI (Multilateral Agreement in Investment).

Theresa J. Wolfwood (Canada) is Director of the Barnard-Boecker Centre Foundation, Victoria. Her research and writings concern peace, social justice and women's issues. She is an activist at rallies, seminars and conferences in Canada, Europe, Asia, Africa and Latin America, a human rights observer in Guatemala and Mexico, and a solidarity worker in Nicaragua, Kenya, Mexico and Eritrea.

Introduction

Despite the barrage of claims to the contrary to which we have been ruthlessly subjected over the past two decades, each of the sixteen chapters in this volume proves in its unique way that *there is an alternative* to globalization and the neo-liberal model that has propelled it into such a dominant position in contemporary politics, economy and society. As a whole, this book convincingly demonstrates that there is not just one alternative, but a multitude of alternatives to the version of corporate domination over our lives that is usually referred to by the deceivingly progressive-sounding term 'globalization'. These alternatives are as numerous and diverse as the contributors to this work, who approach this question from the widest possible range of geographic and experiential backgrounds.

Striking similarities emerge, however, from this rich and varied collection of stories about successful resistance to corporate globalization. All are inspired by a renewed sense of the indivisible whole to which our bodies, minds, souls, spirits and means of production and reproduction belong, despite centuries of patriarchal scientific and religious programming that has attempted to atomize these fundamental aspects of our existence in order to construct false dichotomies, such as body vs mind or subjectivity vs objectivity. Beyond the rejection of these illusory binarisms, each contributor to this volume reaffirms that a necessary condition for effective resistance to corporate globalization is the re-establishment of our sense of individual and collective power over our bodies, beliefs, communities, land, food, markets and so on in order to redirect our labour towards the creation of use value, abundance, fertility and life and away from the production of exchange value, scarcity, violence and death.

We can therefore say that in spite of the fact that the people who contributed to this work have fascinatingly different stories to tell and use equally distinct voices to communicate their experiences, all have come to share a perspective, that is, an understanding of the fundamental problems that we face at the beginning of the twenty-first century and a sense of where viable solutions can and cannot be found. This perspective corresponds to the *Subsistence Perspective* which has been developed during the last thirty years by Maria Mies and her colleagues.

Professor Mies has dedicated her life's work to the liberation struggle of what she calls the three colonies of capital: Women, the Third World and Nature. In her voluminous and influential writings, she has consistently argued that a key element of this struggle is an economy based on sub-sistence. As an effective and tireless activist at the international level as well as locally in her native Germany, Professor Mies is a co-organizer and founder member of numerous resistance networks, campaign initiatives and alternative projects for social change. Professor Mies's work has pro-vided essential theoretical and practical points of reference as well as invaluable inspiration to all of those who wrote the various contributions to this book. She is in many respects responsible for the fact that there is now a critical mass of people around the world who are in a position to formulate a common theoretical framework of resistance to corporate globalization, as well as to recognize and participate in the construction of alternatives to it. For this reason, this volume is dedicated to Maria on the occasion of her seventieth birthday in February 2001.

This book is divided into three parts: Part I deals with the theoretical underpinnings and implications of current struggles against corporate globalization; Part II examines these struggles in detail; while Part III focuses on old and new forms of subsistence in practice.

Part I begins with an interview which was skilfully constructed and conducted by *Ariel Salleh*, in order to allow Maria Mies herself clearly and concisely to explain both the origins and the main aspects of the subsistence perspective as well as much of the rest of her theoretical work. Next, *Claudia von Werlhof* presents an ingenious new analysis of capitalism as an 'alchemical system', which pursues the patriarchal goal of the total trans-formation and ultimate replacement of human beings, especially women as mothers, nature and society by a new, 'improved' male creation. She specifically targets our misplaced belief in the 'progressive' nature of this project to explain why no action is taken against the violent destruction of all the foundations of life that it entails. In Chapter 3, *Saral Sarkar* conclusively demonstrates with facts and figures how the terms 'sustainable development' and 'sustainable growth' are currently used to perpetuate the environmentally destructive colonialism of the bankrupt development policies of the past and how nothing short of the abandonment of the growth model in favour of a more subsistence-oriented eco-socialist model can save our planet.

Part II starts with a superbly argued critique of the 'green revolution' and patent-driven corporate bio-piracy in India by *Vandana Shiva*, showing how globalized agribusiness-led destruction of natural and cultural diversity has created scarcity, hunger and poverty and will continue to do so, in hypocritical contradiction to its stated goals and the new 'ethical' image being projected by transnationals such as Monsanto. Next, *Nicholas G. Faraclas* turns many of our received notions on their heads by citing the existence of thousands of viable indigenous subsistence-oriented societies in Melanesia at the dawn of the twenty-first century as living proof of the fact that there is nothing normal, natural, inevitable or progressive about corporate globalization. He then goes on to give evidence of how the 'enlightened' and 'self-critical' policies and 'alternatives' recently put forward by the World Bank and some other Bretton Woods institutions are a sham and have been used to enlist the Big International Non-Governmental Organizations (BINGOs) in the ongoing recolonization of the Majority World. In Chapter 6 *Susan Hawthorne* continues on the theme of the unique contributions that indigenous peoples have to make to the theory and practice of the subsistence perspective by using extensive source materials to contrast the holistic, reciprocal and respectful notions of science and the earth held by autochthonous peoples in Australia, the Pacific, Latin America and Africa, with the objectified, violent, invasive and colonizing notions that typify the forces of corporate globalization, which are accelerating their wholesale plunder and destruction of indigenous societies through genetic research, gene technology and patents. *Renate Klein* then lucidly and convincingly reveals how several of the key assertions and demands made by the international women's movement over the past forty years, such as women's control over their bodies ('Our Bodies – Ourselves') have posed such a danger to the patriarchal project that deceptive new discourses of 'choice', 'empowerment' and 'improvement' along with the entire machinery of the philosophical paradigm shift to postmodernism had to be mustered to co-opt successfully and enlist many women and many women's organizations to support the accelerating efforts by the proponents of reproductive technologies eventually to eliminate women and women's power from the reproductive process.

In Chapter 8, *Terisa E. Turner* and *Leigh S. Brownhill* provide a riveting account of the astounding strength of women's resistance movements in Kenya, brilliantly characterized by the authors as a 'fight for fertility' in which women use their collective organizational skills successfully to thwart the forces of corporate globalization and to establish 'civil commons' which they perceive as the basis of a 'subsistence political economy'. *Silvia Federici* then refutes the commonly held assumption that 'ethnic tension' is the main cause of the violence that has recently plagued many countries in Africa. She goes on to present ample and incontrovertible evidence that points the finger instead at the inherently violent nature of the sheer human misery caused by the Bretton Woods institutions' structural adjustment programmes (SAPs) and 'free' trade policies and the destruction and disruption of subsistence food production by the 'food aid', 'relief' and 'peacekeeping' missions of the United Nations and the BINGOs. She then demonstrates how all of these factors pave the way for the enclosure of the land and labour of Africa by global agribusiness and resource extraction companies, inevitably leading to war as local communities mobilize to resist. In her conclusion, she draws our attention to the fact that these methods of 'low-intensity warfare' which the forces of corporate globalization are utilizing to continue the very old process of primitive accumulation of capital are now being exported from Africa to the Middle East (Iraq) and Eastern Europe (Yugoslavia). Finally, in Chapter 10, *Theresa J. Wolfwood* reminds us that the USA, Canada and the rest of the Minority World are not exempt from these trends, as 'free' market jargon is routinely used there to disguise more subsidies for arms production and agribusiness. As dramatized in her gripping eyewitness reports from the massive demonstrations against globalization which took place in Seattle at the end of 1999, she contends that the police and other agents of the corporate-controlled state are prepared to use whatever means necessary to crush the incredible power of non-hierarchically organized subsistence/resistance in the North as well as in the South.

At the beginning of Part III, *Gustavo Esteva* generously shares with us the preliminary results of a remarkable attempt to create a vision for the future that has taken place over the past years by broadly based networks of grassroots activists associated with the Zapatistas in Mexico. Among other characteristics of a future society clearly identified as a result of this process are the reaffirmation of an individual and collective sense of 'place' (a locality which belongs to people and to which people belong and over which they have real control), a radical and inclusive pluralism which will entail the creation of 'a Mexico in which many Mexicos can fit', and freedom for all balanced by relations of interdependence and reciprocity. In Chapter 11, *Farida Akhter* eloquently expresses the subsistence vision of a strong network of women united against reproductive technologies and a cultural movement of small ecological farmers in Bangladesh in the most courageous and beautifully succinct terms, by reminding us that subsistence basically means 'a happy life'; a violence to the earth is a violence to ourselves; it is not companies but women and small farmers who feed the world; and 'there can be only one practice' in the sense that 'the strategic decision to resist must be taken up'. Next, *Helena Norberg-Hodge* juxtaposes a very encouraging description of viable subsistence-based food production and marketing alternatives that are being created by communities in the Minority World with a withering criticism of neo-liberal economics, which points out that the current global economic system ultimately benefits no one (not even the rich), that it is based on outdated theories, that it depends on the plunder of the Majority World, and that instead of establishing so-called 'free markets' or a 'level playing field' it gives massive advantages and subsidies to the largest corporations, which are actually less efficient in meeting people's real needs than are small producers.

In Chapter 14, we find a remarkable and thought-provoking description and analysis by *Christa Müller* of the International Gardens movement in Göttingen, Germany, where subsistence labour involving local control over food production and relations of reciprocity and interdependence form the basis for a new lifestyle for and solidarity between refugee women from the Majority World and German women. Dichotomies such as 'assimilation' vs 'ghettoization' which have been constructed by patriarchal social science are shown to be false, mainly because they are not rooted in the everyday survival/subsistence experience of real people. In Chapter 15 *Elisabeth Meyer-Renschhausen* takes us inside the rapidly growing movement for the production, distribution and consumption of organically grown food in Berlin and the former East German state of Brandenburg. She reflects on her long-standing engagement with the groups involved to demonstrate how viable subsistence-based regional linkages have been re-established between a major urban centre and the surrounding countryside. Finally, *Veronika Bennholdt-Thomsen* concludes the book with a compelling challenge to the prevailing assumptions held by urban residents, administrators and politicians that our cities depend ultimately on money for their survival. By using concrete examples she makes it abundantly clear that it is in fact the subsistence activities of their residents, as care-givers for children, the elderly and the physically challenged, as volunteers in all sorts of social and mutual support associations, as operators of small businesses with a loyalty to their local communities, and as protagonists in the daily struggle for survival which provide the lifeblood to urban areas, while big corporate investors act instead as vampires, sucking the vitality out of our municipalities through tax breaks, the destruction of small-scale markets and businesses, and the replacement of secure and well-paid jobs by McDonaldized minimum-waged temporary positions with no health or other social security benefits.

It is the ultimate tribute to Maria Mies and the Subsistence Perspective that nowhere in this volume do we find the monolithic solution to all of our problems or the new dogma or 'catechism' of the 'new vanguard' which our Mexican colleagues have explicitly avoided in the formulation of their vision of a future society. Instead we find a reaffirmation and celebration of the amazingly creative, resourceful and resilient capacity of women, children and men everywhere to satisfy their immediate needs and resist corporate globalization through subsistence in a dazzlingly variegated number of ways. As proponents of the Subsistence Perspective, all of the authors who have contributed to this work urge us to reject our misguided belief in the ideology, science and technology of patriarchal 'experts' and leaders. Instead we are invited to follow the example of the women of Kenya by looking to ourselves, to our communities and to our everyday existence to find the inspiration, the ideas and the experiences we need to take our present lives back into our own hands in order to create the future of abundance, reciprocity, peace, caring, sharing, enjoyment and love that we all deserve.

Veronika Bennholdt-Thomsen
Nicholas G. Faraclas
Claudia von Werlhof

Part I

On the Theory of Subsistence

Woman, Nature and the International Division of Labour

Maria Mies interviewed by Ariel Salleh

The eco-feminism of Maria Mies stands at the crossroads of the feminist, ecological and colonial liberation movements. Mies attempts to bring Marxian theory face to face with the newly emerging political crises of the late twentieth century. This has involved a heuristic reading of Marx's text in the light of modern anthropology and what she calls 'object-relations'. But Mies is as much an activist as an academic sociologist. Her concerns range from prescriptive essays on methodology in social science, to empirical studies of exploitation among Indian women lace-makers, campaigns against pornography and the reproductive technology industry in West Germany. Ariel Salleh spoke with her in 1987 and formalized this interview by correspondence.

Commodification and Violence

ARIEL SALLEH: Plainly, feminism is in crisis: Third World workers are divided from middle-class western housewives, and both of these from the feminist movement per se. The feminists, in turn, are split between the socialists and those who would organize autonomously. But your analysis in *Patriarchy and Accumulation* gives a new unity and coherence to women's struggle world-wide [Mies 1986]. What experiences in your own life brought you to this insight? Or was it already deducible from your reading of Marxism?

MARIA MIES: Well, I don't think that feminism itself is in crisis. The divisions you mention are objectively part and parcel of the capitalist patriarchal 'divide and rule' strategy. Under capitalism, there emerges not only a sexual division of labour, but also a particular social division between private and public and an international division of labour. All these divisions are hierarchically structured and connected, although they appear as autonomous entities. What binds them together is a dependency relationship based on violence, commodity production and money. The dependent sector in each of these divisions I call 'colonies'.

I did not gain these insights by reading Marxism. First came my experience in India, where I worked and lived for six years; second, was my involvement in the German women's movement since 1968. While trying to find a satisfactory explanation for the ongoing exploitation of women here, and the colonies 'down there', I began to read Marx. But, as argued in my book *Patriarchy and Accumulation*, Marxism did not offer an explanation. The central constitutive relationship studied by Marx and Engels was wage labour and capital, and this excludes all non-wage labour relations. The latter are shoved into the realm of 'nature' or called 'pre-capitalist'; it amounts to the same. This is particularly true for the life-giving and life-sustaining work of women.

ARIEL SALLEH: One result of this, which you take up in the book, is the fact that structuralist Marxists shove 'the woman question' into the realm of 'ideology'; the net result being that they are as politically ineffectual as they claim middle-class 'cultural' feminists to be! Is this problem connected with what you describe as the 'biologically loaded' concept of labour in Marx? What do you mean when you say this?

MARIA MIES: The Marxist concept of labour was certainly not intended to be biologically loaded. Following Adam Smith, Marx stresses that the concept of 'productive labour' under capitalism no longer simply means work for the satisfaction of human needs, but rather surplus-producing labour. This concept comes to be the dominant one and all other forms of labour are left outside the realm of capital accumulation. By calling wage labour 'productive' and all other types of non-wage labour 'non-productive' or natural, Marx contributed to what I see as the 'naturalization' of women's work. Women's labour henceforth disappears from the social or human sphere and becomes invisible, locked up in the family, the 'realm of nature' or even the 'realm of death' as Hegel put it.

The problem with this Marxian concept of labour is not only its dualistic division between 'nature' and 'society', but the dominance relation existing between these two poles: society dominates nature, culture dominates nature, man dominates woman, etcetera. Woman now *appears* as a biological category as a result of eighteenth- and nineteenth-century discourse. Marx and Engels did not break entirely with this discourse. In fact, they expected the reconciliation of Man with Nature to arrive from a further extension of men's domination over it through their development of technology and science as productive forces.

ARIEL SALLEH: Now you are not talking about some universal sexism of men behind this, are you? The naturalism of Marx and Engels' *The German Ideology*, say, is itself an expression of the capitalist mode of production, right? [Marx and Engels 1965]

MARIA MIES: Yes, I do not think that there is anything like an inherent sexism in men. I reject Freud's dictum that anatomy is destiny, as much for men as for women. There were long periods in history when men were not sexist, and there are still cultures where men do not dominate women. Patriarchy is a historical and social system, not a biological one. However, when Marx and Engels in *The German Ideology* refer to the 'natural division of labour in the family' or to the 'sheep-like or tribal consciousness' that prevails until a 'division of labour between mental and material labour appears', they uncritically accept the Enlightenment concept of progress. This discourse is based on an ever-growing mastery of the 'masculine' human mind over 'feminine' nature or matter. Before there was 'industry and exchange' there was rape, robbery and loot. Capitalism would not have emerged without the destruction of self-sufficient and self-sustaining subsistence systems in the colonies and Europe, and the Marxian theory of unlimited development of productive forces helps to justify that, I'm afraid.

ARIEL SALLEH: How does all this relate to your argument about differences between men's and women's object-relation to nature, your observation that men and women are productive in different ways?

MARIA MIES: This argument is often misinterpreted as being biologistic, because it starts with the recognition that the human being appears in two sexes and that men and women interact with nature in bodies which are, at least partly, qualitatively different. Biological difference, however, is not only given. Maleness and femaleness are differently defined in each historical epoch, differently interpreted and valued, according to the dominant mode of production. In matrifocal societies, femaleness was interpreted as the paradigm of all productivity and creativity. Capitalist patriarchal society defines femaleness as devoid of productivity, activity, subjectivity, humanity, historicity.

ARIEL SALLEH: Well, let's come at the question of object-relations this way: I think you see men's reliance on 'tools' to mediate their relation with 'external' nature as basic to the logic of an appropriative economy – the predatory model.

MARIA MIES: I do say that men cannot experience their bodies as 'productive' in the same way as women, that they need 'tools' to mediate their relationship with nature as a productive or creative one. But this instrumental relationship of men to their bodies would not have led to an appropriative or predatory economy, if the tools men invented had remained 'productive' in the true sense. With the invention of arms and the monopoly of some men over these arms, the relationship of men to their bodies, to each other, to women and to external nature, changed fundamentally. Arms are not means of production, but means of destruction and coercion. By means of arms, a relationship of exploitation and dominance can be established and maintained. Only as hunters became warriors and where conquest became a regular *economic* activity, could men's productivity, based on a monopoly over arms, appear as an independent process from women's productivity and nature's productivity.

ARIEL SALLEH: Eventually, 'colonization' and 'housewifization' become two faces of the one 'coin' in the rise of international capital, violence against women being essential to the maintenance of this international division of labour. What are examples of this, Maria?

MARIA MIES: Abundant examples can be found in the history of colonialism, in the politics of slavery, in the violent destruction of self-sufficient survival systems, in the process of the witch-hunt in Europe and its accompanying historical counterpart in the colonies. But even today, violence against women is the 'necessary' method for maintaining the exploitative international and sexual division of labour. Housewifization and colonization are part of the world market system. Both are necessary for capital accumulation. In the modern colonies, this violence takes the form of mass rapes, dowry killings, forced sterilization, sex tourism, use of Third World women as guinea-pigs for testing drugs, pro-natal and ante-natal technology by transnational concerns. Another recent example of neo-patriarchal violence against women is the revival of suttee [widow burning] in India.

As I said, these manifestations are neither the result of some inborn sadism in men, nor remnants of feudal backwardness. They are the result of the ongoing process of primitive accumulation of capital, which has always been dependent on direct violence. In this process, the men play the role of agents for capital; the mediators. Most men in the Third World cannot hope to rise to the standard of living of their big white brothers by means of wage labour. But they still want to get access to the consumer goods the world market offers, the TV sets, cars, motorbikes, videos, computers, which all serve as symbols of modernization and progress. Neither individual men nor Third World governments can reach this material level by means of non-violent exchange. The debt trap is one direct outcome of this impossibility.

Governments who have embraced a policy of modernization in the face of actual dependency will have to sell their women, or their land, or both. The case of suttee in India is revealing. As Madhu Kishwar has shown, the men who campaign for the revival of suttee are not 'backward' peasants, but modern, urban, educated young men who want to get rich quickly, supported by powerful industrial interests which invest a lot of money in temples and religion [Kishwar and Vanita 1984]. By burning a widow, a new suttee-shrine can be established, a new cult can be created. Pilgrims flock to the new shrine and bring money. Neo-patriarchy and religious fundamentalism go smoothly together with modernization and capital accumulation: they are not in contradiction. It's not only in the neo-colonies or the South that violence against women is increasing. We all know about its increase in the industrialized countries: wife-battering, rape, pornography. Even the emergence of reproductive technology which turns women into marketable reproductive raw material is not possible without virtual vivisection of the female body.

Culture not Nature

ARIEL SALLEH: You claim that 'naturalization' is the ideological linchpin in this economic process. How does it work?

MARIA MIES: The concept of 'naturalization' cannot be properly understood without its other pole, namely 'humanization' or 'civilization'. Humanization here implies becoming independent from nature by means of science and technology. Domination over 'nature' in this sense is always a destructive and coercive relationship. 'Naturalization' hence means that not only external nature, but also women and the peoples of the 'South', are seen as 'nature'. So defined, they are robbed of subjectivity, spiritual value, dignity and sovereignty. These 'colonies' become mere objects or raw material for the process of 'humanizing' the working class in the western metropolises [Mies et al. 1987]. As my friend Claudia von Werlhof put it, all that is free of costs for capital is defined as 'nature'. It is, however, important to keep in mind that such a concept of nature is already an ideological one; it implies that the integrity of self-sustaining survival systems, our bodies, the fact that women bring forth children, the earth which produces plants and animals, has already been destroyed. Nature has already been subdued and is dominated by 'Man'.

Then, after this destruction, 'nature' gets ideologically reconstructed in a sentimental way. It is both degraded and romanticized. This is true for women – 'good and bad women'; for external nature – 'chaotic and idyllic'; and for colonized peoples – 'good and bad savages'. Those who have been 'civilized' or 'humanized' obviously cannot forget their 'lost paradise'. They yearn for what they have destroyed. Ironically, this very yearning is the strongest motive force for the present round of capital accumulation: Third World sex tourism, eco-marketing, etcetera.

ARIEL SALLEH: The feminist concept of 'gender' unwittingly collaborates in this naturalistic ideology too.

MARIA MIES: Indeed. The feminist concept of 'gender' collaborates with this dualism and reinforces the polarization between 'nature' and 'culture'. It shares in the concept of progress developed by white men, and in the hegemony of culture over nature. It also shares the evolutionist view of this process as inevitable. Because of the distinction made by some feminists between 'gender' and 'sex', it is easy now for reproductive engineers to say that the realm of sexuality and reproduction is only 'biology', hence it is their domain. Meanwhile the symbolic manifestations of these areas are called 'gender' and are said to belong to the social, cultural or truly 'human' sphere.

ARIEL SALLEH: This device of 'naturalization' continues to be important for the self-definition of the male proletariat, doesn't it?

MARIA MIES: Yes, the European labour movement, at least from the second half of the nineteenth century onwards, aspired to reach the cultural level of the bourgeoisie. The leaders of the German Social Democrats, then still strongly influenced by scientific socialism, saw clearly that for the rise of the German working class from a miserable proletarian existence to a civilized one, an industrial nation like Germany needed colonies. Colonies were necessary for the cheap import of more raw materials, of more labour and for an extension of markets [see Luxemburg 1967]. But for the 'humanization' or civilization of the German male proletarian, a decent family was necessary, where the man was breadwinner and woman the housewife. Hence colonial policy and family policy in imperial Germany were basically accepted by the Social Democrats and by the trade unions. In England and other industrialized countries, the situation was more or less the same.

ARIEL SALLEH: I suppose the technological optimism of Marx, Engels and many present-day socialists would be influenced by men's specific object-relation to nature as well ...

MARIA MIES: Today we have reached a stage where we can speak of an ideological convergence of the male proletarian and the capitalist. Both expect more 'progress' from further domination over nature by high tech. Both collaborate in the further destruction of our natural base of existence. The western working class has been strongly opposed to the ecology movement and also to the women's movement. But it's not only the western working class who share this technocratic Utopia with capital. Workers in present-day socialist countries share the same paradigm of technological progress as the key to all happiness. Its theoretical roots are indeed to be found in the technological optimism of Marx, and particularly Engels, who see domination over nature as a precondition for the liberation of mankind from the 'realm of necessity' and for the beginning of the 'realm of freedom'.

ARIEL SALLEH: What would a feminist concept of labour and economics look like, in your view?

MARIA MIES: A feminist concept of 'labour' cannot be based on domination. Women cannot expect liberation to come from continued exploitation of nature and other colonized peoples. One colony cannot be decolonized at the expense of other colonies. A feminist concept of labour has therefore to replace the predatory economic relationship of Man to 'nature' by a co-operative one. The model of a co-operative, reciprocal relationship between woman and nature is also the only way in which women will restore their bodily integrity and wholeness, their dignity and their sovereignty over life processes. A feminist concept of labour has to reject the notion that all 'necessary labour' is a burden that should be done by machines or robots. We have to maintain a concept of labour in which 'enjoyment' as well as the 'hardness' of work are united. This would require a different economy from the one we know today. I have elaborated on this in the last chapter of *Patriarchy and Accumulation*. The main characteristic of such an economy would be an emphasis on the maintenance of self-sustaining survival systems: 'a subsistence perspective'. It would be a 'moral economy', based on principle, not merely on supply and demand.

ARIEL SALLEH: Women have nothing to gain from a continuation of the prevailing 'growth' ethic, have they? By the way, when you developed your subsistence perspective in *Patriarchy and Accumulation*, were you consciously trying to provide a theoretical bridge between eco-feminism and Green politics? Without a thoroughgoing emancipation of both Third World and western women from their sustaining position in the predatory division of labour, Green politics won't even reach first base, will it?

MARIA MIES: I agree that Green politics will not reach first base unless the growth and accumulation ethic is consistently rejected and a 'subsistence perspective' put in its place. However, Green politics in West Germany at present is far from such. When Greens began to enter the parliaments, a process of redefining their goals began. It ended by drastically reducing their criticism of the industrial growth model and talking rather about an 'ecological reconstruction of the industrial system'. This means they expect a solution of the ecological and social crisis to come not so much from a radical change in people's daily life, but from technological innovations, like solar energy, etcetera. But, since the Social Democrats pursue a similar strategy of harmonizing capitalist accumulation with ecological reconstruction, it is possible that the Greens will not even last very long as a parliamentary party. I put my hope not so much on the Greens or any other party but on the broadening movement among people, particularly women who are ready to challenge the growth model by consumer resistance. We need a strategy combining the goals of the ecology movement, anti-colonialism and women's liberation simultaneously.

New Strategies for Feminism

ARIEL SALLEH: In your favour there is the fact that feminism is much more healthy now in Asia, Latin America and Africa. Originally, colonial women were loath to identify with the feminist movement at all. Why the turnaround?

MARIA MIES: While the old prejudice that 'feminists are all single women, lesbians, man-haters and housebreakers' still exists among some Third World women, increasingly they find themselves confronted with the same manifestations of capitalist patriarchy as we do. The rise in violence against women has renewed feminist rebellion in many Third World countries. It can no longer be labelled a western import. Third World sisters also need an answer to the question 'Why has capitalism or modernization not liberated women?' So we are finding a keen interest in feminist theory now among women in Asia, South America and Africa.

ARIEL SALLEH: Recently, in London, I came across the Wages for Housework campaign again, vigorously pursued by migrant women of colour at the King's Cross Women's Centre. How do you feel about the revival of this strategy in the present conjuncture?

MARIA MIES: It is understandable why women who are hit by unemployment, the flexibilization of labour or 'housewifization' of more and more areas of production demand a guaranteed minimum income or 'Wages for Housework'. This strategy has even been adopted in West Germany to some extent by the Christian Democrats. They have granted women with small children a small allowance as 'education money', too little, of course, even to feed them. Though the demand is understandable, as a tactical move, it begs the same strategic questions as the old Wages for Housework campaign. These are:

1. Can the strategy be applied to all women in the world? Is it conceivable that all women in the world can in reality become 'housewives' maintained by a male breadwinner or the welfare state? Is this desirable?

2. As the state has to pay these wages for housework or the guaranteed minimum income, this demand will automatically lead to state control in the sphere of reproduction and livelihood.

3. Would such a strategy not presuppose continuation of the existing international division of labour and the existing world market? It is even conceivable that some women in the West may be paid wages for housework out of debt services paid by the indebted Third World nations. The debt bondage of the Third World can easily be used to feed an increasing number of non-wage workers or unemployed in the metropolises. But it is impossible to feed all the unemployed and all non-wage workers in the world at the same level. If all women should get wages for housework, then none of the indebted nations would be in a position to repay the interests on their loans. This, in turn, would be the end of wages for housework in the metropolises.

ARIEL SALLEH: Changing tack, Maria: I notice that your thesis makes use of Carolyn Merchant's eco-feminist deconstruction of Baconian science. Is the critique of science developed by English-speaking feminists such as Sandra Harding, Evelyn Fox Keller, Hilary Rose and others well regarded in Europe?

MARIA MIES: Carolyn Merchant's and Evelyn Fox Keller's books have been translated and are discussed in Germany by women and men who, since Chernobyl, have begun to criticize the foundations of science and technology [Merchant 1982; Fox Keller 1985]. The critique is spearheaded in West Germany by the women's movement against reproductive and genetic engineering. Women begin to understand that this technology amounts to a revival of the eugenics movement of the Nazis, but now activated on a world scale. In other European countries, the resistance against these developments is not so strong. Recently, I heard French feminists saying: 'After we have rationalized production, we rationalize reproduction.' In France, the faith in instrumentalism is fairly unbroken.

ARIEL SALLEH: Your own assault on patriarchal methodology in social science puts particular emphasis on action research. And this is one of the most impressive aspects of your writing, I think; not only does it bring a vast array of empirical and historical material into synthesis and shows how diverse areas of feminist politics are interrelated, it is clearly informed by a long-standing personal engagement in women's struggle both in the Third World and the 'overdeveloped West'.

MARIA MIES: True, my work follows methodological principles for feminist research first formulated in 1978, integrating research and action, theory and practice. I still use these ideas with my students, in women's and environmental projects, and with other groups. In the present political climate, however, it seems that nothing is more suspect to those powers that maintain the status quo than integration of theory and practice. In West Germany, it is quite all right if you hold courses on Marxist or feminist theory; it is even considered innovative! But as soon as you step out of the confines of academia and link up feminist research and politics, you are suspect. Or you are not seen as a 'good scholar'.

ARIEL SALLEH: Can you tell us a little about the police raids on your German feminist colleagues who are actively opposing reproductive technologies and genetic engineering? This harassment on the part of the state seems to underscore the structural significance of the patriarchal need to appropriate and control women's reproductive labour 'resource'.

MARIA MIES: The December 1987 raids on women in the movement against reproductive and genetic engineering were a reaction to the erosion of public acceptance for these new techniques. Since 1985, our women have mobilized over their anti-woman, indeed anti-human, effects. Industry is keen to launch bio-tech as one of the main 'future technologies', so the police raids were meant to intimidate the protest movement and thus create a better climate for investment here [Mies 1987]. Clearly these new technologies cannot be 'profitable' unless the state steps in to enforce total control over women's reproductive capacities. Here we see the unity of patriarchy and capitalism again. In West Germany, we have always insisted on linking up our critique of reproductive technology to that of genetic engineering and to the issue of population control policy in the Third World. Only by showing the interconnectedness of these areas can we expose the basically racist, sexist and, ultimately, fascist implications of such techniques. [A second congress for Women Against Reproductive and Genetic Engineering was held in Frankfurt in November 1988.]

ARIEL SALLEH: Among the feminists I encountered working with Die Grunen, some have endorsed a Mothers' Manifesto; others are fiercely opposed to what they perceive as the naturalism of that same document. In my view, this 'debate' marks a significant new stage in our developing feminist consciousness. If only the movement will be mature enough to work through the political antinomies posed by the Manifesto.

MARIA MIES: The Mothers' Manifesto group began by pointing out the many grievances of mothers with small children in the women's movement. These grievances are real and there has not been very much solidarity with mothers on the part of our movement. But it is wrong, as the Manifesto women do, to say that the non-mothers are 'career women', or even that a career means emancipation. This position was already rejected quite early by the women's movement. On the other hand, the women who criticize the Manifesto for its 'biologism' are equally superficial. They usually argue that the Nazis also put 'motherhood' on a pedestal with their '*Blut und Boden*' ideology.

I consider both positions wrong. The Manifesto women treat motherhood as an existential antagonism but forget that it is only one part of a woman's life. The anti-Manifesto women, on the other hand, do not take the trouble to go deeper than their anti-fascist rhetoric – a rhetoric by which any new movement in Germany can be denounced. They thus commit the same mistake which communists and social democrats committed in the Weimar Republic, before Hitler came to power. These groups denounced all feelings of discontent centring on topics such as 'nature', 'motherhood', 'land' and 'home' as irrational, out of tune with the modern world. And in doing so, they gave this whole dimension of human reality over to the Nazis. Given its lodgement in Enlightenment discourse, scientific socialism was not able to accommodate these so called 'irrational' yearnings within its theoretical body and policies. However, by basing their Utopia exclusively on rationalization and class struggle, communists and social democrats were not able to understand the 'rumblings under the factory floor', as my late friend Christel Neususs put it. These rumblings stemmed from the emotional alienation of the industrial working class and Hitler exploited these feelings for his own purposes. Yes, I also hope that the discussion around the Mothers' Manifesto will be able to transcend the facile pattern of 'right' and 'left', and come to grips with what lies underneath the rebellion of mothers in the women's movement.

Note

This interview was first published in Australia as Maria Mies with Ariel Salleh, 'Women, Nature and the International Division of Labour', *Thesis Eleven*, 21 (1988), pp. 129–39. It was reprinted in the UK in *Science as Culture*, 9 (1990), pp. 73–87 and in the USA by *Fifth Estate*, 26 (1992), pp. 8–17.

References

Fox Keller, E. (1985) *Reflections on Gender and Science*, New Haven, CT: Yale University Press.

Kishwar, M. and R. Vanita (eds) (1984) *In Search of Answers: Indian Women's Voices*, London: Zed Books.

Luxemburg, R. (1967) *The Accumulation of Capital*, London: Routledge.

Marx, K. and F. Engels (1965) *The German Ideology*, London: Lawrence & Wishart.

Merchant, C. (1982) *The Death of Nature: Women, Ecology and the Scientific Revolution*, San Francisco, CA: Harper.

Mies, M. (1986) *Patriarchy and Accumulation on a World Scale: Women in the International Division of Labour*, London: Zed Books.

— (1987) 'Sexist and Racist Implications of the New Reproductive Technology', *Alternatives*, XII, pp. 323–42.

Mies, M., V. Bennholdt-Thomsen and C. von Werlhof (1987) *Women: The Last Colony*, London: Zed Books.

2

Losing Faith in Progress: Capitalist Patriarchy as an 'Alchemical System'

Claudia von Werlhof

Why is it that we in the West have such a hard time conceptualizing alternatives to corporate globalization, particularly Maria Mies's assertion that 'Subsistence is the Alternative' (SITA)? I contend that the difficulties that we have in imagining alternatives stem directly from the fact that especially women, nature and the colonies have been subjected to domination, exploitation and also to a fundamental *transformation*. The concept that we normally use to refer to this exploitative, violent and sexist history is 'patriarchy' (along with its flipside 'matriarchy'). In my opinion, patriarchy has not yet been fully analysed, and I will therefore attempt to deepen this analysis in this chapter in order to redefine the very concept of patriarchy.

Patriarchy has neither been *systematically* related to other significant phenomena of our society nor has it been interpreted as a system of changing and multifunctional concrete politics in everyday life as well as on a general social level. In a word, it has been *underestimated* as an interdisciplinary historical category and as a reality. Patriarchy has not vanished with progress. On the contrary, it is developing with progress: it is progress itself! Capitalism is only the latest stage of patriarchy and not its contradiction, as many people (especially women) seem to believe today.

My contribution to this theoretical debate consists in the use of the seemingly obsolete historical concept of *alchemy*. In relating alchemy to patriarchy, however, I found the 'key' (the key is the main symbol of alchemy) not only to understanding the history and concrete versions of patriarchy, but also the forms of patriarchal behaviour, of concrete patriarchal politics towards people, women, nature, society and the world in general. In a nutshell: alchemy is the 'method' of patriarchy. Using this method, politicians, technocrats, scientists and experimenters try to transform the world not just into a modern one, but also into a patriarchal one. Therefore, patriarchy has become what I call the 'Alchemical System'.

I will first consider religion, namely Christianity, and how it is related to the violence of capitalist patriarchy. In reality, we believe in violence. The 'Alchemical System' can survive only because people put all their faith in it. Therefore the question is how to rid ourselves of this misguided and self-destructive belief. Only then can our eyes be opened to the real alternatives to the limited choices that global capital is forcing us to accept. I am sure that my friend Maria Mies will welcome this approach as an extension of her own analysis (Mies 1986).

The Thesis

Is it possible to say that our economics and technology, capitalism, are the practical side of our religion, Christianity? Is it possible to say that with capitalism society has assumed the Christian goal and task of proving the existence of God? If so, what would 'God' then be?

From this point of view our economics and technology would actually be a form of religious practice, while our religion would in truth be an economic and technological theory. However, whereas this is not necessarily true for all systems of economics and for all religions, it could nevertheless be true for us in the West (see Weber 1993).

If our hypothesis about such a narrow relationship between capitalism and Christianity is true, then we would need to abandon this faith in order to be able to change the economic and technological order. In the search for real alternatives we therefore are required to liberate ourselves from a set of beliefs. But what is wrong with our beliefs?

If we begin with the results, then we are certainly forced to admit that our modern economic and technological system, capitalism, is in fact systematically destroying the earth; the final outcome having much less to do with 'God', than with the question of ecology (Brown and Ayres 1998).

On the other hand, if we focus on religion, we see, surprisingly, that at least our religious institutions, paramount among them the Church, are apparently not at all opposed to this destruction. In any case, the Church seen as the centre of a world power has until now said or done very little about the ecological problem (with exceptions: see Drewermann 1991). Of course, this is not true for many Christian grassroot movements around the world or for feminist theology; but these groups did not succeed in changing the attitude of the 'leaders' of the Church. At first glance this might seem surprising because it is 'God's creation' which is being destroyed, and we would expect the Church as such to stand up and say, 'Stop! We can't do this'. Yet this seldom happens, and still less is it followed by concrete political acts. In my opinion this is tantamount to saying that the Church, along with most other institutions – like the majority of governments, political parties, trade unions, entrepreneurs and social movements – is in agreement with what is happening. The real question is 'Why?' We must take the Church's response very seriously, and we cannot make excuses by saying that the Church has only forgotten to respond, or does not properly understand that the earth is gradually being destroyed, or that a distinction must be made between the Church and Christianity, or between the Church and its members.

Thus I have to conclude that the Church – in theory and in practice – is in agreement with the destruction of the earth by modern economic and technological systems (see Hunke 1987). So, to have faith either in religion or in capitalist progress is to have faith in the destruction that corporate globalization is visiting on the earth.

The Patriarchal Project

From this perspective, the Church and Christianity on the one hand and the capitalist system on the other hand appear to be one and the same project. I call it the 'patriarchal project'. But what is it that both are attempting to achieve, and by which practical method? How can this explain the negative results for most of us and our planet?

I will hereafter refer to this common denominator of Christian religion and capitalist system as 'patriarchy'. Thus, for me, the first and most central question is, what is patriarchy really? As of yet there has been no proper definition of patriarchy which can offer an explanation for the observable relationship between Christianity and capitalism.

'Pater' and 'arché' If we examine the word patriarchy from a literal viewpoint – and this is always a good starting point, because the names of things are no accident – we see that it is a combination of the words *pater* and *arché*. *Pater* means 'father', and *arché* basically means 'origin', 'beginning', and, in a concrete sense, 'uterus'. Over the centuries the meaning of *arché* has shifted to include 'power, rule, domination', which of course is something rather different. We generally think only of this second meaning when we see the word *arché*, thus patriarchy and matriarchy are defined as 'rule of fathers' and 'rule of mothers'; accordingly, we wrongly think of matriarchy as a society ruled by mothers/women. This, however, is a condition which has never existed; there is no evidence of it in pre-patriarchal societies anywhere on our earth (see Weiler 1993; Lerner 1991; Göttner-Abendroth 1988; Meier-Seethaler 1992; Eisler 1993). Correspondingly, many people wrongly explain and justify patriarchy as the logical reverse of mothers/or women's rule.

Much of this confusion can be eliminated if we return to the older meaning of *arché*, according to which 'matriarchy' simply means 'in the beginning the mother' (Göttner-Abendroth 1988). All life originates from and is born of mothers. This is and always has been simply the state of things here on earth, a fact which may seem banal at first glance but which has potentially paradigm-shattering implications. With that in mind, the idea that 'patriarchy', means 'in the beginning the father' seems strange. This would be like saying that fathers give birth. Suddenly patriarchy, *pater arché*, becomes a more complicated and difficult concept than *mater arché*, or matriarchy, because it is not referring to any concrete event, fact or state of things. Therefore *pater arché* cannot be the reverse of *mater arché*, simply because it does not exist.

The second problem arises from the transformation of the meaning of *arché* from 'origin' to 'rule, domination'. First, a 'right to rule' is deduced from the fact of origin. This could mean the power of the body of the mother, of the female (e.g. Mühlmann 1984), or mother-power (Canetti 1986), or 'mother-right' (Bachofen 1978). But in this case there is no 'rule'. Perhaps what is meant is that the maternal power, which by nature is necessary for nurturing, protecting and accompanying new life until it is able to take care of itself, is replaced by a father's 'right to rule'. Either the father 'rules' and assumes the power of the mother while she is giving birth, or the father makes his claim to the power because he himself is the one giving birth. This would mean a kind of 'father-power'. However, since fathers are not (yet) able to give birth and thus are not by nature 'powerful' in this sense, we still have the problem of explaining which non-maternal birth and non-maternal ruling power we are talking about here.

Things are just as difficult when we look at the word *pater*. In the discussion on patriarchy it is often not taken into account that the word father did not even exist in pre-patriarchal society, and when it finally appears with patriarchy, it does not mean any of the things that we usually associate with it. When the concept of father appeared in history, it did not mean the physical father who takes care of his children; from the beginning it was an abstract institutional concept of hierarchy, rule and domination (e.g. Braun 1990). The father appears from the beginning in connection with the concept of domination, the lawful ruler, God, something superhuman (see Freud 1974). It did not necessarily mean physical fatherhood, and it did not originate in the sensual culture of the matriarchy (here and elsewhere in the text I will use the term 'matriarchy' with the concrete pre-patriarchal meaning 'in the beginning the mother' rather than the mythical 'rule of the mothers'). Only with this in mind can we understand that the concept of father is a purely *Utopian* concept, in the sense that the 'rule' of the 'father' is: (a) possible; (b) desirable; (c) so all-comprehensive that it could even include the maternal, real origin, the birth event; and/or (d) no longer needs the maternal, because it has completely 'replaced' it.

Patriarchy as Utopia And so patriarchy is basically the expression of a *social Utopia* which states that it is the father and not the mother, in the abstract institutional form of 'fatherhood' (i.e. as a supposed God or his 'law', or even a 'natural law'), who creates life, or who ideally one day will be able to do so.

Thus, for me, patriarchy is in the end an unimaginable, incomprehensible, almost inexpressible claim totally unattached and abstracted from the concrete conditions of earthly existence, going far beyond anything as banal as some sort of 'birth-envy'. Its goal is nothing less than the transformation of the birth-giving female body into an all-producing and universally re-producible thing, to replace the birth-giving body with a non-bodily, non-female machinery and claim this machinery to be the goal and end of human history. Patriarchy thus means 'motherless society' and ends in the policy of attempting to replace the concrete mother with the abstract father. Only when we realize this can we really understand why patriarchy begins with matricide (see Weiler 1991; Tazi-Preve 1992; Wolf 1994), with the subjugation of maternal culture, and ends by trying to replace it with an artificial social 'design'. This attempt at substitution is a true obsession which continues to haunt us and whose menace is as immediate and threatening as ever. Accordingly, as long as there are real, concrete mothers in this world, patriarchy is not complete and does not really even exist. And so there is a continuous, repeated need to prove over and over again that the Father, as the Also-Mother, lording over the world, i.e. God, as presented in all monotheistic religions (not just Christianity), really exists. Thus, from a religious point of view, the real 'sin' of women is simply the fact that they still are needed as mothers because of the fact that life comes into the world only through their bodies. In Christian (or monotheistic) religion, all women are by nature sinners, unless, like Mary, they are mothers without sensual bodies or nine-month pregnancies. This is because in patriarchy a 'spirit' does what is normally done by female bodies, a spirit which does not inhabit the body and which enters it from outside in the form of a masculine godly act, an act which also calls the latest reproduction technologies to mind, not to mention the many sperm theories in the history of breeding (Treusch-Dieter 1990). In any case, this vision presupposes the separation of body and mind, matter and spirit, 'mater' and life.

Just as Mary was the ideal image of a patriarchal Yet-Mother, we are also in possession of an even older image of the father as Also-Mother, namely the Egyptian pharaoh Echnaton, who, as the founder of the first monotheistic religion, Aton, is said to be also the founder of Judaism (see Freud 1974). The god Echn-Aton appears as a pregnant man (see Wolf 1994). Thus, from the very beginning of monotheistic religion we witness the claim of the Father uniting all into one, God as the 'One and All'. The 'One and All' is no longer the cosmic all-mother, the goddess Nut who, interestingly, had her name stolen and used – spoken backwards (A-Tun) – as the name of the new reversed father religion. The so-called Father was established in her stead, a completely unnatural artificial being placed in (and above) the world as a political theory about the goal and end of history. So, long before our present economic and technological systems developed, the political theory of monotheism was accompanied by the politics of despotism, which from then on defined and determined the practical, daily methods for the realization of the patriarchal obsession of replacing the mother. And the ideological part of this system is that which we refer to as monotheistic religion (see Girard 1992).

Patriarchy is the concept of a utopian system which goes hand in hand with monotheistic religion. Patriarchy wants to construct a form of society which not only makes a claim, but also in the course of time attempts to prove it. This claim is none other than the assertion that the better, more divine world is the one inhabited by the *pater arché*, the 'birth-giving' and thus legitimately ruling Father-God, or his Father-Law instead of the 'natural right' of the mother (see Werlhof 1996). But since the political theory of patriarchy, the rule of the birth-giving-origin-father, is purely a claim, it requires a whole system of proofs while at the same time calling for the actual realization of its Utopia. This is necessary, because in the long run a whole civilization cannot be based on something which does not exist and which contradicts everything that our daily experience teaches us.

Patriarchy as violence Thus it becomes necessary for patriarchy to attempt to construct its own reality that speculates upon rather than explains existing reality. This speculation goes along with a sort of 'violent thinking' (Ernst 1986) which is formative for the reality it constructs. From that point on, 'violent thinking' is permanently connected to a politics of brute force that will ruthlessly remake anything in its way which does not fit its theory. This practice of force and violence also turns up in science and technology, as well as, last but not least, in economics. From then on there is a constant effort to turn the world upside down, to transform nature, which is no longer regarded as female-maternal, into something male-paternal (see Böhme 1988; Merchant 1987).

Modern technology gives us a very clear picture of this. In particular, reproductive technology 'reproduces' not so much actual life itself as the ideal process of life 'production': the pregnancy machinery, or birth machine, in the true sense of the word, which in the end would function without the female body, or at least without parts of it (see Rifkin 1983). This even goes so far as to include the fiction of the pregnant man (no matter how simple, stupid and ugly this fiction might be), into whom birth-giving organs can be implanted. The perverse idea of an artificially pregnant man goes all the way back to the pharaoh Echnaton.

Still, today not *all* thinking takes place along purely patriarchal lines, but those who are busy shaping our destinies certainly do think in this way, as is evident by their constant, unmitigated thirst for power and money, a fact for which we would otherwise have no explanation (see Werlhof et al. 1996).

We thus can say that the patriarchal project is both an ideological (religious, philosophical) and a practical (technological, political, economic, cultural) attempt to convert the entire world into its opposite, a world which would then be 'better', more 'divine' and more in line with what is assumed to be its own, real 'evolutionary' tendencies. For this reason, from a religious as well as from a technological and economic perspective, the world appears as a place in need of improvement, an imperfect, 'evil', 'unclean', worthless, low or somehow insignificant place. Thus there is always a basic need for redemption or salvation – not only *of* the world, but also *from* the world (see Kippenberg 1991). In patriarchal religions (beginning with the Gnosis: see Sloterdijk and Macho 1991; and also Buddhism) the world, all earthly existence, is seen as a form of suffering, the most important difference between them being the way salvation is to be attained. From a pre-Socratic viewpoint (see Ernst 1997), the world was originally a Garden of Eden that was later lost; for we have been driven from Paradise. It is also believed that, although we might be able to construct a new paradise, we can never go back to the old one. And this is the point where the new concept of economics and technology comes into play. We can never be satisfied with the way the world (supposedly) is, with nature as it (supposedly) is; we can never be satisfied that nature is something 'maternal', that life comes from the female. No, for us this seems to be something almost outrageous, even diabolical. This is why, from the religious point of view, all women are seen as automatically 'low' and 'bad'. This fundamentalist damnation of all that is female and/or natural stems from the belief that only God, the Father should bring forth life. In reality, nevertheless, heterosexual intercourse and sexual desire are necessary to the life-process, as well as to the entire scope of bodily, spiritual, intellectual and sensual experience, all the things which are capable of uniting men, women and children in a completely non-patriarchal way, in a this-worldly, erotic community (see Schubart 1989). Patriarchy's task is thus to break the power of the senses, the power of sense, and to get rid of the entire bodily sphere, along with all life-celebrating emotions and sensibilities. What is meant is the dulling of the senses and the replacement of the sensual world, of sense itself, with an unsensual, sense(s)less, non-sensical world, a world in which all sensibility has been lost, a world which makes no sense (see Kutschmann 1986).

Thus we can explain why the patriarchal project, beginning with its very basic concept of '*pater arché*', is such a thoroughly violent one, making use of the most systematic, all-inclusive and thoroughgoing violence in all of known history; why it has grown to such insane proportions and spread itself globally; and why it is a thoroughly irrational project. Rationality itself is used as a tool to turn the entire globe upside down along with all previous culture, changing nature into something which it is not. And this is what women-kind, or people in general, still do not grasp: the perpetrators of this system are deadly serious, *they really mean it.*

What we are dealing with here is not the denial of the testing or of the development of something new, as many voices perhaps would say. What needs to be recognized is that this something new which patriarchy is seeking is really something thoroughly *opposed* to the world, something inimical, perverted and destructive. We cannot seriously wish for everything non-patriarchal to be destroyed and eventually be prevented from existing at all (Deschner 1994; Ullrich 1980; Paczensky 1970; Illich 1982, 1983).

In the meantime we quietly assume that the new is better than the old, no matter how, why or at what cost this 'new' is constructed. Where living beings are constantly suffering injury, we ought to be hearing alarm bells but we do not; destruction supposedly has a creative aspect, or will be followed by 'creation'. See, for example, the world-renowned Austrian economist Joseph Schumpeter who speaks of 'creative destruction' (Schumpeter 1962). All that religious guilt, so present otherwise, is gone here, because Christianity is not concerned with any of these questions. Instead, the crimes against nature, against women, matricide, the murder of the 'sweet and wise body', the murder of women's culture and of Eros – these are the very goals of the patriarchal project and the prerequisites for its achievement. Thus the persecution of witches has never really stopped – it just changed shape (Kimmerle 1980) – yet no one seems to feel very guilty about it, either in the Church or among men in general. So, the murder of women appears as a somehow normal and understandable event in criminal history (see Trube-Becker 1987). From the logic of this point of view it is, on the contrary, sinful to love women and not to punish them.

Patriarchy and 'improvement' ('evolution', machinery) The patriarchal Utopia could therefore not be realized unless women/nature did not exist, except in some 'improved', i.e. perverted, form which has nothing at all to do with the reality of nature or of women. When everything is seen as evil – the human being, especially women and nature – then this legitimizes the right to 'improve' them, make them 'ripe' for civilization, or to 'cleanse' the world of them. This principle of human 'evolution' is very obvious if we look at all sexist, racist and especially educational practices (Dressen 1982; Hammer 1997). To this end the human being, the world, nature and women, must – first – be *transformed* into something evil, a dirty, low or bad matter, not only ideologically but also empirically, in reality. This is the initial task of religion, technology, politics and economy. Without first undergoing degradation, there would be no need for 'improvement'. However, the original act of degradation, of making something out to be bad, leaves some irreversible results, so that afterwards almost anything would seem to be an improvement. We see the same thing happening in the destruction of the rainforest, in land erosion and desertification due to modern farming and mining techniques, or in the 'breeding' of 'ennobled' species and 'races' (Chargaff 1988).

After the world and its beings have been degraded, there is a justification for their improvement or even replacement. Investment in 'human capital' seems to liberate us from the 'risks' living beings pose to the system. It seems to be able to produce a purified, healthy, happy and perfect life 'free' from suffering (Bergmann 1992); a life which has been transformed by machinery. In this way we have become accustomed to accepting a new primitiveness, brutality and irrationality, combined with a planned ignorance – the totalitarian outcome of 'violent thinking'.

Thus economics, in conjunction with technology, appears to be the secular arm of the patriarchal project, as originally formulated in religion and in politics. Despite its claims to have left all its irrational and religious aspects behind it, it seems that capitalism today, in parallel with religious patriarchal thought, is attempting to take that very same religious patriarchal Utopia and turn it into reality: to prove the existence of One (male) God and to create a 'divine' world as the realization of Utopia, the 'good', the 'beautiful' and the 'true' world, a new Paradise on earth (cf. Plato 1962).

Patriarchy as scarcity It thus becomes apparent why our modern system defines itself in terms of the task of overcoming scarcity (Illich 1982; Gronemeyer 1988; Sachs 1993). There are, however, two interesting aspects to this scarcity. One of these, which as far as I can discover has never been examined, is the scarcity of patriarchy. There simply are no birth-giving fathers, nor are there any real substitutes for nature, or any natureless, motherless worlds. We can thus say that patriarchy itself is in fact scarce, extremely scarce. What is utopian about patriarchy is that it is presented as normal, as anything but scarce, and in order to do this it has to be plentiful. This results in huge sums of money and exessive quantities of commodities becoming involved in a literal 'production-battle'; it also produces 'great' men (Godelier 1987) and many small 'lords'; and it puts forward theories about conception and fertilization, claiming that it is only the male sperm which carries life, and that women are merely 'boxes' for transformation and growth (see Treusch-Dieter 1990). It constructs a 'second nature', one that is put upon or forced into nature, an artificial un- or anti-nature. Like Ernst Bloch we could say, patriarchal civilization moves in the world like 'an army in the enemy's territory' (Bloch 1967). In the meantime, even women see their bodies and their ability to give birth as something unimportant, ugly or old-fashioned, to the point that they themselves campaign for its abolition and replacement through industry (see the 'gender' approach of Firestone 1975 to Haraway 1995).

There is also a second aspect to the overcoming of scarcity through capitalism, one which has been well documented. I am referring to the fact that scarcity, i.e. need, which the economic system is supposed to free us from, is actually created by it through policies of monopolization, accumulation and destruction (see Bergfleth 1992; Mies and von Werlhof 1999). On the one hand we possess an entire artificial armoury of means and products, and on the other hand we see an unbearable, artificially produced scarcity of these very means and products, as well as the supposed lack of any alternatives to them. This becomes especially obvious when we look at the means and products which are basic and essential for life (see Werlhof 1983; Krieg 1980; Mies and Shiva 1993). Economics presents itself as the saviour, but it actually creates the problem it is supposed to save us from (see George 1980; Imfeld 1985). This is essential for a general acceptance of the economic programme. Only then, when misery, disaster, infertility and destruction, i.e. a scarcity of paradise, really do exist, is it also necessary to construct a better world with less scarcity, a new paradise; but this time it is assumed the paradise will never disappear – as 'evolution'.

Patriarchy as metaphysics This cynical production of scarcity through accumulation and destruction leads to a *delusion*: that it is possible and desirable to construct a new world. In the final analysis, this world would be a metaphysical one, beyond physics, beyond the body, matter, the mother (*physein* in Greek also means to give birth), i.e. beyond all of nature (Shiva 1989). The incredible strength of our faith in this patriarchal religion is revealed in our acceptance of the nihilistic notion that the existing world must first be destroyed in order to get a better one; for what happens if this self-generated natural catastrophe, this apocalypse, ends only in a big 'self-made' Nothing? And much seems to point to this eventuality (see Schütz-Buenaventura 2000). It is an incontestable fact that there is not even a shred of evidence for any credible replacement for this Nothing on the horizon. The project of the supposed conquest of nature, originally expressed in religious terms as God's instruction to Adam to 'rule over the earth', has ended in her accelerating retreat (see Colburn et al. 1996).

Despite this, our behaviour towards nature and women remains the same, and the legitimization of this behaviour remains the same, although everyone knows what a lie it is. The 'valuation' of nature means the destruction of its value, its transformation into waste. Patriarchal thinking has 'penetrated' our consciousness so deeply that it is nearly impossible for us to imagine anything other than the destruction and subsequent improvement of the world, even when we see that this is not possible. For example, the mention of the 'curse' of technology is always countered with mention of its apparent 'blessings', which are nothing but short-lived illusions of 'improvement' that can be sustained only if we manage to ignore the violence and degradation that was necessary to produce them. There is only one real alternative to this dire situation: the acceptance of nature as it is, and a relationship with it based on this acceptance (see Mességué 1989). This acceptance is a prerequisite for any co-operation, but this sort of reasoning has not been possible in our 'reasonable' age and civilization. We are no longer even capable of recognizing what nature is, and even less capable of knowing who women are.

The Method of Patriarchy: Alchemy

In this section I deal with the methods used to set up the patriarchal utopian dream as a 'concrete' utopian world and to prove the existence of this 'new world' through religion and, particularly, through economics and technology. That there must be such a method clearly follows from the fact that patriarchy, as a utopian theory, does not exist; it is a 'wannabe'. Patriarchy as a social system must remain unproven as long as reality does not conform to the theory or to the Utopia. Patriarchy is always in need of a proof, especially over the longer term, for we have often seen that terror and lies will not work for ever to keep people in bounds, and intimidation and deception alone will never turn them into true believers in patriarchy. All over the world we can still hear women laughing – those who still are able to laugh – at the male patriarchal version of how life is created and of what a tremendous role they play in it (see Diotima in Plato 1985). Moving beyond the religious or ideological expressions of patriarchy, people have always felt the need to put its theory into practice through politics, technology, science and economics, in order to prove the correctness of its hallucinations. And in fact, from the beginning, in all of patriarchy's theories, even in philosophy and in other supposedly non-religious disciplines, we have seen the attempt to formulate patriarchy's perverted train of thought in such a way as to expand the *faith* in the correctness of its claims, although (or perhaps because) there can be no real *knowledge* of these claims (see Hunke 1987). And so we have here a system of belief which is considered as particularly divine and which must be maintained over and against everything we know. This faith begins where there is no knowledge, and where knowledge cannot exist. The absurd can only be believed, it cannot be known: *credo quia absurdum*. In the long term, however, the problem of the practical realization of the theory becomes increasingly important. How can a patriarchal world really be brought about, so that faith in it, permanently precarious, can be replaced by 'concrete' knowledge of it?

After examining various natural sciences and the history of technology, I have gradually come to the conclusion that the method for the realization of patriarchy was and still is *alchemy*. Alchemy, as a kind of all-inclusive theology and technology, is the key to the question of *how* patriarchy puts its theory into practice, in all areas and at all levels of society.

The word 'alchemy' goes back to the Arab word *keme*, the black mud of the Nile. The annual flooding of the Nile left behind thick layers of this black mud on its banks, making them fertile. Through nature's chemistry of mixing water and earth new life was created. Alchemy must originally have been the attempt to observe this natural phenomenon, to understand it, to help it along, and to imitate it. This is most likely the phase of the pre-patriarchal alchemy of gardeners and peasants, of men and women who wished to help this process along and co-operate with this natural phenomenon, without changing the principles behind it (e.g. the early notion of the Garden of Eden or the famous 'Hanging Gardens' of Semiramis).

Alchemy is known to us through the history of religion and of technology. It has existed throughout the world in many forms. Most certainly alchemy had its origins in ancient matriarchal cultures and over time became more and more patriarchalized and perverted – turned into its opposite. There is much evidence of alchemical practices and theories in China, India, Africa, the Middle East, and throughout Europe, especially in Eastern and south-eastern Europe (see Eliade 1980; Jung 1985; Binswanger 1985; Bologne 1995; Gebelein 1996; Biedermann 1991). But as far as I can discover, there have been no attempts until now to examine alchemy from the perspective that I have suggested here. Thus I am crossing into new territory, at least subjectively. However, the time appears ripe to attempt an initial thesis on the role of alchemy in patriarchy and vice versa, and later to substantiate these beginnings with further research (Werlhof 2000a).

Whereas our economy, the 'capitalist world system' (Wallerstein 1974; 1986; 1989), appears to be the practical side of our religion with the goal of achieving patriarchy by adding 'In the beginning was the father' to the idea of 'paradise', then alchemy, according to the thesis, is the concrete method for achieving this goal.

Let us examine what the method of alchemy is. The central concept in Egyptian alchemy, going back more than 5000 years, is the key (Binswanger 1985). Egyptian alchemy actually saw itself as the key to deciphering the world. I will similarly use alchemy as the key to the interpretation of the method for constructing patriarchy.

Patriarchal alchemy   The principles of nurturing and co-operation in early alchemy are entirely different from those of patriarchal alchemy, such as the production of the so-called '*materia prima*' or '*massa confusa*' or '*nigredo*' on the one hand, and of 'dissolve and combine' (in Latin '*solve et coagula*') on the other hand. The *materia prima* is the outcome of a process in which the alchemist wants to go back to the origins of matter. For this purpose he has to 'blacken' all matter, mostly by using fire, producing the so-called *nigredo* which is supposed to be the all-inclusive substance of matter. In other words, the alchemist starts with bringing death to matter. This process is called 'mortification' (from latin *mors* = death) (Bologne 1995). It is no coincidence that blacksmiths and all forms of pyro-techniques played a special role in alchemy (Eliade 1980), and that women, seen as witches, were burned.

After that, according to the principle of 'dissolve and combine', individual elements are then separated from the *materia prima* and from each other by using 'purification' techniques to isolate the different 'elements' (such as sulphur, mercury and, in the last instant, gold) which later are recombined. It is the same process which in the social sciences we refer to as 'divide and rule'. This is also the principle of patriarchal technology. The raw material first undergoes the process of abstraction, filtering and isolation. The abstracted substances are then combined with other abstracted substances (see Ernst 1993). This method anticipates machine technology (Mumford 1977) which, although appearing much later, does the same thing (see Bammé et al. 1983). Machine technology shares with alchemy this principle of separation and purification (see the experiment in sciences), as well as the principle of producing raw materials primarily as 'resources' first of all. Here we have a context, a common ground, reaching through various epochs and expressing itself in the development of various periods of patriarchal thought, intention and practice. Thus alchemy shows up right within the capitalist system, despite the fact that our modern world claims to have left the superstitious and ignorant or naive method which alchemy is labelled to be far behind it.

The central principles of blackening and of dissolve and combine are those of force and violence. They require sacrifice, that of matter, e.g. nature, and that of people, especially women (Eliade 1980). The isolation of so-called 'pure' substances (characteristic of modern chemistry as well) comprises the 'construction' and later destruction of the *materia prima*, reducing it to essences which do not occur in nature. Alchemy goes about its work of producing new, 'improved' substances and materials by combining these 'pure' substances. The alchemist completes his 'great work' through the so-called 'chemical' or 'holy marriage' of the materials. 'Holy marriage' is a metaphor taken from matriarchal culture. Whereas holy marriage originally was the coming together of the goddess and her hero in a great celebration of Eros from which all life springs and is confirmed (see Weiler 1993), in alchemy it appears as a connection between, and forced upon, artificially abstracted substances characterized as either male or female (i.e. gender as a truly 'social construction'; see Jung 1985). For example, the blacksmith was often responsible for circumcision, thus producing 'pure' sexes (see Wolf 1994). The ceremony is no longer one of the mixing of the natural polarity of materials as a 'great work' of nature; it is the forced putting together of artificial opposites (see Ernst 1993; 1996), from which the 'great work' of the alchemists springs. The alchemist sees himself here as the true creator, as the procreator of a completely new kind of life; he sees himself as a kind of new 'great mother' or, rather, God, who, like the priest at a wedding, completes the holy ritual in the 'sacrament' of bringing the couple together. From this established act of bringing together (and, correspondingly, the first sexual act is permitted only following this ceremony) springs something entirely new, in particular – so it is supposed – new life ('heterosexual reproduction'), and this life is based on the sacrifice of women's life.

However, the whole principle of the combination of pure substances seems all the more puzzling in that 'pure' substances are essentially dead ones, from which no life is very likely to grow. And so patriarchy is in principle *barren* (see Colburn et al. 1996; this fact is gradually being noticed by modern chemistry which has begun mixing its pure substances with 'impure', living ones). But this supposedly new life is meant to come into being in a way that makes the alchemist, rather than nature or women, appear to be the 'divine creator'. And above all, the alchemist's goal is to construct not just any old new life, but rather a very special new form of life which is not only better, but which also leads to the discovery of the so-called 'philosopher's stone' – the 'tincture', the 'elixir', the 'powder', all terms for the 'quintessence', the fifth or final essence, with which all matter can be transformed into the most valuable of all matter: gold, meaning 'life'. Finding life in its 'pure' form is the ultimate goal of all alchemical filtering.

The purpose of alchemists, however, is not to promote and protect life and fertility. It needs the philosopher's stone in order to get hold of the 'essence of life' which is thought to be lurking somewhere inside all matter. Here, the pre-patriarchal belief in the unity of matter and mind is still maintained. But the eventual rejection of this unity is foreshadowed by the attempt made by the alchemist in this instance to separate them, which is an act of violence against matter in order to convert it into something deteriorated, subdued, 'female' in a patriarchal sense. In contrast, the supposedly separate mind from now on appears to belong to something 'higher', 'holier' and 'male' in a patriarchal sense. 'Pure mind', the mind without matter, then, seems to be the pure power of life, with which one is believed to be able to produce living beings even beyond nature and women: the so-called 'homunculus', the small human often depicted as sitting in a test tube. Homunculus would be, so to speak, the first successful test-tube baby, a creation of the alchemist experimenter – something that has never happened or existed. For example, Paracelsus, the famous alchemist and physician of the sixteenth century, still tried to produce new life by combining male sperm with human (female?) blood (see Paracelsus 1990). Similar experiments using alchemical methods have taken place through the centuries up until the present day (Worms 1988).

Unlike earlier, pre-patriarchal alchemy with its principle of co-operation with nature, what we see here is an attempt at the *usurpation* of the female pregnancy and birth process, not only in theory, but also in *reality*, an attempt to 'improve' them and replace them with something else. This is what we have previously referred to as the attempt to prove the existence of God: the proof that a male, omnipotent creator *above* matter really does exist. For previously there were only female gods and female creators *within* matter. And nothing has changed. Using alchemical principles scientists are still attempting the same thing today, because they have never succeeded in proving the existence of God and have never brought about a 'male' creation of new life. In this sense alchemy has been a failure, but it has in its current form (better known as chemistry) effectively retained all of its former goals and methods.

Alchemy, capitalism (speculation) and individual identity Let us now turn to alchemy as the patriarchal method in the field of economics itself. The Swiss economist Hans Christoph Binswanger, in his book *Geld und Magie* (Money and Magic) (1985), discusses the connection between modern economics and alchemy – without, however, any reference to patriarchy. For Binswanger, Goethe's Faust symbolizes modern capitalist economics as an alchemical process. The goal is a new creation out of nothing, which in the end is supposed to be possible as a pure abstraction. Whereas previous alchemists attempted to reduce matter to its basic essence, to reduce its form to gold, i.e. to suggest that gold, the 'pure metal', is the ultimate essence of matter (this would be a good place to apply the term 'essentialism'), modern economics for its part starts with the belief that gold is the ultimate value and most convincing symbol of wealth and power. After the invention of paper money, this belief changes from 'having gold equals having (power over) life' to 'having money equals having (power over) life' (see *Beiträge zur feministischen Theorie und Praxis* 1985). This way the belief is changed into speculation: the belief in a piece of paper. This means an attempt to change even paper, or just 'information', as today, back into money or gold, be it now or in the future. Whereas in alchemy real materials served as the basis, today the belief in the potential of paper (currency notes) or information must suffice to serve as the claim to the treasure (gold). And thus, in our economic system, money, even more so than gold itself, is raised up as the philosopher's stone, and its existence then, logically, represents the proof of the existence of God.

In the real world, money, as the philosopher's stone, itself appears to be the means for turning everything else into money as well. Money appears to be life itself, or the cosmic life power, which can incite or force the continual production of something new, something previously unknown. Money 'is born' through the 'alchemical' mixing of land and labour, later increasing even more by being mixed again with capital, itself the 'product' of labour and land. Capital, soil and labour are filtered out of the world as 'pure substances'. As such they exist in the form of the 'labourer', the cultivated field, *Blut und Boden*, machinery. They amalgamate to form new 'life', the commodity as fetish (see Marx 1974). The commodity, rather than any other 'antiquated' form of life, seems to guarantee, even to be, a new and 'better' form of life. Later, the same increasingly applies to machines, which today are referred to as 'beings' (this is the 'essentialism' of the 'postmodern' discourse), while human beings are conversely regarded as (post-human) 'systems' (see Weizenbaum 1978).

Money really does begin to seem like a kind of philosopher's stone, because it keeps this process in motion, in particular by mobilizing people as labour and placing them at the service of the alchemical process of turning (their) life into money/capital while at the same time succeeding at keeping them faithful to the beliefs that underpin the system. The separation (abstraction) of humans from their surroundings by so-called 'original accumulation', i.e. their separation from land and other means of production, forces them to concentrate all their productive capabilities on to the production of pure 'human material', the 'labour power', and to reduce all their hopes and desires to the goal of making money like a modern alchemist, or of placing themselves at his disposal like the 'pure substance'. And the women have to play the part of the *materia prima*, having been transformed from witches to 'housewives' and having to sacrifice themselves, or being sacrificed in the process of patriarchal 'life-production'; going all the way from mothers to 'mother-machines', ideally being in the end replaced by machines. This would be the ultimate sacrifice of women.

The *homo oeconomicus* and *femina domestica* (Illich 1982) are the product of a total mobilization in service of the artificial uterus, and become themselves a kind of philosopher's stone which each individual in the economic melting pot has created in, for and of himself ('self-realization'). Nowadays everybody has become his/her own alchemist (see the truly alchemical notion of 'gender'). Individualization seems to mean 'alchemization'. It is the *generalization* of alchemy instead of its retreat from the world.

Today, the stated goal is to do anything for money, to be eternally 'prepared' for money, in order to have a God-fearing, 'self-determined', modern 'piece of life' (Duden 1991). And the necessity of this goal, including faith in it, is what defines the person as a *homo christianus*; a 'good Christian', someone to be found especially among the prosperous who are the God's chosen ones. According to Calvin, to have money is proof of the proper faith in God's existence, for He has provided those riches, and He does not do the same for everyone. Faith in God and faith in money become one and the same thing. It becomes a matter of, a proof of, faith when the individual spends all his time and thought on nothing other than making money. Otherwise he is regarded as wastrel (see also especially Weber 1993; Foucault 1977; Dressen 1982; Schütz-Buenaventura 1996). Faith itself, Christianity, through its connection with modern economics, becomes a kind of philosopher's stone. For, where there is a (permanent) lack of money, this lack is replaced by faith, which assumes the task of calming the poor and the losers while at the same time motivating them to continue doing exactly that which caused their misery in the first place.

The fact that everyone is busy doing the same thing, searching for the same 'main thread', is characterized later by Adam Smith as being God's secular will set in motion and directed by the great 'invisible hand' (see Smith 1823). It is as if the new co-operation between economics and religion were a holy act, although it should more appropriately be regarded as a black mass or conjuring the devil. And thus the murderous egoism of each individual, which is thus systematically brought to the fore, appears afterwards to be beneficial to society, socially good, socially valuable, part of a good or godly society, in any case as a part of the best of all possible worlds. What other social system and religion has ever managed to view humankind as bad, literally to make them bad, and to push this fact off as an *improvement* or as 'evolution' of humankind, as the triumph of humankind over nature (e.g. Hobbes 1984; Locke 1970)? How is it possible that the 'mind who wants the evil' (violent thinking), nevertheless 'creates the good'? The answer is: It has not been possible!

With the *great alchemical reversal*, we finally have the explanation for modern Europe's success in (and through) its colonization of most parts of the world. Who else among the world's peoples were individually and collectively as mobile, labourious, arrogant, active, unscrupulous, merciless, violent, convinced of their mission to bring real, i.e. patriarchal, civilization to the entire world; united, like an army, oriented towards a single goal, everywhere, permanently, and without needing even a command from above (see Todorov 1980)? The alchemy of patriarchy, especially in the mixture of Christianity and capitalism, has transformed the entire world, has turned it upside down. After all, it possessed 'pure' Christian faith and 'pure' cold economic calculation – God and Money – as 'pure', abstract 'substances', both originally separate things (and they still are made to appear as such today). And then they were put together in an unholy marriage built upon the decline of nature and women's culture: transformed into 'capital' – money, command, machinery – as the proof of God's existence. The other result of this mixture is, however, not the noble Civilized Man and Paradise on Earth; on the contrary, the result rather resembles something like hell on an earth serving as a home for Dr Jekyll and Mr Hyde. Evil, the devil, sin, 'scarcity', all those things from which religion claims to free us and which economics claims to improve, are really produced by them, and then systematically spread throughout the world. Alchemy has not generated any jolly homunculus, or any gold; it has generated a menagerie of freaks and monsters, e.g. the god-fearing exploiter, the honourable mass murderer, the gentleman conqueror, the salvation-bringing missionary, the torturer in the service of a good cause, the innocent rapist, and the creative maker of the atom bomb; it has invented such marvels as 'creative destruction', war as the 'father of all things', the 'ethics' of degradation, the 'morale' of repression, education to self-destruction, 'modesty' as toleration of domination, violence in sexuality, cynicism as the 'normal' intellectual posture, and war as a 'humanitarian' act (Chossudovsky 1996; Klöss 1985; Daly 1970; Theweleit 1977; Easlea 1986; Sloterdijk 1983).

And yet, in patriarchy, none of this is considered as evil, sinful or diabolical, because, in contradiction to what really has taken place, patriarchy regards itself as the one and only instrument, the 'weapon', against evil, sin and the devil which it sees lurking everywhere in nature, in life, in everything feminine, sensual and erotic, and ultimately in the very world itself. This is the *real distortion* of things.

The alchemical system, with its goal of patriarchy, has in the meantime become so internalized and is so strongly present in the back of the mind that for humankind, driven from its 'paradise', there generally is no need of any external force for one to be squeezed into the alchemical purification process. The modern person continually 'alchemizes' himself by transforming his 'passions' into 'interests' (see Hirschman 1987). And although his empirical experience tells him that his life does not seem to be improving, nor is it becoming 'precious', or attaining a special 'identity' or 'individuality', but is in the end wasted, his life is being hardened into something dead (see Marx's concept of capital as 'past', 'dead' labour), he still hangs on to his alchemical superstition without knowing that the whole process is, as it always has been, nothing but a swindle (see Werlhof 1983).

Even women, who ought to know better because it is still they through whom self-creating life enters the world without the assistance of any alchemy, have begun to believe this dangerous patriarchal non-sense. They, too, now wish to be 'equal' with patriarchal men, as labourers, individuals, as possessors of commodities, sexuality, power and money. They want to catch up with men's supposedly more advanced development to make this development generally accessible, copy it, rather than to see to it that the insane notion of a 'better' life be exposed as the deadly illusion it is. Many of them even accept the new reproductive technologies dealing with pregnancy, birth and maternity, not realizing that the goal of these technologies is the final, last possible (or impossible) step towards their total removal from the 'power to be', as well as the replacement and destruction of the last remaining form of life and subsistence which has not yet been split asunder. Many women today act as if they did not know what this means, as if the patriarchal attempt to construct a motherless world were possible, even desirable (Butler 1991).

In the final analysis, of course, there is no such thing as the philosopher's stone. Money, God, the male 'creator' and the faith in these things are all illusions. The belief in the philosopher's stone is the superstition that blinds us all to the strength and power with which we are naturally endowed from birth, the erroneous belief that drives us to seek strength and power instead in God, in money, in dead objects (capital) or in political 'power'. Indeed, we cannot imagine finding strength and power within ourselves unless and until our lives have somehow been 'cleansed' of everything living. Thus we seem not to object in the slightest to sacrificing either ourselves or others, because we believe that it is all in the cause of the improvement of humankind and of the world. This explains the paradox of 'progress' demanding sacrifices (Gambaroff et al. 1986). And from a theological point of view it seems that the sacrifice and further 'existence' of Christ is seen as the 'model' for our own alchemical transformation. Christ himself appears as 'Christus lapis' (Jung 1985) as the 'philosopher's stone' for the redemption of humanity.

In the modern world we maintain the illusion of the effectiveness of the so-called philosopher's stone only because pure substances have been mixed not only with other pure substances – as in pre-modern patriarchal alchemy – but have also been combined with living ones, with life itself. Just as in chemistry: as long as the artificial fertilizer is not put into the fields, it will never have any effect; as long as no one uses those machines, they are only heaps of junk; and the artificially fertilized egg still needs a uterus for the embryo to develop. Without impure life there is still no outcome at all. This is of course why so much money is being spent on research in such areas as plant growth without earth, self-producing and self-maintaining systems – so-called artificial intelligence – as well as artificial birth machines. In the meantime it has become obvious that patriarchal 'new life' (beyond a simple cell combination!) – if any 'new' life should ever come into being in this way – is not a better form of life at all, but a weak, susceptible, monotonous, dependent, primitive, reduced form of life, life without spirit/mind, machine-'life', life without a future – not to mention the ecological destruction which generally seems to go hand in hand with it (see Chargaff 1988; Dahl 1989; Shiva 1992).

Paradoxically, this is becoming even more apparent in the next phase of alchemy, the combination of different, but living substances in genetic engineering and all sorts of bio-technology (called 'algeny' by Rifkin 1983). This is essentially because artificial life can in a way 'be made', but it would never be able to 'replace' born life. (And, maybe, they don't even want it!)

Alchemy without matter? The power of money to force all of life into prostitution and to present this perversion as a quasi-religious act makes our system out to be a kind of Christian pimping, or, in other words, reveals procuring to be the real kernel of the patriarchal economic system, especially of capitalism.

Where money is concerned, the alchemical procedure still appears to be a success. It is no accident that the word for a return on money is 'interest'. The money which comes to exist in the alchemical process of the modern economic system, capitalist money, appears to 'give birth' to more money. Money has children and grandchildren, i.e. simple interest and compound interest. It really does seem to appear almost out of nowhere, from pure abstraction. In the earlier stages of alchemy, as long as someone had to work in order to produce simple and compound interest, this was not the case. However, we can observe how interest is meanwhile being paid out on future, not yet accomplished, supposedly potential, production and services whose eventual realization we are required simply to believe in. Interest thus is actually coming out of a temporary nothing, a not-yet, it is a mortgage on the future which will soon be due for payment. Today, in the sphere of floating speculation – i.e. faith – capital is no longer directly connected to actual production processes (see Kennedy 1990). The material alchemical transformation process of economics is in a certain sense no longer applicable, and is being temporarily replaced by an invisible, 'non-material' alchemy, alchemy without matter (see Werlhof 1997). It is alchemy none the less, although on a 'purely spiritual', truly 'theological' level. For, certainly, the images of the goose who laid the golden egg, or of water transformed into wine, without anyone lifting a finger, amazingly still do not appear to arouse people's doubts. On the contrary, alchemy appears to have finally reached its goal of creating a world in which milk and honey flow (for no reason); as if the self-creating original nature has finally been replaced by 'pure' money, the 'pure' spirit, the one-and-all God. It even appears as if the 'postmodern' economic system has only need of imaginary services in order finally to arrive at the philosopher's stone, which itself in the end seems to be made of only 'pure thought'. What progress for alchemy! Thought alone is now all that is needed. This is then seen as 'intellectual development'. And is not non-substantial alchemy the best proof that God, the Creator, patriarchy, really exist? And is alchemy without matter not the best proof that producing Nothing is no problem at all but, on the contrary, even that the Nothing is God himself? One simply assumes that it will all work out in the end, for everyone, and for ever. What a rude awakening is in store for the true believers!

The Necessary Failure of the 'Alchemical System'

We can say that in contrast to former times alchemy as a method of thinking and acting has been expanded to all spheres of society, all sorts of production processes and all people living under these conditions. Therefore it is justified to speak of the existence of an alchemical system today. Alchemy has progressed by means of generalization and 'globalization' (see Werlhof 2000b). Its methods of usurpation/negation, mortification/ degradation, abstraction/isolation, perversion/'improvement', construc-tion/production and speculation/nihilism seem to leave us without any alternative. After 5000 years of the alchemical implementation of the patriarchal project, we feel incapable of imagining that the world could function in any other way.

Meanwhile, it is finally becoming obvious that the project of constructing patriarchy, of creating the *pater arché*, is a true catastrophe. Our belief in alchemy is being shaken as we come to realize that countless human and non-human beings are being pushed towards their destruction and driven to extinction. Alchemy has never produced a better form of life, nor has it come up with anything with which to replace the original form. The construction of patriarchy as an empirical fact rather than as a Utopia has still not succeeded and is further from success than ever. And it cannot succeed, because the world is being ruined in the process. There is nothing after the devastation. From nothing comes nothing. The 'scarcity', the waste, the loss of faith are all pointing to this fact. It makes room for a different, 'dissident' world view, the scope of which is no longer anthropocentric (androcentric). The 'Goddess comes back', the women say, but only to a world in which not only 'holy water' is holy, but all water.

The first decisive step beyond the nihilistic-tautological forms of patriarchal thinking and doing would therefore be finally to stop believing that the destruction of the earth is not such a terrible thing after all, or will even lead to our redemption from nature; it is believed that the world will be followed by something better, a 'post-natural', 'post-worldly' paradise.

Seen world-wide, I think that we are already approaching the 'critical mass' needed to rid ourselves of the alchemical belief in deadly miracles. Let us restore our view of the world by putting our feet back on the earth and turning our reality rightside-up again. Let us begin to celebrate the liberation of our earth, our bodies, our minds and our souls from the destructive faith in patriarchy, alchemy and corporate globalization!

Translated by Danny Lewis (based on Werlhof 1997)

References

Bachofen, J. J. (1978) *Das Mutterrecht*, Frankfurt: Suhrkamp.

Bammé, A. et al. (eds) (1983) *Maschinen-Menschen, Mensch-Maschinen, Grundrisse einer sozialen Beziehung*, Reinbek: Rowohlt.

Beiträge zur feministischen Theorie und Praxis (1985), Geld oder Leben?, 15/16.

Bergfleth, G. (1992) 'Perspektiven der Antiökonomie', *Niemandsland. Zeitschrift zwischen den Kulturen*, 4, 10/11 (Tugendterror), pp. 251–9.

Bergmann, A. L. (1992) *Die verhütete Sexualität, Die Anfänge der modernen Geburtenkontrolle*, Hamburg: Aufbau.

Biedermann, H. (1991) *Lexikon der Magischen Künste. Die Welt der Magie seit der Spätantike*, Munich: Heyne.

Binswanger, H. Ch. (1985) *Geld und Magie*, Stuttgart: Weitbrecht.

Bloch, E (1967) *Das Prinzip Hoffnung*, Frankfurt: Suhrkamp.

Böhme, H. (1988) *Natur und Subjekt*, Frankfurt: Suhrkamp.

Bologne, J.-C. (1995) *Von der Fackel zum Scheiterhaufen. Magie und Aberglauben im Mittelalter*, Solothurn and Düsseldorf: Walter.

Braun, C. von (1990) *NichtIch, Logos-Lüge-Libido*, Frankfurt: Neue Kritik.

Brown, L. and E. Ayres (1998) *The World Watch Reader on Global Environmental Issues*, New York and London: W. W. Norton.

Butler, J. (1991) *Das Unbehagen der Geschlechter*, Frankfurt: Suhrkamp.

Canetti, E. (1986) *Masse und Macht*, Frankfurt: Fischer.

Chargaff, E. (1988) *Unbegreifliches Geheimnis, Wissenschaft als Kampf für und gegen die Natur*, Stuttgart: Klett-Cotta.

Chossudovsky, M. (1996) *The Globalization of Poverty*, London: Zed Books.

Colburn, Th. et al. (1996) *Our Stolen Future*, London: Abacus.

Dahl, J. (1989) *Die Verwegenheit der Ahnungslosen. Über Gentechnik und andere schwarze Löcher des Fortschritts*, Stuttgart: Klett-Cotta.

Daly, M. (1970) *Gyn/Ökologie*, Munich: Frauenoffensive.

Deschner, K.-H. (1992) *Das Kreuz mit der Kirche: Eine Sexualgeschichte des Christentums*, Munich: Heyne.

— (1994) *Kriminalgeschichte des Christentums*, 1–4, Reinbek: Rowohlt.

Dressen, W. (1982) *Die pädagogische Maschine. Zur Geschichte des industrialisierten Bewußtseins in Deutschland*, Frankfurt, Berlin and Vienna: Ullstein.

Drewermann, E. (1991) *Der tödliche Fortschritt. Von der Zerstörung der Erde und des Menschen im Erbe des Christentums*, Freiburg: Herder.

Duden, B. (1991) *Der Frauenleib als öffentlicher Ort. Vom Mißbrauch des Begriffs Leben*, Hamburg and Zurich: Luchterhand.

Easlea, B. (1986) *Die Väter der Vernichtung. Männlichkeit, Naturwissenschaftler und der nukleare Ruestungswettlauf*, Reinbek: Rowohlt.

Eisler, R. (1993) *Kelch und Schwert. Von der Herrschaft zur Partnerschaft. Männliches und weibliches Prinzip in der Geschichte*, Munich: Frauenoffensive.

Eliade, M. (1980) *Schmiede und Alchemisten*, Stuttgart: Klett-Cotta.

Ernst, U. M. (1997) *Die Schrift der Göttin*, in U. M. Ernst et al. (eds), *Ökonomie (M)macht Angst*, Frankfurt, New York and Paris: Peter Lang, pp. 147–74.

Ernst, W. W. (1986) *Legitimationswandel und Revolution, Studien zur neuzeitlichen Entwicklung und Rechtfertigung politischer Gewalt* (esp. Introduction), Berlin: Duncker & Humblodt.

— (1993) 'Zu einer Phänomenologie von "Fest-Setzung" und "Gegen-Stand"'. in H. Reinaltter (ed.) (1993) *Vernetztes Denken – Gemeinsames Handeln. Interdisziplinarität in Theorie und Praxis*, Thaur, Vienna and Munich: Kulturverlag, pp. 195–207.

— (1996) 'Metapsychologie und "egologisches Subjekt"', in C. von Werlof (ed.), *Herren-Los. Herrschaft-Erkenntnis-Lebensform*, Frankfurt etc: Peter Lang, pp. 80–110.

Firestone, S. (1975) *Frauenbefreiung und sexuelle Revolution*, Frankfurt: Fischer.

Foucault, M. (1977) *Überwachen und Strafen, Die Geburt des Gefängnisses*, Frankfurt: Suhrkamp.

Freud, S. (1974) *Der Mann Moses und die monotheistische Religion: 3 Abhandlungen* [1939], in *Fragen der Gesellschaft – Ursprünge der Religion*, Frankfurt: Fischer, pp. 455–581.

Gambaroff, M. et al. (1986) *Tschernobyl hat unser Leben verändert. Vom Ausstieg der Frauen*, Reinbek: Rowohlt.

Gebelein, H. (1996) *Alchemie. Die Magie des Stofflichen*, Munich: Diederichs.

George, S. (1980) *Wie die anderen sterben. Die wahren Ursachen des Welthungers*, Berlin: Rotbuch.

Girard, R. (1992) *Das Heilige und die Gewalt*, Frankfurt: Fischer.

Godelier, M. (1987) *Die Produktion der Großen Männer*, Frankfurt: Campus.

Göttner-Abendroth, H. (1988) *Das Matriarchat I: Geschichte seiner Erforschung*, Stuttgart, Berlin and Cologne: Klett-Cotta.

Gronemeyer, M. (1988) *Die Macht der Bedürfnisse*, Reinbek: Rowohlt.

Hammer, S. (1997) *Humankapital. Bildung zwischen Herrschaftswahn und Schöpfungsillusion*, Frankfurt, Paris and New York: Peter Lang.

Haraway, D. (1995) *Die Neuerfindung der Natur. Primaten, Cyborgs und Frauen*, Frankfurt and New York: Campus.

Hirschman, A. O. (1987) *Leidenschaften und Interessen, Politische Begründungen des Kapitalismus vor seinem Sieg*, Frankfurt: Suhrkamp.

Hobbes, Th. (1984) *Leviathan oder Stoff, Form und Gewalt eines kirchlichen und bürgerlichen Staats,* ed. Iring Fetscher, Frankfurt: Suhrkamp.

Horkheimer M. and Th. W. Adorno (1988) *Dialektik der Aufklärung, Philosophische Fragmente*, Frankfurt: Fischer.

Hunke, S. (1987) *Glauben und Wissen. Die Einheit europaeischer Religion und Naturwissenschaft*, Hildesheim: Olms.

Illich, I. (1982) *Vom Recht auf Gemeinheit*, Reinbek: Rowohlt.

— (1983) *Gender*, New York: Pantheon.

Imfeld, A. (1985) *Hunger und Hilfe*, Zurich: Rotpunkt.

Jung, C. G. (1985) *Erlösungsvorstellungen in der Alchemie*, Solothurn and Düsseldorf: Walter.

Kennedy, M. (1990) *Geld ohne Zinsen und Inflation*, Steyerberg: Permakultur.

Kimmerle, G. (1980) *Hexendämmerung. Zur kopernikanischen Wende der Hexendeutung*, Tubingen: Konkursbuch.

Kippenberg, H. G. (1991) *Die vorderasiatischen Erlösungsreligionen in ihrem Zusammenhang mit der antiken Stadtherrschaft*, Frankfurt: Suhrkamp.

Klöss, E. (1985) *Die Herren der Welt. Die Entstehung des Kolonialismus in Europa*, Cologne: Kiepenheuer & Witsch.

Krieg, P. (1980) Filmscript, *Septemberweizen*, Freiburg.

Kutschmann, W. (1986) *Der Naturwissenschaftler und sein Körper*, Frankfurt: Suhrkamp.

Lerner, G. (1991) *Die Entstehung des Patriarchats*, Frankfurt and New York: Campus.

Locke, J. (1970) *Gedanken über Erziehung*, Stuttgart: Reclam.

Marx, K. (1974) 'Der Fetischcharakter der Ware und sein Geheimnis', in K. Marx *Der Produktionsprozeß des Kapitals (Das Kapital Band I)*, in Marx/Engels-Werke, 23, Berlin: Dietz, pp. 85–98.

Meier-Seethaler, C. (1992) *Ursprünge und Befreiungen, Die sexistischen Wurzeln der Kultur*, Frankfurt: Fischer.

Merchant, C. (1987) *Der Tod der Natur, Ökologie, Frauen und neuzeitliche Naturwissenschaft*, Munich: Beck.

Mességué, M. (1989) *Das Gesetz der Natur*, Frankfurt and Berlin: Ullstein.

Mies, M. (1986) *Patriarchy and Accumulation on a World Scale: Women in the International Division of Labour*, London: Zed Books.

Mies, M., V. Bennholdt-Thomsen and C. von Werlhof (1987) *Women: The Last Colony*, London: Zed Books.

Mies, M. and V. Shiva (1993) *Ecofeminism*, London: Zed Books.

Mies, M. and C. von Werlhof (eds) (1999) *Lizenz zum Plündern. Das Multilaterale Abkommen über Investitionen – MAI – Globalisierung der Konzernherrschaft – und was wir dagegen tun können*, Hamburg: Rotbuch EVA.

Mühlmann, W. E. (1984) *Die Metamorphose der Frau, Weiblicher Schamanismus und Dichtung*, Berlin: Dietrich Reimer.

Mumford, L. (1977) *Mythos der Maschine*, Frankfurt: Fischer.

Paczensky, G. von (1970) *Die Weißen kommen. Die wahre Geschichte des Kolonialismus*, Hamburg: Hoffman & Campe.

Paracelsus (1990) *Die Geheimnisse, Ein Lesebuch aus seinen Schriften*, ed. W.-E. Peuckert, Munich: Knaur.

Plato (1962) *Politeia*, in Werke, III, Reinbek: Rowohlt.

— *Das Trinkgelage. Über den Eros*, Frankfurt: Suhrkamp.

Rifkin, J. (1983) *Algeny*, New York: Viking.

Sachs, W. (ed.) (1993) *Wie im Westen so auf Erden*, Reinbek: Rowohlt.

Schütz-Buenaventura, I. (1996) 'Die Vergesellschaftung des destruktiven Konstruktivismus', in C. von Werlhof et al. (eds), *Herren-Los*, Frankfurt, Paris and New York: Peter Lang, pp. 270–301.

— (2000) *Globalismus contra Existentia. Das Recht des ursprünglich Realen vor dem Machtanspruch der Bewußtseinsphilosophie*, Vienna: Passagen.

Schubart, W. (1989) *Religion und Eros*, Munich: C. H. Beck.

Schumpeter, J. A. (1962) *Capitalism, Socialism, and Democracy*, New York: Harper.

Shiva, V. (1989) *Das Geschlecht des Lebens. Frauen, Ökologie und Dritte Welt*, Berlin: Rotbuch.

Shiva, V. (1992) *Monocultures of the Mind*, London: Zed Books.

Sloterdijk, P. (1983) *Kritik der zynischen Vernunft*, Frankfurt: Suhrkamp.

Sloterdijk, P. and T. Macho (1991) *Weltrevolution der Seele, ein Lese- und Arbeitsbuch zur Gnosis von der Spätantike bis zur Gegenwart*, 2 vols, Gütersloh: Artemis und Winkler.

Smith, A. (1823) *Eine Untersuchung über Natur und Wesen des Volkswohlstandes* (An Inquiry into the Nature and Causes of the Wealth of Nations [1776]), Jena.

Tazi-Preve, I. (1992) *Der Mord an der Mutter*, Innsbruck, Diplomarbeit.

Theweleit, K. (1977) *Männerphantasien*, Vol. 1, Frankfurt: Roter Stern.

Todorov, T. (1980) *Das Problem des Anderen*, Frankfurt: Suhrkamp.

Treusch-Dieter, G. (1990) *Von der sexuellen Rebellion zur Gen- und Reproduktionstechnologie*, Tubingen: Konkursbuch.

Trube-Becker, E. (1987) 'Sexuelle Misshandlung von Kindern', in H. Faessler (ed.), *Das Tabu der Gewalt*, Innsbruck: Eigenverlag, pp. 186–94.

Ullrich, O. (1980) *Weltniveau*, Berlin: Rotbuch.

Wallerstein, I. (1974) *The Modern World System I: Capitalist Agriculture and the Origins of the European World-Economy in the Sixteenth Century*, New York: Academic Press.

— (1980) *The Modern World-System II: Mercantilism and the Consolidation of the European World-Economy, 1600–1750*, New York: Academic Press.

— (1986) *Dad moderne Weltsystem: Kapitalistische Landwirtschaft und sie Entstehung der europäischen Weltwirtschaft im 16. Jahrhundert*, Frankfurt: Syndikat.

Wallerstein, I. (1989) *The Modern World-System III: The Second Era of Great Expansion of the Capitalist World-Economy, 1730–1840s*, New York: Academic Press.

Weber, M. (1993) *Die protestantische Ethik und der 'Geist' des Kapitalismus*, Bodenheim: Athenäum-Hain-Haustein.

Weiler, G. (1991) *Der enteignete Mythos, Eine feministische Revision der Archetypenlehre C. G. Jungs und Erich Neumanns*, Frankfurt: Campus.

— (1993) *Eros ist stärker als Gewalt. Eine feministische Anthropologie I*, Frankfurt: Campus.

Weizenbaum, J. (1978) *Die Macht der Computer und die Ohnmacht der Vernunft*, Frankfurt: Suhrkamp.

Werlhof, C. von (1983) 'Zum Natur- und Gesellschaftsbegriff im Kapitalismus', in M. Mies et al., *Frauen, die letzte Kolonie*, Reinbek: Rowohlt, pp. 138–61.

— (1988) 'On the Concept of Nature and Society in Capitalism', in M. Mies et al. (eds), *Women: the Last Colony*, London: Zed Books, pp. 96–112.

— (1996) 'Das Rechtssystem und der Muttermord', in C. von Werlhof *Mutter-Los*, Munich: Frauenoffensive.

— (1997) 'Ökonomie, die praktische Seite der Religion. Wirtschaft als Gottesbeweis und die Methode der Alchemie', in U. M. Ernst et al. (eds), *Ökonomie (M)macht Angst*, Frankfurt, Paris and New York: Peter Lang 1997, pp. 95–121.

— (2000a) 'Patriarchat als "Alchemistisches System". Die (Z) ErSetzung *des* Lebendigen', in M. Wolf (ed.), *Optimierung und Zerstörung. Intertheoretische Analysen zum menschlich-Lebendigen*, Innsbruck: STUDIA Universitätsverlag, pp. 13–31.

— (2000b) '"Globalization" and the "Permanent" Process of "Primitive Accumulation": The Example of the MAI, the Multilateral Agreement on Investment', in G. Arrighi and W. L. Goldfrank (eds), *Festschrift for Immanuel Wallerstein, Part II, Journal of World-Systems Research*, VI, 3, Fall/Winter.

Werlhof, C. von, A. Schweighofer and W. Ernst (eds) (1996) *Herren-Los, Herrschaft-Erkenntnis-Lebensform*, Frankfurt, Paris and New York: Peter Lang.

Wolf, D. (1994) *Was war vor den Pharaonen? Die Entdeckung der Urmütter Ägyptens*, Zürich: Kreuz.

Worms, A. von (1988) *Das Buch der wahren Praktiken in der göttlichen Magie*, ed. Jürg von Ins, Munich: Diederichs.

3

Sustainable Development: Rescue Operation for a Dying Illusion

Saral Sarkar

Development, or economic growth, has since long been seen as the key element in the resolution of two old conflicts: that between the rich and the poor in every society and that between the nations of the North and the South. In the late 1960s, however, some doubts arose. The contradiction between industrial economy and ecology could no longer be overlooked. Nevertheless, even after Meadows et al. (1972) had pointed out the limits to growth, governments throughout the world continued with the same economic policies, while establishment economists brought forward many arguments to deny both the existence of any limits to growth and any contradiction between economy and ecology. But since about the mid-1980s, most establishment economists, politicians and political thinkers have been compelled to concede that there is a problem; it has become impossible for them to ignore global ecological degradation any longer. Some among them have realized that they cannot carry on as before, but they are not prepared to change course substantially, and they cannot, for reasons I shall elaborate below. So they invented a new term; they are no longer preaching development and growth, pure and simple. They are now preaching sustainable development or sustainable growth.

Three Illusions

I am not absolutely sure that they are consciously deceiving people; perhaps they are only suffering from delusions. The result, though, is the same. First, in the early phase of the controversy, some economists denied that there was any resource problem, even in respect to non-renewable resources. Professor Wilfred Beckerman (1972), then head of the department of economics at the University of Oxford, very confidently asserted that there were enough resources in the world to sustain continued economic growth for the next 100 million years (see also Simon and Kahn 1984).

Others believed that all rare materials could be substituted by more abundantly available materials such as iron and aluminium. Some even believed that we could produce plastics by processing carbon dioxide in the air (Daublebski 1973). As recently as 1993, the president of the Japanese Council of Sciences, Professor Jero Kondo, suggested that, in order to solve the problem of global warming, both the surplus carbon dioxide in the air and the carbon dioxide escaping through chimneys should be captured by means of solar energy and converted into useful industrial chemicals! Such is the degree of delusion that has infected the discourse on sustainable development (Schmidt-Bleek 1993: 80).

This primitive form of the illusion is no longer popular. Since about the mid-1980s, some protagonists of sustainable development have believed that, thanks to developments in science and technology, economic growth can continue in spite of drastic reductions in resource consumption (WCED 1987) or that at least the present-day standard of living in the industrial societies can be more or less maintained through 'a new model of prosperity' (Weizsäcker 1994; Schmidt-Bleek 1993; Friends of the Earth Netherlands 1992).

Second, again on the basis of naive faith in the development of science and technology, most of them have believed that the pollution problem can be solved if only we devote sufficient resources to this task. And third, all of them believe that their goal can be achieved within the framework of a capitalist market economy.

The Reality

I am one of the small number of sceptics. In this section, I shall examine the above assertions and hopes and try to explain why I think that they, and their more sophisticated variations, are illusions.

The issue of resources   Let us ignore people like Beckerman, Simon and Kahn, who do not even feel it necessary to advocate sustainable development. But even some of those who demand that resource consumption should be drastically reduced say the main problem is not that of resources shortage, at least not in the foreseeable future, but that of environmental degradation (e.g. Schmidt-Bleek 1993: 48). For instance, some assert that shortage of energy is not the problem; the real problem is global warming due to too much CO_2 in the atmosphere. This is a gross error. At present there is no shortage of resources for Western Europeans and North Americans, so they think there is no resource problem. But in other countries of the world, especially in the countries of the South, resource shortage – e.g. availability of arable land and fresh water – is already a big problem. And there is shortage of petrol even in Nigeria, a country that exports oil, so much so that large numbers of Nigerians bore holes in pipelines to steal a few buckets of the fuel and risk their lives in the process. Because the poor of the world do not have the money to go to the world resources markets as purchasers, most economists are not aware of the problem.

Nevertheless, the proponents of sustainable development have realized that general environmental degradation is proportional to overall resource consumption. So they think, to protect the environment, it is necessary to reduce resource consumption drastically. And they think that is possible without having to sacrifice economic growth or the western standard of living. In 1987, the authors of the Brundtland Report claimed to have noted 'favourable trends' that allegedly proved that 'future patterns of agriculture and forestry development, energy use, industrialization, and human settlements can be made far less material-intensive, and hence both more economically and environmentally efficient' (WCED 1987: 89–90). In Chapter 8, entitled 'Industry: Producing More With Less', it cites some supporting data from the 1960s to the middle of the 1980s. Since the beginning of the 1980s, we have been hearing of an 'efficiency revolution' that is expected to increase the resource productivity of industrial economies through technological progress. More recently, in their book entitled *Factor Four – Doubling Wealth, Halving Resource Use*, Weizsäcker et al. (1997) gave many examples of particular products to show that such an efficiency revolution has already begun.

Other researchers, however, who have focused on *macro-economic data* instead, have noted a contrary trend. F. E. Trainer (1985: 211) cites comparative data from the post-war period till the end of the 1970s to prove just the opposite; namely, that returns to technology in the form of resource productivity are in general going down. Dennis Meadows corroborated this in 1998 when he said in an interview: 'We already have to spend more and more capital to get access to the raw materials' (*Die Zeit*, 19 February 1998). For example, between 1963 and 1977, annual investment in the US mining industry increased by 130 per cent (in constant dollars), but output measured by tonnage increased only by 38 per cent (Trainer 1985: 51). In industrialized agriculture, more and more fertilizer and non-renewable energy are necessary to produce the same quantity of grain. In 1950, the use of one additional tonne of fertilizer yielded an average of 14.8 additional tonnes of grain, but in 1980 this additional grain yield fell to only 5.8 tonnes (Brown 1984: 179). More recently, Fred Luks (1997) calculated that if, in the industrial countries, resource consumption in the next fifty years is to go down by a factor of 10, as demanded by Schmidt-Bleek (1993) and many others (e.g. Loske et al. 1998), and the economy is to grow simultaneously at the rate of 2 per cent annually, then resource productivity in this period must rise by a factor of 27. How realistic is that?

Explaining the economic difficulties of the former Soviet Union, Abel Aganbegyan, then chief economic adviser to Gorbachev, wrote in 1988 that:

> In the 1971–75 period, the volume of output of the mining industry increased by 25% but only by 8% in 1981–85. This decline in growth […] was mainly connected with the worsening of the geological and economic conditions of mining […] the Soviet Union is rapidly exhausting the most accessible of its natural resources […] it is necessary to dig deeper, to discover new deposits and to transfer to less favourable fields. The fuel and raw material base in the inhabited regions […] is already unable to meet our requirements […] It is necessary […] to construct transport lines, to create new towns and develop territories and attract population there. (Aganbegyan 1988: 8)

Actually, this is economic common sense. No doubt, stopping wastage alone increases resource productivity. And occasional ingenious inventions and innovations can also raise it in some particular technologies. But normally, sooner or later, all technologies attain their optimum. Thereafter, the law of diminishing returns comes into operation. We may invest as much as we want in research and development, but we shall never have a car engine that does not need any fuel. We cannot wish away the laws of physics, chemistry and biology.

In the past, technological progress was driven by two 'motors': the intellect and abundant use of resources, especially of fossil fuels. A pneumatic hammer, for example, which is far superior to an ordinary hammer in terms of rate of work, embodies not only some high-class inventions, it also requires many more resources for its production and operation than the latter. But the theory of sustainable development stipulates that total resource consumption in the advanced industrial societies be drastically reduced; i.e. doing without the second car, so to speak. Of course, much can be achieved with only one car. Mainly through the work of intellect, the computer has become much smaller and can process more data than before. Yet, to produce a small personal computer, 15–19 tons of material have to be processed (Malley 1996). Moreover, one cannot live in a computer and eat data.

A few isolated successes can delude us about the overall situation. A motorcar today needs less petrol per kilometre than it did, say, fifteen years ago. But the US oil industry today must consume more energy and material to extract and transport Alaskan oil than it had to do for Pennsylvanian oil. As a result, its energy input–output ratio is worsening.

Let us look at another aspect of so-called energy-efficient cars. VW corporation has developed a car that consumes only 3 litres of petrol per 100 km. It has been made lighter by using aluminium and magnesium. For producing these light metals, much more energy and materials have to be consumed than for producing steel. 'All people are only staring at the fuel consumption and are not noticing at all how they are causing the gigantic merry-go-round of raw materials consumption to rotate ever faster [...] That simply will not work' (Schmidt-Bleek quoted in Wille 1999).

Such people, however, notice car prices, which reflect *inter alia* energy and raw materials consumption in the production process. Common to all highly energy-efficient car models is that they are much costlier than comparable conventional models (Geissler 1999; Petersen and Diaz-Bone 1998). On the hypercar model of Amory Lovins, Geissler writes: 'The revolutionary hypercar model – an ultra-light car with a small electro-motor attached to each wheel – which is claimed to need just 1 litre of petrol per 100 km, is still like a mirage' (Geissler 1999). And Greenpeace explains why it considers such concepts to be totally illusory. Commenting on a similar dream of VW chief Piech, Greenpeace traffic expert Günter Hubmann says: 'At the present level of technology, such an ideal car would cost more than 100,000 deutschmarks (DM)' (*Kölnische Rundschau*, 22 September 2000).

Limits to recycling   There are also limits to recycling. Of course, metals can, in many cases, be recycled easily, but they are often used in such a dissipative way (e.g. zinc in paint) that no recycling is possible. In many other cases, recycling is possible but requires too much energy and materials consumption to be economic. On an average, according to the authors of a report to the Club of Rome, about 70 per cent of the annual production of metals is lost after one use. Of the 30 per cent that are recycled, only 0.1 per cent remain in use after ten 'life cycles' (Gabor et al. 1976: 144–5). Of course, the recycling rate can be improved through technological development and rising prices, but recycling can only postpone the problem, not solve it.

The myth of the information society and the service society   We often hear researchers say that in the advanced industrial societies economic growth has been uncoupled from growth in resource consumption. Indeed, in the early 1980s it was pointed out in support of the above view that in the USA 60 per cent of employed people only processed information in some form or other (Naisbitt 1982: 14). All such statistics are supposed to prove that sustainable growth is possible. Apart from the fact that the concept 'GNP' is highly problematic, because fictitious transactions, and even disasters and the money spent to repair the damage are included in it, we should not overlook the fact that the old high-energy and raw-materials-consuming branches of the economy can be (and are in fact being) shifted away from the advanced industrial countries to developing or East European countries. The advanced industrial economies can then grow more through sectors such as banking, insurance, data-processing, research and development, selling and licensing of patents than, say, through mining and steel production. But it is a zero-sum game. This way, of course, their balance (ratio of energy and raw materials input to GNP) may look better, but the balance of the world economy remains unchanged. The same applies to environmental degradation.

What is more, if we cease to stare only at the production side and also consider the consumption side, the balance of the highly developed economies would appear very bad. For one unit of need satisfaction (say, quenching thirst), a data-processing US citizen consumes many times more resources (Coca-Cola in a can) than an average citizen of India (a glass of water from the tap). This has also been realized by the authors of the Brundtland Report. They write: 'even the most industrially advanced economies still depend on a continued supply of basic manufactured goods. Whether made domestically or imported, their production will continue to require large amounts of raw materials and energy' (WCED 1987: 217).

Environmental protection through technological fixes The realization that resource consumption must be drastically cut in order to protect the environment is quite recent and not very widespread. Most people, even many environmentalists, do not see the connection. They believe what is needed to protect the environment is simply to devote a larger portion of the expected and normally growing GNP to this task, to invest more in conventional environmental technologies. The more modern among them demand that large amounts of money be invested in research into renewable resources, which are assumed to be totally clean, and that more money be spent on developing and promoting such resources and the relevant technologies. They believe that renewable resources can fully replace all the non-renewables we consume today. I shall examine the latter belief in the next section. Here I point out the fallacies of the former.

It is conceivable that in the initial phase of a new technology (or a new branch of industry), environmental impact per unit of production can be reduced through its further development – through new ideas and without more expenditure of resources. But as in the case of resource consumption per unit of production, also in regard to environmental impact, at some point the optimum will be reached and the technology will attain maturity. After that, increases in production will be accompanied by proportional or even over-proportional increases in environmental degradation.

The conventional technological environmental protection policy is not oriented towards the overall ecological context. It is limited to selective and peripheral interventions, which can provide only short- or middle-term relief in respect of particular problems. In most cases, they only shift the problem. Pollutants are shifted from the medium air into the media water and ground or the other way round. Or they are thinly distributed over a large area, e.g. through very high chimneys. Or they are diluted by adding fresh air or water. Or they are only intercepted, collected and dumped somewhere, often in Third World and Eastern European countries. In the long run, and from a global standpoint, such 'successes' are of no use. This is common knowledge among those who are in charge of executing this policy. For example, in 1976, the then president of the West German Federal Bureau of Environment, von Lersner, characterized his job as 'a Sisyphean task'. He said: 'By the time we have brought one pollutant under control, another one has become a problem' (*Der Spiegel*, 40, 1976, p. 62).

The filters and other equipment used in technological fixes for environmental protection are all industrial goods. Their manufacture and operation require, as with all industrial products, considerable expenditure of resources. That also causes pollution (and resource depletion), only somewhere else and of some other kind. For instance, sulphur dioxide emissions from a thermal power plant can be largely eliminated, but that requires a chemical plant that consumes 3 per cent of the production of the power plant. That would mean that more coal would have to be burnt which would entail more carbon dioxide emission. Someone who has understood this would also realize that the recent fashionable talk about an emission-free car driven by hydrogen fuel cells is just a bluff. The production of both hydrogen and fuel cells generates a lot of polluting emissions, only somewhere else. Moreover, all filters and other equipment have a limited lifespan. They must be replaced every ten, fifteen or twenty years. Technological environmental protection thus becomes a regular industry, causing more resource depletion and more pollution.

The Search for Renewable Resources

Many environmentalists believe that renewable resources are potentially so abundant that all the current consumption needs of all humanity could be easily fulfilled. Hermann Scheer, president of Eurosolar, and a famous apostle of a 'solar world economy' writes: 'For an unimaginable length of time the sun will be bestowing its energy on humans, animals and plants. And that in such a prodigal quantity that it would be able to meet the most sumptuous energy needs of even drastically growing populations of humans, animals, and plants' (Scheer 1999: 66).

Scheer and thousands of solar energy enthusiasts derive this hope from the fact that every day the sun supplies the earth with 15,000 times as much energy as the total daily commercial energy consumption of the human population at present. Under the term 'solar energy' they subsume all sources of energy except the fossil and nuclear ones: the energy of sunshine, wind energy, energy of falling water, energy from biomass etc. Some of them believe that from biomass we could get raw materials for almost everything: houses, cars, every kind of chemical, and so on. And all such materials could finally be composted (Alt 1993: 6–8).

Now, if these are the facts, why have we not yet been able to solve all the problems of humanity? After all, generating electricity by photovoltaic technology was invented as early as in 1954, biomass energy has been used since time immemorial, wind energy has been harnessed for a few thousand years, and the energy of flowing water for many centuries. It is therefore necessary to examine these beliefs.

If we burn wood to get energy or use only wood for building a house, we can be sure we are using a non-polluting resource. But when we convert biomass into electricity or biodiesel, we use modern industrial equipment, the manufacture and use of which need non-renewable resources and cause environmental degradation. The same is the case when we use wind energy or sunshine to produce electricity.

So far as the quantity is concerned, it is one thing to know that sunshine is an abundant *source* of energy, and it is another thing to make it *available* in the desired forms, namely electricity and liquid fuel. So far, all efforts to make solar electricity cheap enough to replace electricity from coal and uranium have failed. The production cost of electricity from coal in central Europe is DM 0.08 per kilowatt-hour (kWh). Statements on the production cost of 1 kWh photovoltaic electricity in central Europe vary between DM 1.50 and DM 2.00. That is roughly twenty times the figure for coal-based electricity. If this exorbitantly costly solar electricity is used to produce hydrogen from water and then to liquefy it, how much will liquid hydrogen, supposedly the fuel for the cars and aeroplanes of the future, cost?

It is not just a question of price. Idealists may be willing to pay a higher price to protect the environment. And others may be prepared to pay a high price for energy in order to get a different product, e.g. light in the evening. But if we produce only energy (electricity) by using energy (electricity), then it makes sense only if the output is more than the input, in other words, if the energy balance is positive. It is very doubtful that it is so in the case of photovoltaic technology. The reasons for this scepticism are as follows: at present, the lifespan of a photovoltaic module is at the most twenty years. Statements on the energy pay-back time of this technology – that is, the time a photovoltaic module needs to produce the amount of energy that was needed to manufacture and install it – in central Europe range between 1.2 and 10 years. This incredibly wide range alone gives rise to doubts about the seriousness of the calculations. I have discussed this question in detail elsewhere (Sarkar 1999: 103–10). Here I can only state that I doubt that the photovoltaic enthusiasts have added up all the energy that goes into the production of a photovoltaic module. Nicholas Georgescu-Roegen (1978), who first raised this doubt, wrote that in order to come to the correct energy-input figure we should add up all proportionate expenditures of energy beginning with the energy that was needed to build the factory that produced the excavator that was used to dig up sand that was used to produce silicon, and so on. This is standard procedure when calculating the *money cost* of production of 1 kWh of electricity; but this is not done when calculating the *energy cost* of production of 1 kWh of photovoltaic electricity. That explains the astonishing discrepancy between the high money cost of production of photovoltaic electricity and the alleged low energy pay-back time of a photovoltaic module. If we accept Georgescu-Roegen's demand, then we would be likely to come to the conclusion that the energy balance of photovoltaic or any other technology for the direct use of solar energy is negative. And that is the explanation for the fact that not even a pilot project has until now tried to produce photovoltaic modules by using photovoltaic energy instead of conventional energy.

Georgescu-Roegen differentiated between 'feasible' and 'viable' technologies. Technologies for the direct use of solar energy are feasible, but not viable, because they cannot reproduce themselves. That is, they are parasites; they can exist as long as conventional energy can be used for producing the necessary equipment. To illustrate the point, the first bronze hammer was made by using stone hammers. Thereafter, all bronze hammers were hammered by bronze hammers. Georgescu-Roegen thought the problem might be beyond solution. Because the energy intensity of sunshine on the surface of the earth is very low – and that is a cosmological constant beyond our control – a large area must be covered with collectors (photovoltaic modules or aluminium mirrors) to gather and concentrate this energy. That requires a large expenditure of energy (and materials) and makes the energy balance of such technologies negative. In contrast, fossil fuels are solar energy that has been collected and concentrated by nature over millions of years, which is the explanation for their high energy intensity.

If we accept the claim that the energy pay-back time of photovoltaic technology is seven to ten years, will that – after meeting all or a part of our other needs – leave us with enough surplus energy for running all the industries necessary to reproduce the photovoltaic power plants every twenty years? I doubt very much that it will. It is too easy to say that a technological breakthrough will come soon. It may or may not come. In any case, we cannot place our hopes at present on an elaborate vision of 'a solar world economy' (Scheer 1999) on the basis of that expectation.

So far as wind, water and biomass energy (biomass also as raw material for all purposes) are concerned, they have proved their worth in the past. Of course, in contrast to earlier societies, an industrial society needs electricity and liquid fuel, not just mechanical or heat energy. But the fact that the cost of production of wind and biomass electricity is on average roughly between 0.17 and 0.20 DM (hydroelectricity is much cheaper) indicates that their energy balance is positive. However, it should be borne in mind that, unlike coal and uranium, neither sunshine nor wind with sufficient velocity is always available, and the reservoirs of hydropower projects are not always full. Surpluses available during certain periods cannot be easily stored, and liquid hydrogen is too costly – both in money and energy terms – as a storage medium. As regards biomass, its availability is restricted by the fact that we need land for food production, building houses, roads and so on. And the other species of the planet need land too for their survival.

Taking all these things into consideration (for a detailed discussion see Sarkar 1999: ch. 4), it seems safe to predict that in a future sustainable economy neither energy nor raw materials will be as cheap as they are today, nor will their quantity be as large as the sum total of all the non-renewable and renewable resources is today. The need to reduce resource consumption drastically will be compelling, not only for protecting the environment but also because there simply will not be enough to maintain today's average standard of living for a world population of 8–10 billion. The world economy must therefore shrink. The economies of the advanced industrial countries must shrink, as Schmidt-Bleek demands, by a factor of ten if the peoples of the South are to get a chance to satisfy their basic needs.

Sustainability

The conclusion that must be drawn from the above exposition of the problem is that sustainable development or sustainable growth is not possible, unless we understand by the term 'development' something other than industrialization, economic growth and industrial society. Herman Daly and John B. Cobb Jr differentiate between growth and development: '"Growth" should refer to quantitative expansion in the scale of the physical dimensions of the economic system, while "development" should refer to the qualitative change of a physically nongrowing economic system in dynamic equilibrium with the environment' (Daly and Cobb 1990: 71).

In other words, 'growth' means using up more and more resources, whereas 'development' means to increase the benefits derived from the use of the same quantity of resources. Of course, we can say that the economy should grow, like a tree, up to a certain point and not beyond that. Daly and Cobb write: 'Any physical subsystem of a finite and nongrowing earth must itself also eventually become nongrowing. Therefore growth will become unsustainable eventually and the term "sustainable growth" would then be self-contradictory. But sustainable development does not become self-contradictory' (Daly and Cobb 1990: 72). This is all correct. But then it is better and clearer to speak of a 'steady-state economy', as Daly does in an earlier book (1977), rather than of sustainable development. Or we may speak of a sustainable economy or society.

Since logically and by definition, 'a sustainable society is one that can persist over generations' (Meadows et al. 1992: 209), it is right to conclude that it cannot be based on the industrial economy as we know it, because such an economy relies mainly on the consumption of non-renewable resources, which will be exhausted sooner or later. Logically, the economy of a sustainable society must be based, if not exclusively, then at least mainly, on renewable resources.

All the conditions of sustainability discussed until now mean that at the least the economies of the industrial societies, in order to become sustainable, must shrink to become low-level steady-state economies. Will that be possible within the framework of capitalism? All protagonists of sustainable development believe it will be. I think it is impossible.

Eco-Capitalism Cannot Help us

One of the articles of faith of capitalism is that the welfare of society will result automatically if everybody cares for his/her interest only (Adam Smith). It may have proved up to now to be partially true, that is, in respect of wealth creation, although this wealth did not always increase the welfare of society as a whole. But with respect to the protection of the health of the environment, both the natural and the social, it has had the opposite effect. Moreover, capitalism limits the time horizon of the participants in the economy to their own lifespan. At the most, it allows them to think of the interests of their own children. But the project of creating a sustainable human society demands of us that we care for the interests of all coming generations and of all peoples of the world. This is incompatible with the spirit of capitalism. The aphorism 'What has posterity done for me that I should do something for it?' is not a joke, but the modus operandi of capitalist society.

The most serious defect in capitalism that makes it an enemy of sustainability is its growth dynamics. It is not just that the greedy capitalists *want* to have more and more. Competition *compels* them to want to have and accumulate more and more. Expand or perish is a powerful motto in capitalism. Since no entrepreneur wants to perish, it generates a growth compulsion. Moreover, because of the ever larger investments that they are compelled to make to remain competitive, they must search for and create ever larger markets. In capitalism, all firms can make profits if the economy as a whole grows. This dependence on expansion is so strong that even a growth rate below 2 per cent is perceived as a crisis. But sustainability requires economic shrinking. Capitalists are willing to contribute to environmental protection by producing more and more filters, sewage treatment equipment and so on, but they can never be interested in any form of contraction of the economy.

It is surprising that many theorists of sustainable development believe that economic growth will be possible in spite of a drastic reduction in resource consumption, e.g. Schmidt-Bleek (cf. Wille 1999). I have always wondered how they could believe such an absurdity, but now I think that I have an explanation. They confuse growth in *benefits* with economic growth. Daly and Cobb's differentiation between growth and development quoted above is close to what I mean. If, for example, the quality of the air improves because fewer resources are being consumed, then, of course, benefits to people would grow, they would enjoy the good air and would no longer fall sick as often as before. But capitalists as capitalists are not interested in such growth in benefits to society; they are interested only in increasing their sales so that they can make more profit. Similarly, they are not interested in reducing the social costs of production, but only in reducing their own costs of production. Increase in sales can come either from selling more goods and services or from higher prices. But the system of competition generally does not allow any entrepreneur to make profits by selling less at a higher price. Long-lived and easily repairable products are therefore generally of little interest to entrepreneurs who produce them, although a businessman who uses a product to sell a service, e.g. a taxi owner, might be interested in a long-lived product. Built-in obsolescence is therefore rational policy in capitalism. Schmidt-Bleek speaks of growth in 'service units' that can be had from a 'service-supplying product' (1993: 118). That is exactly what we get from long-lived products that are so disliked by most capitalists.

A policy of drastically reducing resource consumption would, first, entail a massive destruction of capital in the mining industry. Not, of course, the machines, but capital in the financial sense, share value, would be destroyed. That would, second, – through a chain reaction referred to by economists as the multiplier and accelerator effects – lead to a general crisis in the economy. What factories, machines and workers in all other branches of the economy actually do is to transform raw materials and energy into goods and services, which are sold at a profit. If they are now allowed to process only one-fourth or one-tenth of the hitherto processed quantities of raw materials and energy, then a proportional quantity of factory, machine and labour capacity would become superfluous. That would create a great depression.

Competition also results in the compulsion to automate and rationalize production. A firm that does not accept this will perish. That is why it is not possible to solve the problem of unemployment within the framework of a capitalist economy – not even if it is a growing one, let alone if it is compelled to stop growing. Also, the current dismantling of the welfare state is the result of a particular kind of competition: in the context of globalization, national industrial locations compete with each other to woo transnational capital. Without questioning this system, we cannot halt or even object to this 'race to the bottom'. Societal sustainability is impossible within the capitalist system.

Conclusion: Eco-Socialism for Sustainability

Eco-capitalism is, therefore, a misnomer. We cannot have both sustainability and the growth dynamics of capitalism. Whether we try green taxes or pollution certificates or depletion quotas, a shrinking *capitalist* economy would mean a disaster for the whole society. No capitalist can willingly accept a low-level steady-state economy. So the *state* must take up the task and organize the retreat.

It must be a *planned* retreat, otherwise there will be terrible chaos and calamity. In order to be able to plan and organize this retreat, the state must *nationalize* at least all large enterprises. In addition, *equality* in terms of the material conditions of life would be necessary, so that the necessary sacrifices are shared by all and accepted by the majority of the people. All this points to eco-socialism as the only solution to the ecological and social crises humanity faces today (for a detailed discussion of eco-socialism see Sarkar 1999).

References

Aganbegyan, Abel (1988) *The Challenge of Perestroika*, London: Hutchinson.

Alt, Franz (1993) 'Heilung für den blauen Planeten – Schilfgras statt Atom', *Wegweiser*, 4.

Beckerman, Wilfred (1972) 'Economists, Scientists, and Environmental Catastrophes', *Oxford Economic Papers*, November.

Brown, Lester R. (1984) 'Securing Food Supplies', in L. R. Brown et al. (eds), *State of the World 1984*, New York and London: W. W. Norton.

Brown, Lester R., et al. (1984) *State of the World 1984*, New York and London: W. W. Norton.

Daublebski, Peter (1973) 'Technologie und Entwicklung', in H. von Nussbaum (ed.), *Die Zukunft des Wachstums*, Dusseldorf: Bertelsmann Universitätverlag.

Daly, Herman E. (1977) *Steady-State Economics*, San Francisco, CA: W. H. Freeman.

Daly, Herman E. and John B. Cobb Jr (1990) *For the Common Good*, London: Green Print.

Friends of the Earth Netherlands (Maria Buitenkamp et al.) (1992) *Sustainable Netherlands – Action Plan*, Amsterdam.

Gabor, Denis, et al. (1976) *Das Ende der Verschwendung*, Stuttgart: Deutsche Verlags-Anstalt.

Geissler, Max (1999) 'Drei-Liter-Fata-Morgana', *Frankfurter Rundschau*, 5 January.

Georgescu-Roegen, Nicholas (1978) 'Technology Assessment: The Case of the Direct Use of Solar Energy', *Atlantic Economic Journal*, December.

Loske, Rainer, et al. (1998) *Zukunftsfähiges Deutschland*, Basel, Boston and Berlin: Birkhäuser Verlag.

Luks, Fred (1997) 'Der Himmel ist nicht die Grenze', *Frankfurter Rundschau*, 21 January.

Malley, Jürgen (1996) 'Von Ressourcenschonung derzeit keine Spur', *Politische Ökologie*, 49, November–December.

Meadows, Denis, et al. (1972) *The Limits to Growth*, London: Chelsea Green.

Meadows, Donella H., et al. (1992) *Beyond the Limits*, London: Chelsea Green.

Naisbitt, John (1982) *Megatrends – Ten New Directions Transforming Our Lives*, New York: Broadway Books.

Nussbaum, H. von (ed.) (1973) *Die Zukunft des Wachstums*, Düsseldorf: Bertelsmann Universitätsverlag.

Petersen, R. and H. Diaz-Bone (1998) *Das Drei-Liter-Auto*, Basel, Boston and Berlin: Birkhäuser Verlag.

Sarkar, Saral (1999) *Eco-Socialism or Eco-Capitalism? – a Critical Analysis of Humanity's Fundamental Choices*, London: Zed Books.

Scheer, Hermann (1999) *Solare Weltwirtschaft*, Munich: Verlag Antje Kunstmann.

Schmidt-Bleek, Friedrich (1993) *Wieviel Umwelt braucht der Mensch?*, Berlin, Basel and Boston: Birkhäuser Verlag.

Simon, Julian L. and Herman Kahn (1984) *The Resourceful Earth*, Oxford: Basil Blackwell.

Trainer, F. E. (1985) *Abandon Affluence*, London: Zed Books.

WCED (World Commission on Environment and Development) (1987) *Our Common Future*, Oxford: Oxford University Press.

Weizsäcker, Ernst Ulrich von (1994) *Earth Politics*, London: Zed Books.

Weizsäcker, Ernst Ulrich von, Amory B. Lovins and L. Hunter Lovins (1997) *Factor Four – Doubling Wealth, Halving Resource Use*, London: Earthscan.

Wille, Joachim (1999) 'Die Maschinisten des Wachstums', *Frankfurter Rundschau*, 5 October.

Part II

On Resistance to Globalization I:
Fighting the New Colonialism

4

Globalization and Poverty

Vandana Shiva

Recently, I visited Bhatinda in Punjab because of an epidemic of suicide among farmers. Punjab used to be the most prosperous agricultural region in India. Today, every farmer is in debt and despair. Vast stretches of land have become waterlogged desert. And as an old farmer pointed out, even the trees have stopped bearing fruit because the heavy use of pesticides has killed the pollinators – bees and butterflies.

Punjab is not alone in experiencing this ecological and social disaster. Last year I was in Warangal, Andhra Pradesh, where again farmers have been committing suicide. Farmers who traditionally grew pulses, millets and rice had been lured by seed companies into buying hybrid cottonseeds referred to as 'white gold', which were supposed to make them millionaires. Instead they became paupers.

Native seeds have been replaced by new hybrid varieties which cannot be saved and need to be purchased every year at a high cost. Hybrids are also very vulnerable to pest attacks. Spending on pesticides in Warangal has increased 2000 per cent from $2.5 million in the 1980s to $50 million in 1997. Now farmers are consuming the same pesticides as a way of killing themselves so that they can escape permanently from unpayable debt.

The corporations are currently trying to introduce genetically engineered seed which will further increase costs and ecological risks. That is why farmers like Malla Reddy of the Andhra Pradesh Farmers' Union uprooted Monsanto's genetically engineered Bollgard cotton in Warangal.

On 27 March 2000, twenty-five-year-old Betavati Ratan took his life because he could not pay back debts for drilling a deep tube well on his 2-acre farm. The wells are now dry, as are the wells in Gujarat and Rajasthan, where more than 50 million people face a water famine. The drought is not a 'natural disaster'; it is man-made. It is the result of mining of scarce ground water in arid regions to grow thirsty cash crops for exports instead of water-prudent food crops for local needs.

It is experiences such as these which tell me that we are so wrong to be smug about the new global economy. Here I will argue that it is time to stop and think about the impact of globalization on the lives of ordinary people. This is vital if we want to achieve sustainability.

Seattle and the World Trade Organization (WTO) protests last year forced everyone to think again. People often refer to different aspects of sustainable development while taking globalization for granted. For me it is now time radically to re-evaluate what we are doing, for what we are doing to the poor in the name of globalization is brutal and unforgivable. This is particularly evident in India as we witness the unfolding disasters of globalization, especially in the vital areas of food and agriculture.

Who feeds the world? My answer is very different to that given by most people.

It is women and small farmers working with biodiversity who are the primary food providers in the Third World and, contrary to the dominant assumption, their biodiversity-based small farm systems are more productive than industrial monocultures.

Rich diversity and sustainable systems of food production have been destroyed in the name of increasing food production. However, with the destruction of diversity, important sources of nutrition disappear. When measured in terms of nutrition per acre, and from the perspective of biodiversity, the so called 'high yields' of industrial agriculture do not imply more production of food and better nutrition.

Yield usually refers to production per unit area of a single crop. Output refers to the total production of diverse crops and products. Planting only one crop in the entire field as a monoculture will of course increase its individual yield. Planting multiple crops in a mixture will have low yields of individual crops, but will have high total output of food. Yields have been defined in such a way as to make the food production on small farms by small farmers disappear. This hides the production by millions of women farmers in the Third World – farmers like those in my native Himalaya who fought against logging in the Chipko movement, who in their terraced fields grow jhangora (barnyard millet), marsha (amaranth), tur (pigeon peas), urad (black gram), gahat (horse gram), soy bean (glycine max), bhat (glycine soya), rayans (rice bean), swanta (cow peas), koda (finger millet). From the biodiversity perspective, biodiversity-based productivity is higher than monoculture productivity (Shiva 1996; Rosset and Altieri 1999). I call this blindness to the high productivity of diversity a 'Monoculture of the Mind', which creates monocultures in our fields.

The Mayan peasants in Chiapas are characterized as unproductive because they produce only 2 tons of corn per acre. However, the overall food output is 20 tons per acre when the diversity of their beans and squashes, their vegetables and fruit trees are taken into account (J. Lutzen-berger, personal communication).

In Java, small farmers cultivate 607 species in their home gardens, with an overall species diversity comparable to that of a deciduous tropical forest.

In sub-Saharan Africa, women cultivate as many as 120 different plants in the spaces left alongside the cash crops, and this is the main source of household food security.

A single home garden in Thailand has more than 230 species, and African home gardens have more than sixty species of trees.

Rural families in the Congo eat leaves from more than fifty different species of trees.

A study in eastern Nigeria found that home gardens occupying only 2 per cent of a household's farmland accounted for half of the farm's total output. Similarly, home gardens in Indonesia are estimated to provide more than 20 per cent of household income and 40 per cent of domestic food supplies (FAO 1998).

Research done by the FAO (Food and Agricultural Organization, UN) has shown that small biodiverse farms can produce thousands of times more food than large industrial monocultures (Shiva 1996).

Diversity is the best strategy for preventing drought and desertification.

What the world needs to feed a growing population sustainably is biodiversity intensification, not chemical intensification or genetic engin-eering. While women and small peasants feed the world through bio-diversity, we are repeatedly told that without genetic engineering and globalization of agriculture the world will starve. In spite of all empirical evidence showing that genetic engineering does not produce more food and in fact often leads to a net decline in yields, it is constantly promoted as the only alternative available for feeding the hungry (Shiva 2000; 1998a).

That is why I ask, who feeds the world?

This deliberate blindness to diversity, the blindness to nature's pro-duction, production by women, production by Third World farmers, allows destruction and appropriation to be projected as creation.

Take the case of the much touted 'golden rice' or genetically engineered vitamin A rice as a cure for blindness. It is assumed that without genetic engineering we cannot remove vitamin A deficiency. However, nature gives us abundant and diverse sources of vitamin A. If rice was not polished, rice itself would provide vitamin A. If herbicides were not sprayed on our wheat fields, we would have bathua, amaranth and mustard leaves as delicious and nutritious greens.

Women in Bengal use more than 150 plants as greens: hinche sak (*Enhydra fluctuans*), palang sak (*Spinacea oleracea*), tak palang (*Rumex vesicarious*), lal sak (*Amaranthus gangeticus*), champa note (*Amaranthus tristis*), gobra note (*Amaranthus lividus*), ghenti note (*Amaranthus tennifolius*), banspata note (*Amaranthus lanceolatus*), ban note (*Amaranthus viridis*), sada note (*Amaranthus blitum*), kanta note (*Amaranthus spinosus*), bethua sale (*Chenopodium album*), brahmi sak (*Bacopa monrieri*), sushin sak (*Marulea quadrifolio*) – to name but a few (Deb 1999; Bhatt 1999). But the myth of creation presents bio-technologists as the creators of vitamin A, negating nature's diverse gifts and women's knowledge of how to use this diversity to feed their children and families.

The most efficient means of bringing about the destruction of nature, local economies and small autonomous producers is to render their production invisible. Women who produce for their families and communities are treated as 'non-productive' and 'economically inactive'. The devaluation of women's work, and of work done in sustainable economies, is the natural outcome of a system constructed by capitalist patriarchy. This is how globalization destroys local economies and the destruction itself is counted as growth.

Women themselves are devalued. Because much of their work in rural and indigenous communities is undertaken in co-operation with nature, and is often contradictory to the dominant market-driven 'development' and trade policies, and because work that satisfies needs and ensures sustenance is devalued in general, there is less nurturing of life and life-support systems.

The devaluation and invisibility of sustainable, regenerative production is most glaring in the area of food. While patriarchal division of labour has assigned women the role of feeding their families and communities, patriarchal economics and patriarchal views of science and technology magically make women's work in providing food disappear. 'Feeding the World' becomes disassociated from the women who actually do it and is projected as dependent on global agribusiness and bio-technology corporations. However, industrialization and genetic engineering of food and globalization of trade in agriculture are recipes for creating hunger, not for feeding the poor.

Everywhere, food production is becoming a negative economy, with farmers spending more buying costly inputs for industrial production than the price they receive for their produce. The consequence is rising debts and suicides in both rich and poor countries.

Economic globalization is leading to a concentration of the seed industry, the increased use of pesticides and, finally, increased debt. Capital-intensive, corporate-controlled agriculture is spreading into regions where peasants are poor but, until now, self-sufficient in food. In the regions where industrial agriculture has been introduced through globalization, higher costs are making it virtually impossible for small farmers to survive.

The globalization of non-sustainable industrial agriculture is evaporating the incomes of Third World farmers through a combination of devaluation of currencies, increase in costs of production and a collapse in commodity prices.

Farmers everywhere are being paid a fraction of what they received for the same commodity a decade ago. In the USA wheat prices dropped from $5.75 to $2.43 a bushel, soya bean prices have dropped from $8.40 to $4.29, and corn prices have dropped from $4.43 to $1.72. In India, from 1999 to 2000, prices for coffee have dropped from Rs 60 to Rs 18 per kilogram, while prices of oil seeds declined by more than 30 per cent.

The Canadian National Farmers Union put it like this in 2000 in a report to the Senate:

> While the farmers growing cereal grains – wheat, oats, corn – earn negative returns and are pushed close to bankruptcy, the companies that make breakfast cereals reap huge profits. In 1998, cereal companies Kellogg's, Quaker Oats, and General Mills enjoyed return on equity rates of 56%, 165% and 222% respectively. While a bushel of corn sold for less than $4, a bushel of corn flakes sold for $133. In 1998, the cereal companies were 186 to 740 times more profitable than the farms. May be farmers are making too little because others are taking too much. (National Farmers Union 2000).

A World Bank report has admitted that 'behind the polarisation of domestic consumer prices and world prices is the presence of large trading companies in international commodity markets' (Morisset 1997).

While farmers earn less, consumers, especially in poor countries, pay more. In India, food prices doubled between 1999 and 2000, and consumption of food grains dropped by 12 per cent in rural areas, increasing the food deprivation of those already malnourished and pushing up mortality rates. Economic growth through global commerce is based on pseudo-surpluses. More food is being traded while the poor are consuming less. When growth increases poverty, when real production becomes a negative economy, and speculators are defined as 'wealth creators', something has gone wrong with the concepts and categories of wealth and wealth creation. Pushing the real production by nature and people into a negative economy implies that production of real goods and services is declining, creating deeper poverty for the millions who are not part of the dot.com route to instantaneous wealth creation.

Women, as I have said, are the primary food producers and food processors in the world. However, their work in production and processing has now become invisible. According to the McKinsey corporation: 'American food giants recognise that Indian agro-business has lots of room to grow, especially in food processing. India processes a minuscule 1 per cent of the food it grows compared with 70 per cent for the US, Brazil and Philippines.' It is not that we Indians eat our food raw. Global consultants fail to see the 99 per cent food processing done by women at household level or by small cottage industries because they are not controlled by global agribusiness. Ninety-nine per cent of India's agro-processing has been intentionally kept at the household level. Now, under the pressure of globalization, things are changing. Pseudo-hygiene laws, which shut down the food economy based on local small-scale processing under community control, are part of the arsenal of global agribusiness for establishing market monopolies through force and coercion, not competition.

In August 1998, small-scale local processing of edible oil was banned in India through a 'packaging order' which made sale of open oil illegal and required all oil to be packed in plastic or aluminium. This shut down tiny *ghanis* or cold pressed mills. It destroyed the market for our diverse oil seeds – mustard, linseed, sesame, groundnut and coconut. The takeover of the edible oil industry has affected 10 million livelihoods. The takeover of *atta* or flour by packaged branded flour will cost 100 million livelihoods. These millions are being pushed into new poverty. Moreover, the forced use of packaging will increase the environmental burden of millions of tonnes of plastic and aluminium.

The globalization of the food system is destroying the diversity of local food cultures and local food economies. A global monoculture is being forced on people by defining everything that is fresh, local and hand-made as health hazards. Human hands are being defined as the worst con- taminants, and work for human hands is being outlawed, to be replaced by machines and chemicals bought from global corporations. These are not recipes for feeding the world, but for stealing livelihoods from the poor to create markets for the powerful.

People are being perceived as parasites, to be exterminated for the 'health' of the global economy. In the process, new health and ecological hazards are being forced on Third World people through the dumping of genetically engineered foods and other hazardous products.

Recently, because of a WTO ruling, India was forced to remove restric- tions on all imports. Among the unrestricted imports are carcasses and animal waste parts that create a threat to our culture and introduce public health hazards such as BSE (mad cow disease).

The US Center for Disease Control (CDC) in Atlanta has calculated that nearly 81 million cases of food-borne illnesses occur in the USA every year. Deaths from food poisoning have more than quadrupled due to deregulation, rising from 2000 in 1984 to 9000 in 1994. Most of these infections are caused by factory-farmed meat. The US slaughters 93 million pigs, 37 million cattle, 2 million calves, 6 million horses, goats and sheep and 8 billion chickens and turkeys each year. Now the giant meat industry of the USA wants to dump contaminated meat produced through violent and cruel methods on India.

The waste of the rich is being dumped on the poor. The wealth of the poor is being violently appropriated through new and clever means like patents on biodiversity and indigenous knowledge. Patents and intellectual property rights are supposed to be granted for novel inventions. But patents are being claimed for rice varieties such as the basmati for which the Doon Valley (where I was born) is famous, or pesticides derived from the neem tree which our mothers and grandmothers have been using for centuries. Rice Tec, a US-based company, has been granted Patent no. 5,663,484 for basmati rice lines and grains.

Basmati, neem, pepper, bitter gourd, turmeric and every aspect of the improvement embodied in our indigenous food and medicinal systems are now being pirated and patented. The knowledge of the poor is being converted into the property of global corporations, creating a situation where the poor will have to pay for the seeds and medicines that they have cultivated, developed and used to meet their needs for nutrition and health-care. Such false claims to creation are now the global norm, with the Trade Related Intellectual Property Rights (TRIPS) Agreement of the WTO forcing countries to introduce regimes that allow patenting of life-forms and indigenous knowledge.

Instead of recognizing that commercial interests build on nature and on the contribution of other cultures, global law has enshrined the patriarchal myth of creation to create new property rights to life-forms just as colonialism used the myth of discovery as the basis of the takeover of the land of others as colonies.

Humans do not create life when they manipulate it. Rice Tec's claim that it has made 'an instant invention of a novel rice line', or the Roslin Institute's claim that Ian Wilmut 'created' Dolly the sheep denies the creativity of nature, the self-organizational capacity of life-forms, and the prior innovation of Third World communities.

Patents and intellectual property rights are supposed to prevent piracy. Instead they are becoming the instruments of pirating the common traditional knowledge from the poor of the Third World and making it the exclusive 'property' of western scientists and corporations. When patents are granted for seeds and plants, as in the case of basmati, theft is defined as creation, and saving and sharing seed are defined as theft of intellectual property. Corporations which have broad patents on crops such as cotton, soya bean and mustard are suing farmers for seed saving and hiring detective agencies to find out if farmers have saved seed or shared it with neighbours.

The recent announcement that Monsanto is giving away the rice genome for free is misleading; Monsanto has not made a commitment to stop patenting rice varieties or other crops.

Sharing and exchange, the basis of our humanity and our ecological survival, have been redefined as crimes. This makes us all poor.

Nature has given us abundance, women's indigenous knowledge of biodiversity, agriculture and nutrition has built on that abundance to create more from less, to create growth through sharing. The poor are pushed into deeper poverty by being made to pay for what were their resources and knowledge. Even the rich are poorer because their profits are based on theft and on the use of coercion and violence. This is not wealth creation but plunder.

Sustainability requires the protection of all species and all people and the recognition that diverse species and diverse people play an essential role in maintaining ecosystems and ecological processes. Pollinators are critical to fertilization and generation of plants. Biodiversity in fields provides vegetables, fodder, medicine and protection to the soil from water and wind erosion.

As humans travel further down the road to non-sustainability, they become intolerant of other species and blind to their vital role in our survival.

In 1992, when Indian farmers destroyed Cargill's seed plant in Bellary, Karnataka, to protest against seed failure, the Cargill chief executive stated: 'We bring Indian farmers smart technologies which prevent bees from usurping the pollen.' When I was participating in the United Nations Biosafety Negotiations, Monsanto circulated literature to defend its Round-up herbicide resistant crops on the grounds that they prevent 'weeds from stealing the sunshine'. But what Monsanto calls weeds are the greens that provide vitamin A and prevent blindness in children and anaemia in women. A world view that defines pollination as 'theft by bees' and claims that biodiversity 'steals sunshine' is a world view which itself aims at stealing nature's harvest by replacing open, pollinated varieties with hybrids and sterile seeds, and destroying biodiverse flora with herbicides such as Monsanto's Roundup. The threat posed to the Monarch butterfly by genetically engineered basmati crops is just one example of the ecological poverty created by the new bio-technologies. As butterflies and bees disappear, production is undermined. As biodiversity disappears, with it go sources of nutrition and food. When giant corporations view small peasants and bees as thieves, and through trade rules and new technologies seek the right to exterminate them, humanity has reached a dangerous threshold. The imperative to stamp out the smallest insect, the smallest plant, the smallest peasant comes from a deep fear – the fear of everything that is alive and free. And this deep insecurity and fear is unleashing violence against all people and all species.

The global free trade economy has become a threat to sustainability and the very survival of the poor and other species is at stake not just as a side effect or as an exception but in a systemic way through a restructuring of our world view at the most fundamental level. Sustainability, sharing and survival are being economically outlawed in the name of market competitiveness and market efficiency.

I want to argue here that we need urgently to bring the planet and people back into the picture.

The world can be fed only by feeding all beings that make up the world. In giving food to other beings and species we maintain conditions for our own food security. In feeding the earthworms we feed ourselves. In feeding cows, we feed the soil, and in providing food for the soil, we provide food for humans. This world view of abundance is based on sharing and on a deep awareness of humans as members of the earth family. An awareness that, in impoverishing other beings, we impoverish ourselves, and in nourishing other beings, we nourish ourselves is the basis of sustainability (Shiva 1998b).

The sustainability challenge for the new millennium is whether global economic man can move out of the world view based on fear and scarcity, monocultures and monopolies, appropriation and dispossession and shift to a view based on abundance and sharing, diversity and decentralization, and respect and dignity for all beings.

Sustainability demands that we move out of the economic trap that is leaving no space for other species and most humans. Economic globalization has become a war against nature and the poor. But the rules of globalization are not god-given; they can be changed. We must bring this war to an end.

Since Seattle, a frequently used phrase has been the need for a rule-based system. Globalization is the rule of commerce and it has elevated Wall Street to be the only source of value, and as a result things that should have high worth – nature, culture, the future – are being devalued and destroyed. The rules of globalization are undermining the rules of justice and sustainability, of compassion and sharing. We have to move from market totalitarianism to an earth democracy.

We can survive as a species only if we live by the rules of the biosphere. The biosphere has enough for everyone's needs if the global economy respects the limits set by sustainability and justice.

As Gandhi reminded us: 'The earth has enough for everyone's needs, but not for some people's greed.'

References

Bhatt, V. (1999) *Case Study —Himalaya*, New Delhi: RFSTE.

Deb D. (1999) *Case Study – Bengal*, New Delhi: RFSTE.

FAO (1998) 'Women Feed the World', World Food Day, Rome, 16 October.

Morisset (1997) *World Bank*, New York, April

National Farmers Union (2000) *The Farm Crisis, EU Subsidies, and Agribusiness Market Power*, paper presented to the Senate Standing Committee on Agriculture and Forestry, Ottawa, Ontario, 18 February.

Rosset, P. and M. Altieri (1999) *The Productivity of Small Scale Agriculture*, IFA White Paper.

Shiva, V. (1996) *Biodiversity-based Productivity*, New Delhi: RFSTE.

— (1998a) *Betting on Biodiversity: Why Genetic Engineering Will Not Feed the Hungry*, New Delhi: RFSTE.

— (1998b) *Globalization, Gandhi and Swadeshi: What is Economic Freedom? Whose Economic Freedom?* New Delhi: RFSTE.

— (2000) *Stolen Harvest: The Hijacking of the Global Food Supply*, Boston: South End Press.

5

Melanesia, the Banks, and the BINGOs: Real Alternatives are Everywhere (Except in the Consultants' Briefcases)

Nicholas G. Faraclas

Globalization for Corporations, Not for People

Corporate globalization is presented to us as inevitable. But must we accept as an inevitable fact of life the mortgaging of the lives of future generations of entire nations in the form of debt to the banks and the profiteers who invented corporate globalization? Corporate globalization is discussed in the media as if it were a natural phenomenon. But can the most massive transfer of wealth in the history of humanity from the poor to the rich sponsored by the World Bank/International Monetary Fund (WB/IMF or 'the Bank') and enforced by the World Trade Organization (WTO) under the agenda of corporate globalization be considered natural? We are told that corporate globalization is the next logical step in the evolution of the world economy. But is there anything natural or logical about the premature death of our planet, which corporate globalization looks certain to bring about?

There is nothing natural, normal or inevitable about either corporate globalization or the 'alternatives' to it proposed by the WB/IMF, bilateral aid agencies, the Big International Non-Governmental Organizations (BINGOs) and the rest of the development establishment. Despite what the media, governments, schools, churches and economists say, human beings did not always live like this. Your ancestors and mine had control over their productive and reproductive processes, which they utilized to serve the interests of their communities as a whole, rather than those of a small minority. In fact, it is only in a few aberrant societies and only during the past few thousand years that the land, work, communities and cultures that once were controlled by all and used to satisfy the needs of all were enclosed, appropriated, diverted and distorted to feed the insatiable greed of a system that serves profits, not people. Unfortunately, these aberrant societies have perfected the technologies of illusion, addiction and death in such a way as to impose their system of profit and domination on most of the peoples of the earth.

Melanesia and Alternatives to Corporate Globalization

Indigenous Melanesians make up more than 95 per cent of the 4.5 million inhabitants of Papua New Guinea, the Solomon Islands and Vanuatu. The constitutions of the three nations recognize the power of indigenous peoples and their customary laws over the 90 per cent of their national territory that has not yet been registered under 'western'-style land legislation. In most of the rest of the world, the collective power over land that all of humanity once enjoyed has long ago been ceded to the state, in exchange for a few individual land-ownership rights. This has not yet happened to the vast majority of the indigenous peoples of Melanesia, who consequently enjoy the full food, housing, employment and land security that not so long ago all humans enjoyed. While the remarkable developmental achievements of traditional Melanesian societies fill transnational companies and WB/IMF consultants with bewilderment or disgust, they have the potential to inspire the rest of us to reconstruct our collective pasts and take back control over our common futures.

The battle over alternatives to corporate globalization is indeed a crucial one, but it will not be fought with money or guns or political machines. Instead, it will be fought with ideas, beliefs and community work. We ignore this fact at our own peril. The multinational companies certainly do not ignore it. Before land and labour can be enclosed in the interests of profit, people's minds and beliefs need to be enclosed. For this reason, there are more missionaries per capita in Melanesia than anywhere else on the earth today. Melanesians do not yet believe that it is normal for one person to have enormous wealth and another to have nothing, for people to be forced into suffocating sexual roles or nuclear families, or for someone else to control their land or their labour. But the combined forces of missionary preaching and company advertising that have invaded even the most remote villages are preparing yet another indigenous nation for submission to a patriarchal God who demands blind obedience, addiction to substances that require wage slavery to obtain, and the expropriation and exploitation that inevitably follow.

Popular Education, Alternative Pasts and Alternative Futures

At present, the debate over corporate globalization is effectively dominated by the profit system, working through international agencies such as the WB/IMF which are wholly dedicated to the propagation of the gospel of neo-liberal economics. The WB/IMF has quite successfully enlisted governments to adopt and implement its vision of corporate globalization, while at the same time co-opting non-governmental organizations to articulate its vision of 'alternatives' to corporate globalization. Until we can seriously consider alternative pasts, it is useless to talk about alternative futures. Unless we can effectively reconstruct our own pasts in our own interests, how will we be able to avoid constructing futures that serve only to feed the insatiable greed of the forces which are leading us all to misery and our planet to destruction?

This battle over alternatives must first be inspired by a reawakened memory that things do not have to be this way, then waged with our abundant power to resist and reject the 'alternatives' that are being presented to us now, and finally won with the boundless creativity that we as communities have to influence our futures in our own interests. To accomplish all of this, popular education and awareness are essential. It is not insignificant that among all the 'alternatives' currently being put forward by the preponderant majority of international agencies and BINGOs, few include a programme of genuine popular education or critical awareness. Popular education begins with communities collectively identifying their problems in a radical way, then critically analysing the causes of their problems, and finally formulating transformational solutions to their problems, using their own knowledge, resources and labour as much as possible. Because they lack these essential components, we can say that almost all of the 'alternatives' that are being presented to us today are not alternatives at all, just 'kinder, gentler' ways to sacrifice more land, more labour and more lives to the God of profit.

Corporate Globalization and Recolonization

In order to understand corporate globalization, we need to understand why the Bank and the WTO are promoting it as 'Our Future'. The great depression and the Second World War severely weakened the ability of the dominant classes of the North (especially those of Northern Europe and the United States) to extract profit from the lands and peoples of the Majority World, whether from the militant, unionized workforce of the 'First World', from the socialist states of the 'Second World', or the newly independent nations of the 'Third World'. It should be noted that I consider the Majority World to transcend national boundaries, i.e. most of Brixton and the Bronx are part of the Majority World. The WB/IMF was set up in the 1940s to remedy this situation. Its first major mission, which occupied it until the late 1960s, was to help reconstruct the former colonial powers and their war-ravaged economies.

Colonial economies, though, cannot exist without empires. Therefore, in the 1970s and 1980s the WB/IMF shifted its focus to its second main task, the recolonization of the world. But this form of colonization would not repeat the mistakes of the administrative type of colonialism practised by European governments on their dependent territories in the South since the fifteenth century. Instead, it would follow the much more efficient and insidious debt-driven model imposed since the nineteenth century by British and American banks on the nominally independent states of Latin America. The success of this strategy was phenomenal. By the early 1990s, the neo-liberal advisers from Washington could be said to have seized effective economic and administrative control over nearly every nation of Asia, Africa, Latin America, the Pacific and Eastern Europe.

The system that the WB/IMF and the WTO serve can never be satisfied. It must consume ever greater amounts of land, resources and labour to generate ever increasing rates of profit and regular record highs on the stock markets, or it collapses. Ultimately, it is a system that favours no one. Whatever it can get away with in the colonies, it eventually imposes on the metropoles, and vice versa. So while the WB/IMF was forcing the South to accept structural adjustment, Thatcher, Reagan and their neo-liberal clones such as Blair and Clinton have been imposing similar 'austerity programmes' first on the working classes of Britain and the United States, then eventually on all but a small minority of the peoples of Northern Europe, Japan, Australia and Aotearoa/New Zealand.

So the recolonization of the South is inextricably connected to the repauperization of the North; this is the essence of the corporate globalization which has been codified and made legally binding on all governments under the provisions of the WTO. Corporate globalization has dismantled the welfare state in the former 'First World', state socialism in the former 'Second World', and state sovereignty in the former 'Third World'. All of these worlds are being merged into one global configuration that pits an ever growing majority forced to live in misery against an ever shrinking minority 'enjoying' relative privilege behind barbed-wire fences. Distinctions between North and South and among nation-states are breaking down, with rapidly expanding pockets of Majority World 'underdevelopment' springing up in the former metropoles and corresponding enclaves of Minority World 'development' establishing themselves in the former colonies.

From Arrogance to Feigned Contrition: the Bank's Response to the Movement against Corporate Globalization

Over the past fifty years, an increasingly vocal and articulate movement has emerged in opposition to corporate globalization and the institutions that push it. Up until the massive protests at Seattle in 1999 and Prague in 2000, the WB/IMF systematically and categorically ignored these voices. But now that the WB/IMF's mission has largely been accomplished, some acknowledgement and even some tactical use can be made of such criticisms. It was possible for Robert McNamara to apologize for the WB's lending policies under his presidency only once the majority of the world's population, their children and their children's children had already been effectively enslaved by the debt mechanism unleashed by these same policies. When the WB was still lending money to reconstruct Japan and Germany after the war, these countries were allowed to default on debts and some of their debts were forgiven. But even after McNamara's admission of gross mis-management at the Bank, no country in the South has been able to benefit from such forgiveness. The highly publicized plans for limited debt 'relief' are so restricted and require such complete capitulation to the most draconian form of neo-liberal adjustment that they do not merit consideration here.

The latest, heavily censored *World Development Report*s published by the Bank constitute the closest thing to an apology that can be expected from such a completely unaccountable institution for the unbridled attack that the WB/IMF has made over the past two decades on all forms of state services (excepting police, defence forces, prisons and subsidies for multinational 'investors', of course). In these reports, the Bank has glossed over the structural adjustment-induced 'misery factor' which played a major role in pushing Bosnia, Burundi and Rwanda over the edge. But now that the state has imploded in Liberia, the Democratic Republic of the Congo, Somalia and Sierra Leone under the unbearable pressure of structural adjustment combined with the legacy of the WB/IMF-sup-ported dictatorships of Doe, Mobutu, Barre and the Freetown 'elite', the Bank has been forced to backtrack and take a more moderate position on the potential role of the state.

In this way, Africa has extracted a bitter-sweet revenge for being more or less written off the WB/IMF's development agenda in past editions of the *Report*. But it makes little difference in the final analysis; just as the Bank crucified the state, so it can resurrect it to do its bidding. Now that the governmental apparatus in the great majority of countries is directly or indirectly accountable to the WB/IMF (rather than to their people) and legally bound to structural adjustment under the WTO, the state has become a valuable tool in the extraction of labour and resources for the transnational companies who ultimately determine WB/IMF and WTO policy.

Much more threatening to the forces of corporate globalization is the emergence during the past decade of a very effective system of traditional clan-based self-governance by the people of Somaliland (the former British-administered area in the north of what eventually became Somalia). Despite the fact that Somaliland has one of the best functioning and least corrupt governments in Africa, it has been ostracized by the farcical collection of agencies, governments, BINGOs, and media conglomerates that the companies sell to us as the 'international community'. With a civil service of only 6000 for a population of more than 2 million, no debt, and negligible dependence on the poisonous addiction that is otherwise known as bilateral and multilateral 'aid', Somaliland proves that indigenous systems of government can achieve peace, respect for human rights, and relative prosperity by making the national-state subservient and effectively accountable to a diverse collection of profoundly democratic local-level political and economic structures (Prunier 2000: 14).

The Bank's Defence of Corporate Globalization

As the mountain of evidence attesting to the disastrous consequences of structural adjustment can no longer be ignored, the Bank is finally responding. One response is that the WB/IMF acted with the best of intentions, but corrupt governments were to blame for the problems. Another contends that the plans were made correctly in Washington, but that they were implemented incorrectly on the ground by incompetent governments.

These arguments can be easily refuted by the long list of hopelessly corrupt and incompetent regimes which have been actively supported by the Bank, the longer list of regimes who were corrupted or further corrupted either by the type of money given by the Bank or by the way in which it was given, and the shorter list of relatively competent regimes who seriously attempted to be transparent and accountable to their people, but who were effectively boycotted by the Bank because they didn't adhere to the neo-liberal orthodoxy which has assumed the status of religious dogma in the WB/IMF and the WTO. Because the Bank has set itself up as the gatekeeper for nearly all bilateral and multilateral assistance, its blockades have swept these latter governments into the dustbin of history, with the help of an unsavoury group of mercenaries and Contras assembled by northern governments to defend the interests of the profiteers who call the shots in Washington, Paris, London and Tokyo.

When all other defences fail, WB/IMF officials use the ultimate justification for their policies, namely that there was no possible alternative to their intervention, and if they hadn't acted, things would have been much worse. Under normal circumstances it would be very difficult to argue against such an assertion, given the fact that the proponents claim to have complete knowledge of events past and future in several parallel universes. But in this case, we need only to cite the WB/IMF's sister UN organization UNICEF, which attributes 500,000 childhood deaths per year directly to WB/IMF structural adjustment programmes, not to mention the millions who have perished indirectly through the withdrawal of food subsidies and health services, the victims of the rapid rise in violence, war and genocide that accompanies structural adjustment, and so on. The WB is a profit-making institution. Current debt payments on loans made or brokered by the Bank are responsible for a net outflow of capital from the overwhelming majority of countries in the South to profiteers in the North. It doesn't take a clairvoyant to see that a simple cancellation of part or all of this debt would have landed us in a happier world than the one that neo-liberal economists present to us as 'the way it always was, the way it inevitably has become, and the way it will always be'.

From Marginalization to Co-optation: NGOs and the 'Alternatives Trap'

The WB/IMF is not only responding to criticism, however; it is re-cuperating it and utilizing it to co-opt and buy off its critics. Over the past few years, the WB/IMF has actually come to dominate debates on corporate globalization, not merely by defending the corporate globalist position, but by actively intervening in the construction of arguments on 'both sides' of the question. While the International Monetary Fund still boldly advocates corporate globalization in its pure 'unmanaged' form, the World Bank is putting forward a set of 'alternatives' which amount to nothing more than 'managed' versions of corporate globalization. The hard-line position of the IMF and the revisionist position of the WB create a false polarization that becomes very seductive to erstwhile critics who crave the short-term financial and political advantages of co-operating with the Bank. In Melanesia and elsewhere, transnational mining companies and the World Bank are now entering into partnerships with BINGOs such as WWF, the global environment network, to create 'alternative' programmes in tropical regions which are heavily impacted by mineral and timber extraction. Upon closer examination, however, these programmes turn out to be nothing but band-aid operations that put a 'human face' on the wholesale destruction of communities and habitats.

The World Bank is now funding smaller indigenous NGOs in countries like Papua New Guinea to show that they recognize that NGOs too have a role to play (in carrying out structural adjustment!). More than US$15 million for credit schemes (the flavour-of-the-month, since Grameen), portable sawmills, and the like is flooding into local communities. The WB managed to introduce the funding mechanism in the most divisive way possible, by buying off two prominent NGO leaders to head up two competing facilities for NGO involvement in a WB/IMF-sponsored 'Poverty Alleviation Programme'. The predictable splits over involvement with the Bank occurred in the organizations and networks which had placed their trust in these leaders. Of course, those NGOs that decided to take the money aligned themselves with the two different camps and came to blows over their competing claims.

Several existing NGOs which have financial management problems have put aside their scruples and taken the WB money. For them, the money is a new 'fix', allowing them to put off dealing with the crisis until it grows to such proportions that it destroys them. A significant portion of this money will go to 'mushroom NGOs' that formed only because the funds were available. Most of the money that will not be misused outright will go into 'alternative income generation' which usually means the setting up of one or a few individuals (mostly young men) as local businesspeople, who will disrupt traditional egalitarian political and economic mechanisms, and propagate relations of domination in their communities by becoming the local dispensers of beer, abusers of women and silencers of critics.

Just as it did when it tempted governments to take loans in the 1970s and 1980s, the WB/IMF is now waving money in the faces of NGOs, and a distressing number of former WB/IMF critics are taking the bait. Of course, the Bank will claim in a few years' time that the disintegration of the NGO movement in Papua New Guinea and the rampant corruption and financial mismanagement which followed this reckless disbursal of funds was in no way encouraged or abetted by the WB/IMF! Meanwhile, the 'mushroom NGOs' become the fifth column of the WB/IMF within the NGO movement and the 'local businesspeople' become the shock troops of the profit system within their communities.

Since the WB/IMF has embarked on the alternatives business, it is positioning itself as an 'expert' on the subject. When critics confront the Bank, they are immediately challenged to produce an alternative. This is the ultimate trap. No real alternatives to corporate globalization could ever be designed by the WB/IMF, programmed by governments, brainstormed in the headquarters of BINGOs, or even collectively formulated by indigenous local NGOs. When the Bank asks its critics to come up with alternatives, it is asking them to replicate the relations of domination that keep communities from articulating and implementing their own alternatives, rather than the 'alternatives' that the 'experts' from outside propose for them. The only real alternatives to corporate globalization involve processes of critical, radical and transformational community awareness, analysis and mobilization, not ready-made solutions to unanalysed problems.

Melanesia, Popular Education and Reclaiming the Abundance of Subsistence

The development establishment has reserved its last desperate weapon for those who have managed to avoid the alternatives trap and propose instead popular education processes as the basis for the emergence of real alternatives. The claim is that the popular education process has no basis in the past or the present, but only as part of some utopian dream. In fact, nothing could be further from the truth, and the evidence is to be found everywhere, once we begin to challenge received notions of how it was, is and will be.

In Melanesia, over 1500 languages are spoken by at least that many different ethnic groups. Each of these groups constitutes a society distinct from the others in countless ways, but there are some commonalities that unite them. In general, these societies have traditionally shunned extreme accumulation of wealth, have striven for collective decision-making, have recognized women's power over their own productive and reproductive processes, and have utilized an economy based on subsistence to create an abundance that ensures all of their members food, housing, employment and land. None has opted for the nuclear family, strait-jacketed sexual roles or profit-making as a positively valued social activity. Most importantly, however, these societies have maintained control over their own history, their mechanisms for dealing with problems in the present, and their vision for the future. Critical and democratic identification, analysis and resolution of problems by communities have been the norm rather than the exception in Melanesia. These incredibly significant achievements have been attained by each society in its own unique manner, without forced assimilation or conquest.

In Melanesia we have living evidence of what feminist archaeologists in Europe (Gimbutas 1991) and zoologists working with primates such as the bonobos in Central Africa (McKie 1997: 25) are discovering: that patriarchal society based on violence, repression, scarcity and domination is most probably a very recent phenomenon in human history, establishing itself without conquest or threat of conquest in only one or perhaps a few human populations. The society of domination that neo-liberal economists present to us as normal is therefore quite the opposite. Because they sustain themselves through illusion (like the stock market) and mass addiction (like consumerism) and because they propagate themselves through conquest and technologies of death, societies of domination are the antithesis of any but the most warped concept of what could be considered to be 'natural' or 'evolutionarily advantageous' to our species.

In other words, for all but a short moment of human existence on the planet and in all but a handful of societies, all of our ancestors lived in the abundance of subsistence, in open societies which co-existed in relative peace, fostering and celebrating tremendous diversity, individuality and creativity. This is the past that we can all reclaim, if we dare to reject the version of history that portrays the loss by the vast majority of humanity of our power over our land, labour, communities, history and sense of possibilities during the past few thousand years as some sort of 'progress' into the 'light' from some dark and evil 'primitive' pre-history. We reclaim this past not to idealize it or to try mechanically to replicate it, but to use it as an inspiration for the reinterpretation of the present and the foundation for building a future for people, not for profit.

Resistance and Alternatives to Globalization are Everywhere

Equipped with this re-reading of our past, the present becomes abundantly rich with evidence for resistance to domination and possibilities for transcending it. Despite the fact that a WB/IMF-sponsored genocide has been practised against them, the peoples of West Papua continue to resist and reclaim their power over the land, just as indigenous peoples do worldwide. Despite the mass murder of millions of women as 'witches' to consolidate the patriarchal system in Europe and to make possible the imposition of that system on the rest of the world through missionization and colonization, women everywhere continue to reclaim control over their bodies. In order to survive as a human being in the neo-liberal universe, we are compelled to commit acts of resistance at nearly every moment and constantly to subvert the control that the profit system exerts over our minds, our labour and our lives.

When we remove the blinders of the limited 'alternatives' that the development establishment presents to us as the only possible choices for the future, a vast and almost limitless array of possibilities is open to us. The sense of such possibilities has allowed the indigenous peoples in Melanesia to develop and practise thousands of different but equally effective systems which guarantee equal access to the abundance of subsistence, collective decision-making, equitable relations between the sexes and so on. And this is the future that we can all claim, if we only dare.

References

Gimbutas, Marija (1991) *The Civilization of the Goddess: The World of Old Europe*, San Francisco, CA: Harper.

McKie, Robin (1997) 'Monkey business as science', *Guardian Weekly*, 3 August 1997, p. 25.

Prunier, Gerard (2000) 'Somalia reinvents itself', *Le Monde Diplomatique*, April, p. 14.

6

The Clash of Knowledge Systems: Local Diversity in the Wild versus Global Homogeneity in the Marketplace

Susan Hawthorne

> I not see you long time now, I not see you long time now.
> White fella bin take me from you. I don't know why
> Give me to missionary to be God's child
> Give me new language, give me new name
> All time I cry, they say – 'that shame'
>
> (Johnson, 1985: 35)

Indigenous accounts customarily begin with a reflexive self-identification, and so I want to acknowledge where I am coming from. I grew up on land originally inhabited by the Wiradjuri people of New South Wales, Australia, but which in my school geography classes was referred to as the Western Slopes. The farm on which I grew up had been woodland with mixed callitris pines (cypress family) and eucalypt (box gum and stringybark were common). In the late 1800s a timber mill was set up and the bushland was decimated, leaving a few significant stands. My grandfather moved on to the land in the early years of the twentieth century, grew wheat, oats, and barley and kept sheep.

I lived on this farm until I was sent away to the city as a boarder at secondary school.[1] In my post-secondary years I encountered feminism, alternative health systems, resistance politics, lesbian culture, environmentalism, indigenous women's culture and a host of other challenging social and political movements. In the early 1990s I travelled to Bangladesh and had the opportunity to see some of the devastating effects of structural adjustment programmes (SAPs) and globalization in the Majority World. I began informing myself more thoroughly about the process of corporate globalization.

Indigenous Knowledge Systems

Indigenous peoples have become a global capital resource. Their successful stewardship over the environment, their success in sustaining biodiversity, their extensive knowledge of local ecologies and their considerable skills in the utilization of local resources have all been targeted for further enclosure by the forces of corporate globalization.

The twentieth century has seen a huge shift in perception of indigenous peoples, both from the indigenous point of view (see Bell 1998; Faraclas, this volume; Tuhiwai Smith 1999; La Duke, 1999; Ani 2000) and from the point of view of the colonizing nations.[2] With few exceptions the invading colonizers, whether they came as traders, whalers, missionaries or agriculturalists, dispossessed native peoples of their land, their languages, their cultures and, all too often, their lives. In Australia the histories of 'first contact' are filled with tales of massacre. These include revenge killings of Aborigines for killing and roasting a settler's sheep. There are stories of strychnine poisoning through the distribution of deliberately tainted flour (Reynolds 1990). There are innumerable accounts of women being abducted and raped (Bell 1998) and of children being removed from their families (Bird 1998; Kartinyeri 2000).

Research which takes seriously the knowledge systems of indigenous peoples is a very recent phenomenon. Not until indigenous scholars arrived on the scene was it possible to read about distinctively indigenous ways of knowing and being in literature. Among indigenous scholars there remain huge differences, and that diversity of approach is important in that it has produced a flourishing of scholarship which attempts to throw off the shackles of colonization. Linda Tuhiwai Smith (1999) a Maori scholar from Aotearoa/New Zealand, writes about the way in which the whole project of research itself is 'underpinned by a cultural system of classification and representation [which ...] help determine what counts as real'. Tuhiwai Smith's insights in this regard closely parallel those of Vandana Shiva, who states that: 'The universal/local dichotomy is misplaced when applied to the western and indigenous systems of knowledge, because the western is a local tradition which has been spread world wide through intellectual colonization' (Shiva 1993: 10).

Marimba Ani (2000) in her extraordinary challenge to European thought and behaviour identifies quite precisely the problem of western culture. She posits a driving force for European culture which she calls *asili* (Ani 2000:12–13) that has to do with separation and involves dividing the world from the person. So there is 'the European' and 'the other', there is 'man' and nature, there is truth and falsehood. Such division and dislocation lead to the systematic negation of the existence of 'the other' and the redefinition of 'the other' as having as its sole purpose to serve the desires and needs of 'man'. Ani goes on to describe the construction of thought forms which she calls *utamawazo* (pp. 14–15) and practices within European culture, and attributes this to the inspiration or *utamaroho* of western culture (pp. 15–17) which she identifies as domination. Ani suggests that domination is carved into all of the structures of European culture. It is present in every institution, every sanctioned behaviour, especially those which dispossess 'the other' or which offer a means of control over nature, land and resources. It is present in every institution and every sanctioned behaviour, especially those which dispossess 'the other' or which offer a means of control over nature, land and resources. Ani critiques the way in which western culture has been imposed on peoples all around the world and made out to be a higher and more evolved form of 'civilization', thereby justifying the whole-sale destruction or appropriation of languages and other aspects of culture to which Eva Johnson refers in the quotation at the beginning of this chapter.

The negation of the other as the driving force of western culture is readily evident in the way in which the US patent system works. Dutfield (2000: 65) points out that patent examiners are not required to take into account the traditional knowledge of indigenous peoples unless that know-ledge has been made known in the western global knowledge system of scientific journals and books. Effectively, this means that the local knowledge is considered not to exist[3] even though the literature on it might be substantial (but not in a European language or in a western academic framework). Given that written sources are treated in this way, how much harder is it going to be for cultures whose records are maintained through an oral tradition to have the existence of their traditional knowledges recognized, respected and protected?

Among the most important aspects of indigenous and traditional know-ledge is its depth of understanding about a particular place, a particular environment and its ecology. This situatedness can be invaluable in deter-mining what works and what does not work in terms of sustainable survival. The literature on this is proliferating. La Duke (1999: 139ff) writes of sustainable buffalo ranging in America's Midwest. Langton (1998) discusses the importance of fire in maintaining the Australian landscape. As Dean Yibarbuk writes: 'The secret of fire in our traditional knowledge is that it is a thing that brings the land alive again. When we do burning the whole land becomes alive again. It is reborn' (Yibarbuk 1998: 1).

Anoja Wickramasinghe found that the women of Sri Lanka possessed a 'unique indigenous knowledge' (1994: 93) of the species of trees in the forest and their uses. She suggests that the recognition of women's know-ledge would 'eliminate several years of experimentation and trials' on the medicinal and other useful properties of the trees (p. 94).

Virginia Nazarea has found that women are more likely to be actively involved in conservation because of their connection to 'culturally significant plants' (1999: 101). This aspect of women's knowledge is portrayed in Sinith Sittirak's (1998) study of women and development in which she looks at the way in which her mother is able to use a whole range of plants from her back yard in Bangkok instead of the consumer goods available in the shops. Farida Akhter (1990) identifies similar patterns among the village women of Bangladesh.

Claire Robertson (1997: 259), while doing her research on women farmers in Kenya, and Penelope Schoeffel (1995: 12), while studying women in fishing communities in the Pacific, both witnessed how women's considerable contributions to farming and fishing were rendered non-existent and invisible even when the evidence of women's participation was directly in front of the eyes of men engaged in working in some 'official capacity' (i.e. within the western paradigm) with the local people.

The traditions and knowledge systems of many indigenous peoples around the world are flourishing, but they are increasingly threatened by the globalized mainstream which is pushing further and further into indigenous communities. The attitudes and assumptions of the forces of corporate globalization towards indigenous knowledge in the twenty-first century differ little from those of the European settlers towards the Aboriginal peoples of Australia in the nineteenth century, namely that indigenous knowledge should remain on the margins, and should eventually give way to the 'modern' ideas of the global market economy.

Fantu Cheru challenges this view when he argues that for Africa marginalization may well be a positive force, providing Africans with a chance to redefine their own priorities based on their particular context and meaning. He goes on to argue that 'poor people's knowledge about their own reality [...] counts most' (Cheru 2000: 130), as does 'the process of decolonising the imagination' (p. 123). Respecting people's knowledge means understanding the context of people's lives, respecting the specificities of their histories and their systems of knowledge. This is a view which is shared by Tuhiwai Smith who points to the importance of localizing approaches to critical theory, taking account of the 'specific historical, political and social context' (Tuhiwai Smith 1999: 186; see also Ani 2000).

Veronika Bennholdt-Thomsen and Maria Mies (1999) capture vividly the politics of the marginalization of indigenous knowledge and women's knowledge. In reference to the struggles of the women of Belau against the appropriation of their land and seas by the US government for operations related to nuclear warfare, they conclude:

We learn, if we let ourselves be inspired by the politics of the taro fields, that women in the taro field have a different concept of power from that of the men 'who only talk and talk'. The power of women grows out of their control over subsistence and the means of subsistence, particularly the land. They defended this collective power against their husbands, against the colonial masters[4] and against the US military. (Bennholdt-Thomsen and Mies 1999: 212)

The Clash of Knowledge Systems

The structure of knowledge systems is different across cultures. European culture is based on an objectification of the self, of truth, of nature and of knowledge (Ani 2000). The rhetoric of Western culture is that all knowledge is accessible; however, there are many ways of restricting access to and utilization of particular kinds of knowledge.[5] Furthermore, the separation of 'objective' knowledge which is said to be universally true from 'subjective' experiential knowledge based on connection and context, leads to the commodification of the sources and objects of 'subjective' knowledge, such as land, seeds and other parts of the global commons.

Most indigenous cultures view access to certain types of knowledge as something which is earned or which is secret and impose sanctions on those who spread such knowledge publicly. Legal protection of such secrecy has been included in draft legislation drawn up in the Brazilian Indigenous Societies Act of 1994 (Posey 1996: 14). Access to knowledge also entails community responsibilities. For many indigenous peoples, 'knowledge and determination of the use of resources are collective and inter-generational. No Indigenous population, whether of individuals or communities, nor the government, can sell or transfer ownership of resources which are the property of the people and which each generation has an obligation to safeguard for the next' (COICA/UNDP [1994] in Posey 1996: 10).

This returns us to the core of the problem of exploitation of 'wild' resources. Katerina Teaiwa (1997) provides an interesting critique of the way in which the Body Shop has exploited the resources of the Banaban people of Kiribati in the Western Pacific. She suggests a community response, one which recognizes the importance of 'talk amongst themselves' and an awareness that 'self-determination must come before global participation or we will be swept away by the tide of boundarilessness' (Teaiwa 1997: 8). The type of boundarilessness advocated by the proponents of corporate globalization is not helpful to indigenous peoples whose lands have been colonized. Because their lands have often been proclaimed 'wild and uninhabited' in recent years, many indigenous peoples have had to fight legal battles to reclaim their ancestral domain (see for example Melbourne 1995; Bell 1998; Pryor 2000: 1).

One important aspect of identifying differences in knowledge systems is that it has implications for international law. Darrell Posey concludes that the existing laws on intellectual property rights favour 'industrialized nations rather than the bioculturally rich developing countries' (Posey 1996: 15).

Molecular Colonization

Two projects, the Human Genome Project and the Human Genome Diversity Project (nicknamed the Vampire Project by some indigenous groups), were initiated during the 1990s. These costly projects (trillions of dollars have already been expended on the Human Genome Project alone) are justified on the grounds of finding cures for common and rare diseases, or at the very least of increasing our understanding of human genetics. Laudable as these goals may seem, both projects have been plagued by criticism, in particular with regard to the patenting of human genetic material without the informed consent of the donor.

The theft of land and knowledge on the material and cultural levels is now being paralleled by the theft of body parts (land)[6] and genetic material. Through the collection of individuals' cells (via blood samples) and specimens taken during surgery, pharmaceutical companies are creating cell lines and then patenting the product.

John Moore, an oil worker on an Alaskan pipeline, became an unwilling participant in the Human Genome Project when he was treated for hairy-celled leukemia in 1976. His hugely enlarged spleen was 'harvested' for white blood cells. His doctor then cultivated these cells into an immortal cell line and found that it was capable of producing blood proteins which could be used to treat immuno-suppressive diseases (Vidal and Carvel 1994: 13). Moore then discovered that his doctor and the University of California had applied for – and were granted – a US patent on this 'invention'. At no time was Moore asked for permission to remove a sample from his spleen, nor was he even informed that it was being developed into a cell line. It was not until seven years later that he became aware that a patent had been granted on his own cells. Moore asked some pertinent questions, such as; 'How has life become a commodity?' and he concluded, 'I've been gene raped' (Carvel 1994: 15), and 'I believe that all genetic material extracted from human beings should belong to society as a whole, and not be patentable' (Vidal and Carvel 1994: 13). By 1994 Moore's cell line had earned around US$3 billion for its owners. Moore, of course, received nothing but a small damages settlement out of court.

The Human Genome Diversity Project, which aims to collect material from isolated populations and indigenous peoples, is facing similar problems. In 1995 the US government 'issued itself a patent on a foreign citizen'. The foreign citizen in this case is a member of the Hagahai ethnic group in Papua New Guinea, whose blood was being used without consent to develop new drugs. Similar cases have been reported concerning cell lines from Solomon Islanders, and a Guaymi Indian woman from Panama. Debra Harry, a Paiute from Nevada who is an advocate for indigenous peoples, says: 'Now it's colonialism on a molecular level [...] For us, genes are our ancestry, our heredity and our future generations. They are not to be tampered with' (cited in Horowitz 1996: 34).

At issue, among other things, are two competing world views. The Guaymi of Panama view such commodification as violating 'the integrity of life itself, and our deepest sense of morality' (Shand [1994: 11] cited in Rifkin 1998: 58). Like Ani (2000), the Guaymi see themselves as connected to the whole, not separable into parts, cells or genes. There is no remedy for the degree of violation experienced through these western techniques. On the other hand, the US patent laws specify precisely how life can be owned, patented and 'invented' by scientists and corporations. Like the concept of *terra nullius* enshrined in Australian law until 1992, 'The vacancy of targeted lands has been replaced by the vacancy of targeted life forms and species manipulated by the new technologies' (Shiva 1997: 2).

The Impact of Global Trade Rules in Intellectual Property

The General Agreement on Tariffs and Trade (GATT) first came into effect in 1948 and was developed as one of the 1944 Bretton Woods institutions, which include the World Bank and the International Monetary Fund (IMF). Over the last fifty years the world has changed considerably, and some of the principles on which GATT was based no longer hold. Environmental concerns, for example, are not addressed in the agreement and 'GATT has consistently failed to keep up with the global environmental crisis' (Daly and Goodland 1994: 77).

With the ratification of GATT in 1995 in Marrakech and the subsequent formation of the World Trade Organization (WTO),[7] the economic system advocated by the proponents of corporate globalization became entrenched.[8] The WTO pays little attention to the needs of the people who produce goods but rather focuses on those who benefit most from globalization, namely transnational corporations, international banks and national elites. As Michel Chossudovsky (1998: 35) points out, the GATT agreement 'violates fundamental people's rights, particularly in the areas of foreign investment, bio-diversity and intellectual property rights'.

Trade Related Intellectual Property Rights (TRIPS) were among the last additions to GATT. The adoption of TRIPS means that US patent and copyright laws now apply around the world. And since the US patent laws are much broader than those of Europe, Australia and India (among others) and allow for the patenting of life-forms, they leave the way open to the exploitation of the bio-resources of poorer nations. This is effectively an infringement on national sovereignty which is designed to protect the property of transnational corporations, rather than the labour and knowledge of ordinary people.

In New Zealand Maori activists have been at the forefront of resistance to TRIPS and the Multilateral Agreement on Investment (MAI), which is the logical next step in the process of corporate globalization after the WTO. Aroha Te Pareake Mead, comparing the current wave of colonization with British settlers' felling of indigenous forests, argues that 'what is driving the biotechnology industry is actually more of the same – an obsession to dominate nature and peoples who do not agree with western capitalist models of development: an inability to appreciate nature and the natural order in its "raw-untouched state needing instead to continually manipulate, reconfigure and assert ownership over"' (Mead 1997: 11). As Mahadev G. Bhat (1996: 207) points out: 'Genetic resources that are found to have commercial prospects are commonly found in the wildlands of developing countries whereas commercial manufacturers claiming intellectual property rights to those genetic resources are commonly multinational companies.' This asymmetry[9] between resources and capital is a longstanding one, and its origins go back to the earliest days of capitalism. As with earlier colonial relationships, the push is towards homogenization across cultures, and 'penetration' of dominant cultural values into new environments.

The trend in all these agreements is towards a false universalization of laws applying to trade. This means that all international negotiations of an economic nature follow only one set of laws which blatantly favour the interests of corporations, that these laws are internationally consistent, and that they will not change according to the vagaries of national government policy. That is, the trade rules specifically ignore context and local conditions. It is, effectively, the imposition of a trade monoculture. As I argue elsewhere (Hawthorne 1999: 123), monocultures invariably benefit the powerful and this one is no exception.

Bhat states that: 'Traditionally, the unimproved genetic material or genetic materials that have been partially developed by farmers through field trials and common-sense knowledge are treated as open-access resources' (Bhat 1996: 210). TRIPS follow this 'tradition' because they allow public resources to be used by private companies as the starting point for their research, and when they isolate a component of the genetic resource, it is then privatized and sold to the same farmers who might have developed the original stock. Local access to the stock is lost, and the multinational companies do not even pay royalties to the people who originally developed the resource. The neem tree of India is one example that has led to a successful legal challenge of these principles. But many other plants remain unprotected. Shiva and Holla-Bhar (1993) also cite the endod or African soapberry, a plant widely used throughout Africa as an insecticidal soap, fish intoxicant and spermicidal contraceptive. With commercial uses also in the North American fishing industry, the product of the endod could turn out to be a valuable piece of intellectual property, something which African nations, if they wanted to commercialize the product, could turn into a tradeable commodity of their own.

There is a pressing need to find ways to protect 'wild' resources. In Kenya in the 1980s when an unprotected species, *Maytenus buchananni*, was found to have potential as an anti-cancer drug, the entire adult population of the plant was harvested (Oldfield 1984; Bhat 1996: 212). Collected under the auspices of the US National Cancer Institute, not only was the future existence of the species threatened, but also future research on extracts of the plant. When foreign companies or government institutes move into areas stricken by poverty, the local people will do whatever they can to gain access to cash. As people feel increasing pressures from hunger and poverty and see decreasing possibilities of any future benefit for themselves in maintaining healthy wild stock, they cannot be expected to put conservation above their immediate survival needs.

A host of potential biological resources are currently being screened. If they turn out to be commercially viable, they could return income to their regions of origin, even if the host community had no special use for them. Bhat (1996: 212) points out that wild resources could have 'value for the global community', but at issue is whether the community wants to commodify and commercialize its resources, thereby taking on the western world view of corporate globalization.

Piracy is an unlawful activity. And yet piracy by multinational companies is not only allowed, but enshrined in and protected by international trade agreements policed by the WTO. The universalization of patent laws and the way this is being implemented through the WTO is simply an extension of the old forms of colonization. Visible property, land and the products of culture were destroyed or appropriated by the former imperial powers. These days it is not only the tangible parts of the global commons but also the immaterial goods, the intellectual property, the resources of biodiversity and the spiritual connections of people to their place that are being appropriated by transnational corporations. The process and the players are essentially the same, only the garb differs and the stakes are higher.

Article 8j of the 1992 Convention on Biological Diversity (in Shiva 1993: 166) suggests that innovations that have been developed by particular communities or by indigenous peoples should be given protection. Such protection should ensure open access to seed lines and other resources, as well as the payment of royalties from any wild stock removed from a region. Wild stock and genetic resources are equivalent to bodies and, if marketed, subject to leases and payments to local, state or national governments. But while commercial exploitation may return income to communities, it should not be at the risk of extinction, nor should the communities be forced to participate in the market economy. Just as forests and fishing grounds can be harvested to exhaustion, the harvesting of wild species should be connected to enforceable safeguards, and the integrity of the culture and its world view should be respected.

Industrial diversity and inventiveness is at risk. Access to the products of indigenous plant varieties is at risk. Cultural diversity is at risk. Even our legal frameworks, which have an impact on environmental codes, labour rights and social justice programmes are at risk. Governments of developing countries and former colonies will have a significantly reduced role in the regulation of their own economies. Where does that leave us, the citizens of these countries?

Conclusion

With great prescience, Maria Mies wrote in 1983:

> Subsistence production or production of life includes all work that is expended in creation, re-creation and maintenance of immediate life and which has no other purpose. Subsistence production therefore stands in contrast to commodity and surplus value production. For subsistence production the aim is 'life', for commodity production it is 'money' which produces ever more money, or the accumulation of capital. (Mies 1983, cited in Bennholdt-Thomsen and Mies, 1999: 20)

Maria Mies was thinking ahead of the crowd. Her insight into the momentum and direction of capitalism and her vision for something different have proven to be important tools in developing our understanding of ourselves, and of the destructive impact that western culture and corporate globalization have had on peoples all around the world.

Like her, I long for a vision for western culture which contains something of the spirit of indigenous cultures without appropriating the forms that have been devised by what I call 'the diversity group' who are in the main poor, marginalized and female. Drawing my inspiration from Marimba Ani (2000), I propose a new driving force towards which western culture could move. The driving force for this culture would be the wild. It is what Ani calls the *asili*, the seed (as Shiva would say), life (as Mies would say), *jukurrpa* or dreaming (as the Walpiri of central Australia would say; see Bell 1983). In this new world, biodiversity would become the inspiration for the culture, the defining spirit or what Ani calls *utamaroho*. This spirit would create very different behaviours and institutions, the creations of a particular kind of thought or *utamawazo*. It would mean that people would be incapable of destroying land since the relationship between themselves and the land would be one of connection. It would be impossible to imagine terminator seeds, genetically modified organisms, molecular colonization and bio-technologies which violate women's bodies, since these would be perceived as deeply destructive. The separation of the wild from the tame could not occur and the eradication of cultural diversity would be unimaginable.

Globalization and the homogenization of knowledge, of seeds, of cultures is a one-way route to global destruction. The few (the wealthy and mobile elites) are once again attempting to control the many, that is the diversity group. And it is this diversity group that holds hope for the future, in new ways of thinking, and in the quest for new behaviours and institutions which will hold dear the driving force of wildness.

That these issues are urgent and of wide public concern is evident in the demonstrations which have been held in Seattle, Prague, Melbourne (Melbourne's S11),[10] and around the world against the various incarnations of the WTO.

Notes

1. Over the past few years I have begun to see the sending of children away to school as part of a process of dislocation. In its original European form it enabled Europeans to leave their own countries and colonize others. In its contemporary form it creates a separation from place that enables the privileged to participate happily in the mobility of globalization.

2. Bell (1998) provides an interesting discussion of the continuum of views of the Ngarrindjeri people of South Australia, from the nineteenth-century missionaries, to mid-twentieth-century anthropology, to the developers of the 1990s, and the Ngarrindjeri people themselves.

3. 'Not existing' is a familiar state for many colonized peoples. The declaration of Australia as *terra nullius*, thereby eradicating at least 60,000 years of continuous culture, is one of the more extreme cases of European cultural whitewashing.

4. For an account of women defending their rights against the British colonizers in Nigeria, the story of the Igbo Women's War in 1929, in which the women fought the colonizers with pots and pans, is a marvellous instance of subversive resistance tactics

(for a poetic account see Nwapa 1986: 40–3); see also Shiva's account of the Chipko women (Shiva 1989: 67–77).

5. Doctors and lawyers are the first to protect their ground when alternative systems are offered. An individual may master the knowledge as well or better than many of its practitioners, but without a certificate, diploma or degree it is not possible for that person to make use of the knowledge. This system has been used very effectively to keep women practitioners, for example, out of the system.

6. Vandana Shiva (1989: 41) uses the symbolism of Terra Mater – the Great Mother, Gaia in the Greek tradition, Prakriti (nature) in her Indian tradition – as a core metaphor for her approach to land, a concept which appears in many cultures around the world. In the Ngarrindjeri world view of South Australia the root forms of the words 'land' and 'body' are related. The word for 'land', *ruwi* (sometimes written *ruwe*) shares the same root as *ruwar*, 'body' (Bell 1998: 622). When earth and body are connected in these ways, it becomes more important to take account of the consequences of one's activities in relation to land.

7. Lal Das (2000) provides a detailed guide to the intricacies of the WTO agreements.

8. The recent success of the Neem tree case is to be applauded. Perhaps there is some hope for the continuing 'ownership' of indigenous knowledge. For background see Shiva and Holla-Bhar 1993; Shand 1998; and Dutfield 2000; Shiva 2000.

9. Correa (2000: 1–21) deals extensively with the issue of North–South asymmetry.

10. The S11 protests were held 11–13 September 2000 in Melbourne, Australia. Protesters closed Melbourne's streets around the casino (an appropriate meeting place!) during the World Economic Forum meeting. Protesters were successful in keeping around a third of the delegates from attending the first day of the meeting. It was a peaceful protest marred only by excessive violence on the part of the Victoria police.

References

Akhter, F. (1990) *Women and Trees: Trees in the Life of Women in Kaijuri Village*, Dhaka: Narigrantha Prabartana.

Ani, M. (2000) *Yurugu: An African-Centered Critique of European Cultural Thought and Behavior*, Trenton, NJ, and Asmara, Eritrea: Africa World Press.

Bell, D. (1983) *Daughters of the Dreaming*, Sydney: Allen and Unwin.

— (1998) *Ngarrindjeri Wurruwarrin: The World That Is, Was, and Will Be*, Melbourne: Spinifex Press.

Bennholdt-Thomsen, V. and M. Mies (1999) *The Subsistence Perspective: Beyond the Globalized Economy*, London: Zed Books; Melbourne: Spinifex Press.

Bhat, M. G. (1996) 'Trade-related Intellectual Property Rights to Biological Resources: Socioeconomic Implications for Developing Countries', *Ecological Economics*, 19, pp. 205–17.

Bird, C. (ed.) (1998) *The Stolen Children: Their Stories*, Sydney: Random House.

Carvel, J. (1994) 'He lost his spleen to science; now he vents it', *Melbourne Age*, 10 November, p. 15.

Cheru, F. (2000) 'The Local Dimensions of Global Reform', in J. N. Pieterse (ed.), *Global Futures: Shaping Globalization*, London: Zed Books, pp. 119–32.

Chossudovsky, M. (1998) *The Globalization of Poverty: Impacts of IMF on World Bank Reforms*, London: Zed Books.

Clarke, Tony and Maude Barlow (1997) *The Multilateral Agreement on Investment and the Threat to Canadian Sovereignty*, Toronto: Stoddart.

Correa, C. M. (2000) *Intellectual Property Rights, the WTO and Developing Countries: The TRIPS Agreement and Policy Option*, Penang: Third World Network; London: Zed Books.

Daly, H. and R. Goodland (1994) 'An Ecological-economic Assessment of Deregulation of International Commerce under GATT', *Ecological Economics*, 9, 73–92.

Dutfield, G. (2000) *Intellectual Property Rights, Trade and Biodiversity*, London: Earthscan.

Hawthorne, S. (1999) 'Connectivity: Cultural Practice of the Powerful or Subversion from the Margins?', in S. Hawthorne and R. Klein (eds), *CyberFeminism: Connectivity, Critique and Creativity*, Melbourne: Spinifex Press.

Horvitz, L. A. (1996) 'Vampire Project raises issue of patents for humans', *Insight on the News*, 12.

Johnson, E. (1985) 'A Letter to my Mother', in S. Hawthorne (ed.), *Difference: Writings by Women*, Sydney: Brooks Waterloo.

Kartinyeri, D. (2000) *Kick the Tin*, Melbourne: Spinifex Press.

La Duke, W. (1999) *All Our Relations: Native Struggles for Land and Life*, Cambridge, MA: South End Press.

Lal Das, B. (2000) *The World Trade Organisation: A Guide to the Framework for International Trade*, Penang: Third World Network; London: Zed Books.

Langton, M. (1998) *Burning Questions: Emerging Environmental Issues for Indigenous Peoples in Northern Australia*, Darwin: Centre for Indigenous Natural and Cultural Resource Management, Northern Territory University.

Martinez-Alier, J. (2000) 'Environmental Justice as a Force for Sustainability', in J. N. Pieterse (ed.), *Global Futures: Shaping Globalization*, London: Zed Books, pp. 148–74.

Matsui, Y. (1999) *Women in the New Asia*, London: Zed Books; Melbourne: Spinifex Press; Bangkok: White Lotus.

Mead, A. (1997) 'How are the Values of Maori Going to be Considered and Integrated in the Use of Plant Biotechnology in New Zealand's Sustainability?', *Pacific World*, 46, pp. 10–11.

Melbourne, H. (1995) *Maori Sovereignty: The Maori Perspective*, Auckland: Hodder Moa Beckett.

Nazarea, V. D. (1999) 'Lenses and Latitudes in Landscapes and Lifescapes', in V. D. Nazarea (ed.), *Ethnoecology: Situated Knowledge/Located Lives*, Tucson: University of Arizona Press.

Nwapa, F. (1986) *Cassava Song and Rice Song*, Lagos: Tana Press.

Oldfield, M. L. (1984) *The Value of Conserving Genetic Resources*, Washington, DC: US Department of Interior, National Park Service.

Posey, D. A. (1996) 'Protecting Indigenous Peoples' Rights to Biodiversity', *Environment*, 38.

Pryor, C. (2000) 'New struggle looms after Wik people win six-year land battle', *Australian*, Sydney, 4 October, p. 5.

Reynolds, H. (1990) *The Other Side of the Frontier*, Melbourne: Penguin Books.

Rifkin, J. (1998) *The Biotech Century: Harnessing the Gene and Remaking the World*, New York: Jeremy P. Tarcher/Putnam.

Robertson, C. C. (1997) 'Black, White, and Red All Over: Beans, Women, and Agricultural Imperialism in Twentieth Century Kenya', *Agricultural History*, 71, pp. 259–99.

Schoeffel, P. (1995) 'Women in Fisheries in the Pacific Islands: A Retrospective Analysis', in E. Matthews (ed.), *Fishing for Answers: Women and Fisheries in the Pacific Islands*, Suva, Fiji: Women and Fisheries Network, pp. 7–18.

Shand, H. J. (1998) 'Biopiracy, Biodiversity and People: The Right to Say "No" to Monopoly Patents that are Predatory on the South's Resources and Knowledge', *Human Environment*, V.

Shiva, V. (1989) *Staying Alive: Women, Ecology and Development*, New Delhi: Kali for Women; London: Zed Books.

— (1993) *Monocultures of the Mind: Perspectives on Biodiversity and Biotechnology*, Penang: Third World Network.

— (1997) *Biopiracy: The Plunder of Nature and Knowledge*, Boston, MA: South End Press.

— (2000) 'Global Capital, Local Resources', transcript of a speech given on 10 September, RMIT, Melbourne. www.abc.net.au/specials/shiva/shiva.htm

Shiva, V. and R. Holla-Bhar (1993) 'Intellectual Piracy and the Neem Tree', *The Ecologist*, 23, pp. 223–7.

Sittirak, S. (1998) *The Daughters of Development: Women in a Changing Environment*, London: Zed Books.

Teaiwa, K. M. (1997) 'Body Shop Banabans and Skin Deep Samaritans', in *VIII Pacific Science Inter-Congress Suva*, Fiji: University of the South Pacific.

Tuhiwai, Smith, Linda (1999) *Decolonising Methodologies: Research and Indigenous Peoples*, London: Zed Books; Otago: University of Otago Press.

Vidal, J. and J. Carvel (1994) 'Genetic Harvest', *Melbourne Age*, 24 November, p. 13.

Wichterich, C. (1999) *The Globalized Woman: Reports from a Future of Inequality*, London: Zed Books; Melbourne: Spinifex Press.

Wickramasinghe, A. (1994) *Deforestation, Women and Forestry: The Case of Sri Lanka*, Utrecht: Institute for Development Research Amsterdam.

Yibarbuk, D. (1998) 'Notes on Traditional Use of Fire on Upper Cadell River', Foreword, in M. Langton (ed.), *Burning Questions: Emerging Environmental Issues for Indigenous Peoples in Northern Australia*, Darwin: Centre for Indigenous and Cultural Resource Management, Northern Territory University, pp. 1–6.

Globalized Bodies in the Twenty-first Century: The Final Patriarchal Takeover?

Renate Klein

When, in the late 1960s and early 70s, the second wave of the feminist movement in the twentieth century (the women's liberation movement) burst on the international scene with outrage and passion, one of its first demands in western countries was 'Our Bodies – Ourselves'. This slogan, soon to become the title of an influential book on women's health (Boston Women's Health Collective 1969) and the beginning of an international women's health movement, reflected women's anger that their lives/bodies were defined and controlled by 'experts': patriarchal (male) doctors and scientists who personally and politically had constructed women's social inferiority as based in women's biology. Women, individually and collectively, were fed up with male domination and demanded the end of all social and individual violence, including sexual, medical and psychological abuse. The medicalization of women's lives began to be resisted, feminist self-help groups sprang up like wildfire in countries of the South and the North, and women's liberation promised a women-centred health and sexuality that respected bodily integrity and the dignity of mind/body/spirit/soul.

There was a tremendous hunger for knowledge that could inform actions for (inter)national social justice and solidarity. Women's studies practitioners and feminist researchers, first in the West but soon spreading to the so-called Third World (Committee on Women's Studies in Asia 1994), began their inspirational journeys to produce women-centred knowledge. Not only was it to critique the (ph)allacies of euro- and US-centric 'male subjectivity' (Rich 1979), but this knowledge was to be visionary, daring, challenging, new and emerging from 'a thinking heart and a feeling mind' (Raymond 1986). For, as Maria Mies wrote in her inspirational 'womanifesto', the 'Methodischen Postulate zur Frauenforschung' (1978), 'new wine must not be poured into old bottles' (Mies 1983: 117).[1] Or, as Audre Lorde (1981) was to say shortly after, 'The master's tools will never dismantle the master's house'.

Sisterhood is Diverse and Powerful

During the 1970s and 80s, all issues were declared feminist terrain (Bunch 1981) and, depending on areas of interest and, often, geographical and political location, feminist researchers generated critiques of patriarchy and global capitalism (Mies 1998), compulsory heterosexuality and the institution of motherhood (Rich 1980; 1976) as well as the overwhelming (sexual) violence of racist, classist, international techno-patriarchy (e.g. hooks 1984; Dworkin 1974; 1982; Bunch and Myron 1974). The oppression of women was compared to that of nature (Griffin 1978; Daly 1978; Merchant 1980) and critiques of medicine's control and mistreatment of women emerged (Chesler 1972; Corea 1985a; Scully 1994). Many different 'strands' of feminist theory evolved internationally such as black and lesbian feminism, radical and Marxist/socialist feminism, liberal, post-colonial and eco-feminism, to name just a few. Then, as now, there was often heated disagreement among feminists:[2] liberals worried that radicals were 'going too far' (Morgan 1978), lesbian feminists were concerned that heterosexual women continued to 'sleep with the enemy' (Leeds Revolutionary Feminist Group 1981; Wittig 1992), socialist and materialist feminists became ir- ritated with radical feminists' insistence that pornography and prostitution were at the core of global patriarchy and needed to be theorized and resisted. But in spite of such differences, there was a euphoric belief that mountains could be moved, 'gynaffection' (Raymond 2001) could flourish, and that 'Sisterhood is Powerful' and indeed 'global' (Morgan 1970; 1984). The international feminist mood was one of hope; women's liberation was to foster alliances between strong women whose diversity was their strength, and whose vision and determination to be free individually and collectively would end women's oppression.

Ensuring the integrity of 'Our Bodies – Ourselves' – in the fullest sense of 'body' and 'self', including land, lives, states and politics where the personal is so obviously the political – became one of the central issues in the 1980s that united women of the South with those of the North in emerging discussions of the threat to bodily integrity of (new) reproductive technologies and population control. Following initial and tentative feminist inquiries into whether reproductive technologies such as IVF (in vitro fertilization) were positive developments for women individually and collectively (Arditti et al. 1984; 1985), by the mid-1980s, through the founding of the Feminist International Network on the New Reproductive Technologies (FINRET) in Groningen, Holland, in 1984 (which became the Feminist International Network of Resistance to Reproductive and Genetic Engineering, FINRRAGE, at the 'Emergency Conference' held in Sweden in 1985), feminist interest in these technologies coalesced into a truly international movement. The hypocrisy was glaring: in western countries – and for rich women in the so-called Third World – IVF and other new reproductive technologies were touted as the solution to the heartbreak of infertility;[3] while in Third World countries – and for poor women in the so-called developed world – the same 'techno-docs' and pharmaceutical companies produced harmful contraceptives/abortifacients such as Norplant, the contraceptive vaccine and mifepristone/prostaglandin (better known as the French abortion pill RU486) which, together with enforced sterilization, unashamedly targeted women in the Third World in their racist, western-centred population-control campaigns (Klein et al. 1991; Akhter 1995; Richter 1996; Guymer, 1998; Declaration of People's Perspectives 1993). With the publication of a virtual explosion of books on new reproductive technologies and genetic engineering, and the convening of numerous feminist conferences in, among other places, Germany,[4] Bangladesh, Australia and Canada during the 1980s, an international movement of feminist theorists and activists was created and a groundswell of articles began to permeate the (inter)national 'mainstream' media exposing the violent, woman-hating, eugenic, as well as profit-driven nature of reproductive and genetic engineering and advocating a less fragmented relationship between women and their bodies (Corea 1985b; Hubbard 1985; Corea et al. 1985; Spallone and Steinberg 1987; Scutt 1988; Klein 1989a; 1989b; 1989c, 1992; Spallone 1989; Declaration of Comilla 1991; Rowland 1992; Klein 1992; Raymond).

It is important to note that in addition to pointing out that the infertility/fertility debate – new reproductive and contraceptive technologies – represented two sides of the same coin, feminist writing of that time had already alerted readers to the fact that these technological developments were but stepping stones to a world in which the (re)production of 'perfect' children without women would be firmly in techno-patriarchal hands. Further, these writings foresaw developments such as pre-natal testing, cloning and the deciphering of the human genome and exposed the exploitation of women's fear of producing less than perfect children by techno-docs' promises of a happy world of healthy miracle babies. 'Why do we need all this?', asked Maria Mies (1985), while Jalna Hanmer and Gena Corea called for an international tribunal on medical crimes against women (in Corea et al. 1985: 49). And in 1988 we founded the *Reproductive and Genetic Engineering: Journal of International Feminist Analysis* (published by Pergamon Press).[5]

FINRRAGE became an international resistance movement against heterosexist global patriarchy with its dehumanizing technologies. Through passionate theory-in-action, it galvanized women from a multiplicity of social, sexual, age and ethnic backgrounds into opposing the production of

Man-made Women (Corea et al. 1985) as well as the annihilation of real live poor marginalized (dis)abled women world-wide who do not fit the mould of stereotypical western-defined 'womanhood'. The movement was inspiring and radical; it was deeply threatening to the patriarchal order; and it had to be stopped or at least weakened. The attacks came not only from the international reproductive technology establishment, although they certainly tried their best to discredit our work.[6]

Destabilization

Much of the destabilizing of feminist opposition to reproductive and genetic engineering that took place in the 1990s was due to the 'Zeitgeist' backlash philosophy which, under the guise of 'choice' – the buzz-word of the new libertarians[7] – declared our critique of reproductive and genetic engineering to be 'over the top', simplistic and too radical. We were called cruel and heartless; couldn't we see the suffering of childless people? The promises of reproductive medicine for the sick and disabled? The glory of the coming Gene Age? And patronising: who were 'we' anyway to stop women from using these medical breakthroughs and miracle technologies? Why not produce the supposedly 'perfect' child using pre-natal screening, or give the ultimate gift of love to a sister by offering to become a so-called surrogate mother – 'an incubator, a suitcase really' – or why not try IVF ten or even twenty times because men want their biological lineage continued and women don't want to be 'technological failures' so they never give up, in spite of the damage to their bodies/lives/souls and hearts? In the name of 'doing good' and bringing about 'empowerment', such proponents of choice, who increasingly included international women's health advocates, spread their repro-business gospel internationally.

One sobering experience was the 1994 International Conference on Population and Development (ICPD) in Cairo (see Klein, 1995: ii–v). The conference fostered the myth that population-control programmes would be abandoned in favour of 'family planning' where women's choices would be respected. But in reality only the language had changed; 'choice' still meant coercion, although it would now be promoted as 'empowerment' by international women's health organizations which received huge amounts of funding from the Population Council, one of the world's foremost US-dominated population-control bodies.[8]

Global capital thus accelerated the spread of the globalization virus – deeply inimical to indigenous peoples, women and nature and yet hailed as 'progress' and 'opportunity'. Moreover, in universities around the world the acceptance of postmodern ideology led to the academic glorification of fragmentation, and resistance to anything that appears whole and 'real', such as women's bodies/women's lives. Last but not least, in the 1990s we witnessed the development of the world-wide web phenomenon which, despite its potential for international feminist actions and campaigns,[9] I see as a further destabilizing force for women's sense of self and wholeness, thus contributing to the fragmentation of bodies/minds/spirits/souls.

For all these reasons, while many of us persevere in our opposition to dehumanizing technologies – and none more admirably than Maria Mies who has continued to develop her vision for an alternative future over the last thirty years (e.g. Mies 1998; Mies and Shiva 1993; Bennholdt-Thomsen and Mies 1999) – critical questions about contemporary feminist theories and their connections to the daily praxis of women's lives need to be asked.

- While we now have a women's human rights movement, are women closer to living lives free of bodily bondage in spite of continuing patriarchal notions of 'normalcy': 'normal' bodies, 'normal' minds, 'normal' (in)fertile bodies?
- While we have a veritable industry of postmodern body writing, from 'volatile bodies' to 'sexy bodies', 'unruly bodies', 'post-human bodies', are real live women across the globe, across social class, sexuality, ethnicity and age, free to break rules – or have we become texts without contexts, bodies that can be written, transgressed, invaded, fragmented, augmented, reduced?
- While nation-states begin to dissolve and indigenous groups begin to claim their sovereignty, are indigenous women's connections to, and between, their land and their bodies understood and listened to?
- While we can fly in cyberspace, are women ready to become 're-presentation only': 'cyborgs', eroticized techno-bodies, 'URL bodies', 'metabodies', 'rescued from the limitations of a mortal body' (Moravec 1988: 5)?

To put it bluntly: is this what women's liberation wanted to achieve? Due to limitations of space in what follows I will briefly summarize my concerns about postmodern body writing and cybertechnologies – including their relationship to reproductive and genetic engineering – and reflect on the ramifications for women of the planned annihilation of the organic body. I will finish with some thoughts on embodied feminist resistance which aims to ensure that women's globalized bodies have a chance to survive in the twenty-first century.

Postmodern Body Writings . . .

Postmodern thinking revels in idolizing multiple subjectivities and borderless transgressions. It abhors (universal) truths, connections, identity and, at its extreme, proclaims that 'the author is dead'[10] – all that counts is texts without contexts, words without flesh. Postmodern theorists are particularly keen to deny, destroy, disown, 'disembody' and fragment the body. Indeed, it is not overstating the case that real live bodies – anything that breathes, smells, sighs, laughs and has a heart – are loathed in postmodern writing. Labelled 'essentialist' – and thus banned as having committed the ultimate heresy of postmodernism and replaced by representation only – bodies *are* no longer; bodies exist only 'discursively' and are 'reconfigured' in the production of texts that in jargonistic language dissect and 'disrupt' the body. Without doubt, postmodern body writing has been the growth industry in cultural and literary studies since the late 1980s.

... and Reproductive Technologies

Postmodern (wet) fantasies about fragmented, leaking bodies oozing from the pens of academic theorists are mirrored by the actual feats – and fantasies – of cutters with knives who also revel in fragmentation and alienation: medicos and scientists engaged in reproductive and genetic engineering. Under the guise of helping infertile couples to alleviate their pain of involuntary childlessness, the search is on for the womanless child from the glass; made to order by the 'gods' in the labs. Immature eggs are taken from the ovary of a woman or foetus – dead or alive – matured in vitro, then fertilized with easy-to-get sperm. The resulting embryo is placed in a womb – as of yet still that of a real live woman, though the artificial womb has long been under development – and the designer baby, so the theory goes, makes its sex-selected, disease-screened, monitored and controlled entry into the techno-world.[11] I do not criticize cut-and-paste baby-making because these technologies tamper with 'nature' (the accusation of essentialism again), but rather because they constitute medical violence against women, and will, if continued unabated, remove the decision-making power of whether to have children or not – and how many, and of what sex – from women. It will be techno-docs who are in control, and women's consciousness will be bent to see this as the postmodern responsible 'choice' of baby-making.[12] Moreover, by means of conjuring up any disability as monstrosity – but as preventable – only the 'perfect' child will be allowed to be 'born'; the one whose genes have been checked for existing genetic diseases as well as predispositions to, say, diabetes, manic depression, homosexuality,[13] and, no doubt, the 'correct' race and sex. Worryingly, at the beginning of the twenty-first century, these techno-fix cultures are gaining ground as they mix nicely with the ubiquitous 'do-it-yourself' ideology of the idealized individual which rules supreme in globalization discourse. The emerging cybertechnologies go one step further to facilitate the dissociation of people from 'real' life and encourage 'cyberdreams'.

Cyberdreams: from Cyborgs to Cyberminds[14]

The fragmentary nature of cyberspace builds on the extreme celebration of fragmentation in postmodern ideology as well as in reproductive and genetic engineering which are both concerned with (re)fashioning what constitutes 'bodies' in the postmodern age. What rules supreme is the mind, in complete accordance with man's (*sic*) past, present and future longing for control, and obsession with transcendence and immortality. Similar to reproductive and genetic engineers, cyberenthusiasts conjure up the illusion that bodies are technologically alterable – a cut or a click away – and the motto is 'enhancement' and, above all 'choice'. Cybergurus' dreams are to achieve what religious believers have piously put their faith in for centuries: the cybermind – eternal, bodiless life. Before this ultimate solution, however, the body/machine organism, the cyborg, offers partial liberation from messy *real* bodies that leak blood, guts and gore.

The fascination with physically changing people's bodies has been seized on by cybertheorists who have invented the 'cyborg', an organism that is part-human, part-machine.[15] As Donna Haraway put it: 'The cyborg is a kind of disassembled and reassembled, post-modern collective and personal self. This is the self feminists must code' (Haraway 1991: 163). Thus, Haraway's self is a cut-and-paste body, 'rejoicing in the illegitimate fusion of animal and machine' (p. 176). A self that adds – and sheds – machinic bits so that, according to Haraway, 'communications technologies and biotechnologies are the crucial tools for recrafting our bodies' (p. 164). The cyborg is clearly superior to the human body. As Haraway puts it starkly: 'We don't need organic holism to give impermeable wholeness, [producing] the total woman and her feminist variants (mutants?)' (p. 178).

Digitizing our flesh is the aim of eminent US computer scientist and robotics specialist, Hans Moravec. As outlined in *Mind Children* (1988) and later works, in Moravec's vision, real bodies are relegated to irrelevant 'meat' and 'wetware' (the brain), and the dream of eternal life consisting of ever-changing mind molecules, without the flesh, is writ large. In the 'post-biological' age, we will leave behind our organic bodies made out of proteins (encoded through DNA and RNA). Instead, electronically wired machines of far superior quality – faster and with much more storage and selection/combination capabilities – will take over. In Moravec's words: 'Our culture will then be able to evolve independently of human biology and its limitation, passing instead directly from generation to generation of ever more capable intelligent machinery' (Moravec 1988: 4).

This, Moravec argues, is immense progress as it will do away with the 'uneasy truce between mind and body [... when it] breaks down completely as life ends' (p. 4). The mind, as he goes on to say, will be 'rescued from the limitation of a mortal body' (p. 5). The resulting 'mind children', in Moravec's view, will be perfectly suited to an ever faster pace of life on this planet – and others. The computer as 'head' of a robot body could update the contents of its own mind continuously, adding and deleting, testing components in all kinds of combinations, to keep up with changing conditions (p. 5).[16] Of course these minds could be copied and sold, patented and leased, and cloned – to keep young and fresh on ice – all leading to a burgeoning 'mind industry'.

It is important to emphasize that Moravec is an established scientist who backs up his assumptions with mathematical and computational details. In 1999 he expanded his original vision in *Robot: Mere Machine to Transcendent Mind*. An on-line review published by the John M. Ashbrook Center for Public Affairs at Ashland University (1 February 1999) quotes Moravec as stating:'"[m]achines, which will grow from us, learn our skills, and share our goals and values, can be viewed as children of our minds" [...] In a bid for immortality, many of our descendants will choose to transform into "ex humans," as they upload themselves into advanced computers. We will become our children' (http://www.ashbrook.org/books/moravec.html).

Cyber- and reproductive technology happily married! The annihilation of the organic human body 'of woman born' enthusiastically advocated! By downloading the brain it is hoped, 'we' (which we?) will achieve transcendence. Given the current configuration of cyberspace as overwhelmingly macho, pornographic, (hetero)sexualized and imbued with 'cyberselfishness' (Paulina Borsook in Wertheim 1999: 281; see also Donna Hughes 1999: 'The Internet and the Global Prostitution Industry'), it is quite likely that it will be a white male 'cyberelite' who will invest in cyberimmortality for themselves. Yet at the same time they will need women as real and virtual sex objects as well as menial workers/emotional supporters for their travails/travels in cyberspace. But perhaps the reproductive engineers might come to the rescue: with cloning and the artificial womb perfected and the need for 'hardware' (the hard disk, also called matter, mater, and womb in contemporary cyberwriting; see Dery 1996) diminished, the idea might be to remove women's consciousness from their mat(t)er altogether and have it reside in the cyberskins of robot bodies floating in cyberspace.

Cybermatricide on the cusp of the new millennium as the final patriarchal takeover? What happened to the feminist dream of 'Our Bodies – Ourselves'? It is difficult to assess how much of these (far-fetched?)

scenarios will come true. Like so many other male fantasies, the dream of the bodiless mind that has rendered the woman/body/matter/matrix/mater obsolete might remain just that – a cyberdream. On the other hand, it cannot be denied that computer power is doubling every year, that nanotechnology is advancing rapidly and that, through the use of the world-wide web, information is made available at increasing speed. Similarly, postmodern body theorists, including some feminists, continue to push their 'transgressive boundaries', alienating women (and men) further and further from their own bodies/minds/selves. And uncivil, greedy and selfish globalization rules supreme. However, ever the feminist optimist, I will now turn to some strategies for survival into a feminist future for all.

Bodysense: Reclaiming Wholeness

If feminists are to survive the multiple attacks, it is crucial that the *real* bodies/minds of *real* women remain connected to the environments they live in, and that we reclaim a sense of 'wholeness' that repositions itself at the *centre* of our theory and praxis. German philosopher Annegret Stopczyk (1998) has coined the term 'Leibsinn', a word which resists translation. 'Bodysense' may sound a bit heavy and not very elegant, yet in a way it is precisely such a 'bodysense' that we need to rescue and nurture, a grounded whole/self, resisting fragmentation and dissociation.

The memory of connectivities in indigenous knowledges of body/souls has been lost for many western women but survives in some indigenous cultures. It may be the way ahead to thrive and survive in the postmodern gene- and cyber-age. In her ethnography detailing the lives of the South Australian Ngarrindjeri peoples, *Ngarrindjeri Wurruwarrin: A World that Is, Was, and Will Be* (1998), Diane Bell was told how in Ngarrindjeri culture land and body are fused. The term '*ruwi*' means land and the word '*ruwar*' means body. Thus damage to the land is damage to the body in a very visceral sense (p. 262). Women speak of pegs driven into the land as spiritual wounding (p. 267).

Women have complicated relationships with their bodies. From an early age, the patriarchal messages we get, differing in nuances but not intent, and depending on culture, age, race and social status, are that our bodies are wanting; they are never good enough and thus are in need of ongoing control. Throughout our lives, we are medicalized, our bodies downsized, and our disabilities hidden and all the while we are told that this is 'for our own good'. And we body-modify, from diets to anorexia, from cosmetic surgery to body cutting. There exists an enormous hatred and loathing of female bodies, especially in western cultures around the world, and women are among those who hate their own bodies most. There are always resisters, though, perhaps victims first, but through sheer willpower and insistence – and often theoretical and bodily insight – they are survivors in the end. And there are some wise individuals who manage to live harmoniously from childhood to old age.[17]

In order to survive with our bodies in the 'real' world, with its accelerating pace of 'miracle' technologies aimed at every facet of ourselves, we must, first, be aware of the magnitude of these assaults and the deeply damaging effects they can/could have for women internationally. Second, we have to be aware that to resist these technologies, to insist that we/our children/our pregnancies *are* good enough and that 'perfection' is in the eye of the beholder, is dangerous, and women who resist the dominant ideologies have to pay a price. During the men's 're-naissance', women were burnt as witches. I fervently hope that the twenty-first century will not be another male orgy of oppression and harm to those who are 'other'; who beg to differ from the 'malestream' norms. Our biggest challenge will be to convince young women (and men) to listen to us, to learn from past struggles, to understand how valuable and joyful bodily integrity and dignity of mind/soul/self can be. While some technological developments could and should be welcomed as possible improvements in our 'real' lives, we should never become their – and their masters' – slaves. Should the technical feasibility of scanning one's brain activities on to a computer, or of growing an embryo in an artificial womb, indeed become 'real', we might do well to remember that 'the man [*sic*] on the moon' has not become the norm for woman; and that if we like and enjoy our bodies and ourselves, then the majority of women might not rush to the action. The postmodern, gene- and cyber-enthusiasts' disembodied mind-dreams sound a warning bell and need to be critiqued as a twenty-first century threat to wholeness and body sense.

Those of us who are concerned about the future of the oppressed and marginalized, of women as a social group as well as indigenous peoples and other groups that have kept connections with their mind/body/land/soul, might want to disregard the 'high' disembodied theories that currently plague the minds (maybe even the bodies!) of postmodern techno-docs and cybernerds. Above all, we have to trust that we will find the answers within 'Our Bodies – Ourselves'.

Notes

A version of this chapter was presented at the US National Women's Studies Association Conference, Boston University, June 2000. I am grateful to Deakin University's Faculty of Arts for conference support.

1. The 'Methodischen Postulate zur Frauenforschung' were my first point of encounter with Maria Mies. I remember how deeply impressed, and very intimidated, I was when in 1980 I visited her in The Hague and asked her if Gloria Bowles and I could include this ground-breaking piece in *Theories of Women's Studies* – to which she agreed. The book became a feminist classic, not least thanks to Maria's contribution.

2. These discussions are vividly recounted in recent feminist 'memoirs'; e.g. Rachel Blau DuPlessis and Ann Snitow (1998); Susan Brownmiller (2000); Ann Summers (1999).

3. Infertility can indeed be heartbreaking and in no way do I wish to belittle the very real pain of involuntarily childless women which became all too obvious in my study in Australia of women's experiences with IVF as well as in the international anthology I edited about women's experiences of reproductive medicine (Klein 1989a, b and c). The point is, however, that reproductive technologists exploit this real as well as socially constructed desire for children and use the pain of infertility to justify their use of women as 'living laboratories' (Rowland 1992).

4. Maria Mies and I met again in 1984 at the International Interdisciplinary 'Women's Worlds' Congress in Groningen after a plenary session on reproductive technologies which we called 'The Death of the Female?' After this session, which was packed with hundreds of women, FINRET was founded and an ad hoc committee began planning an 'Emergency' Conference in Sweden in 1985. Also in 1985, German feminists organized the Congress 'Frauen gegen Gentechnik und Reproduktionstechnik' in Bonn where Maria and I were plenary speakers at a forum of 2000 women who loudly proclaimed their opposition to these technologies. Later that year in Sweden, it was largely due to Maria's and other German women's insistence that we included 'genetic engineering' – hence the name change to FINRRAGE. This was the beginning of our long and fruitful co-operation in the struggle against these technologies which led us twice to conferences in Bangladesh and many other places including another International Interdisciplinary 'Women's Worlds' Congress in Adelaide in Australia in 1996.

5. Founding editors were Farida Akhter, Robyn Rowland, Renate Klein, Rita Arditti, Gena Corea with Jalna Hanmer as managing and Janice Raymond as consulting editors. Maria Mies was a member of the editorial board and a frequent contributor and reviewer and the journal profited greatly from her active role in finding German contributors.

6. In Australia, more than once rumours were circulated that Robyn Rowland or I had been locked up in psychiatric institutions and our colleagues at Deakin University were asked how it was to work with 'the psychos'.

7. The growing influence of libertarians, including feminists, who criticized our stance on reproductive and genetic engineering also extended to areas of pornography and prostitution which increasingly became normalized as 'choice': 'Sexwork – a job just like any other'. See Leidholdt and Raymond (1990) on 'sexual liberals and their attack on feminism' and Jeffreys (1997) on prostitution.

8. This money made it possible to pay airfares and accommodation for women delegates in Cairo's luxury hotels. Understandably, but unfortunately, some former FINRRAGE members preferred these arrangements that enabled them to participate in the ICPD. The only grants FINRRAGE was able to distribute came from funds obtained by UBINIG, Farida Akhter's organization in Bangladesh.

9. Contrary to reproductive and genetic engineering where I perceive the technologies as inherently destructive and violent, I can see positive effects for women in the use of cybertechnologies (see Hawthorne and Klein 1999).

10. Ironically, these intellectual feats are attributed to a chorus of prominent,

predominantly French men (see Brodribb 1992), and, in the feminist version, a group of US women – a hypocrisy that I think also pertains to power relations on the net: it is supposed to be democratic and equal-for-all, but it is really the authority of Bill Gates and his competitors that determine our supposedly limitless access to cyberspace.

11. While embryo research and testing have been the *raison d'être* for reproductive scientists since the beginning of their mission to conquer the process of reproduction, a big infertility industry built on hope and despair has certainly aided their quest. Nevertheless, more than twenty years after Louise Brown was born in 1978, the IVF failure rate is still close to 90 per cent per individual woman, which means that the procedure rarely works for more than ten women out of 100. In order to improve on these statistics (in 1999 male infertility accounted for up to half of all clients in fertility clinics) a few, or only one, sperm are injected into an egg of a perfectly fertile woman whose health and indeed life may be jeopardized in the drug-heavy IVF procedure (see Klein and Rowland 1988).

12. A developing gynaecological speciality, adolescent or children's gynaecology (for girls only!) is keen to investigate hormonal and other developmental changes in girls from birth to puberty. To this end they suggest that girls as young as seven be required to attend yearly gynaecological exams. This instils early in a girl's mind the idea that 'doctor' (the expert) knows best. For an illuminating exposé see Schüssler and Bode (1992).

13. I do not for one moment believe in the existence of a gene for homosexuality. Rather, in the age of 'geneticization' (Lippman 1993), socio–biology gets revisited: homophobic pseudoscientific myths browbeat people into accepting science's gospel about their socially constructed sexuality.

14. For more details on cyborgs see Susan Hawthorne's and my chapters on this topic in *CyberFeminism* (Hawthorne and Klein 1999); see also my chapter '(Dead) Bodies Floating in Cyberspace', in *Radically Speaking: Feminism Reclaimed* (Klein 1996).

15. Cyborgs became fashionable in the 1990s, but it was the feminist historian of science and postmodern theorist Donna Haraway who wrote one of the first articles on this topic. Published initially in 1985 and republished many times since then, her 'Manifesto for Cyborgs: Science, Technology and Socialist Feminism in the 1980s' (changed to 'in the late Twentieth Century' in later editions, e.g. 1991), catapulted cyborgs into the limelight as the new feminist icons for 2000 and beyond that were clearly superior to women.

16. In Chapter 4 'Grandfather clause', Moravec (1988) describes in (gruesome) detail how a human mind is 'downloaded' into its new mechanical 'body'.

17. I didn't know Maria Mies when she was a child, but over the last twenty years that I have known her she has certainly come across as a 'wise' woman and I love and admire her for her tenacity to stand her ground, no matter how hard and how hurtful (and stupid!) the attacks.

References

Akhter, Farida (1995) *Resisting Norplant. Women's Struggle in Bangladesh Against Co-ercion and Violence*, Dhaka: Narigrantha Prabartana.

Arditti, Rita, Renate Duelli Klein and Shelley Minden (eds) (1984) *Test-Tube Women: What Future for Motherhood?* London and Boston, MA: Pandora Press.

— (eds) (1985) *Retortenmütter. Frauen in den Labors der Menschenzüchter*, Hamburg: rororo Frauen Aktuell.

Bell, Diane (1998) *Ngarrindjeri Wurruwarrin: A World that Is, Was, and Will Be*, Melbourne: Spinifex Press.

Bell, Diane and Renate Klein (eds) (1996) *Radically Speaking: Feminism Reclaimed*. Melbourne: Spinifex Press; London: Zed Books.

Bennholdt-Thomsen, Veronika and Maria Mies (1999) *The Subsistence Perspective: Beyond the Globalized Economy*. London: Zed Books; Melbourne: Spinifex Press.

Blau DuPlessis, Rachel and Ann Snitow (eds) (1998) *The Feminist Memoir Project. Voices from Women's Liberation*, New York: Three Rivers Press.

Boston Women's Health Collective (1969) *Our Bodies, Ourselves*, New York: Simon and Schuster.

Bowles, Gloria and Renate Duelli Klein (eds) (1983) *Theories of Women's Studies*, London: Routledge.

Brodribb, Somer (1992) *Nothing Mat(t)ers. A Feminist Critique of Postmodernism*, Melbourne: Spinifex Press.

Brownmiller, Susan (2000) *In Our Time: Memoir of a Revolution*, New York: Dell Books.

Bunch, Charlotte (1981) 'The Reform Tool Kit' [1975], in *Building Feminist Theory: Essays from Quest, A Feminist Quarterly*, New York and London: Longman.

Bunch, Charlotte and Nancy Myron (eds) (1974) *Class and Feminism*, Baltimore, MD: Diana Press.

Chesler, Phyllis (1972) *Women and Madness*, New York: Doubleday.

Committee on Women's Studies in Asia (eds) (1994) *Women's Studies, Women's Lives. Theory and Practice in South and Southeast Asia*, New Delhi: Kali for Women; Melbourne: Spinifex Press.

Corea, Gena (1985a)*The Hidden Malpractice. How American Medicine Mistreats Women* [1977], New York: Harper & Row.

— (1985b) *The Mother Machine. Reproductive Technologies from Artificial Insemination to Artificial Wombs*, New York: Harper & Row.

Corea, Gena, Renate Duelli Klein, Jalna Hanmer, Helen B. Holmes, Betty Hoskins, Madhu Kishwar, Janice Raymond, Robyn Rowland and Roberta Steinbacher (1985) *Man-Made Women: How New Reproductive Technologies Affect Women*, London: Hutchinson.

Daly, Mary (1978) *Gyn/Ecology: The Metaethics of Radical Feminism*, Boston, MA: Beacon Press; London: Women's Press.

Declaration of Comilla (1991) *Proceedings of FINRRAGE Conference 1989*, Dhaka: UBINIG, Bangladesh.

Declaration of People's Perspectives (1993) *People's Perspectives on Population 4 and 5*, Dhaka: UBINIG, Bangladesh.

Dery, Mark (1996) *Escape Velocity: Cyberculture at the End of the Century*, London: Hodder and Stoughton.

Dworkin, Andrea (1974) *Woman Hating*, New York: Plume.

— (1982) *Our Blood: Prophecies and Discourses on Sexual Politics* [1976], London: Women's Press.

Griffin, Susan (1978) *Woman and Nature. The Roaring Inside Her*, New York: Harper & Row; London: Women's Press.

Guymer, Laurel (1998) 'Anti-pregnancy "Vaccines": A Stab in the Dark', *Birth Issues*, 7, 3, pp. 87–91.

Haraway, Donna (1991) 'Manifesto for Cyborgs: Science, Technology, and Socialist-Feminism in the Late Twentieth Century', in her *Simians, Cyborgs and Women. The Reinvention of Nature*, New York: Routledge.

Hawthorne Susan (1999) 'Cyborgs, Virtual Bodies and Organic Bodies: Theoretical Feminist Responses', in Susan Hawthorne and Renate Klein (eds), *CyberFeminism. Connectivity, Critique and Creativity*, Melbourne: Spinifex Press, pp. 213–49.

Hawthorne, Susan and Renate Klein (eds) (1999) *CyberFeminism. Connectivity, Critique and Creativity*, Melbourne: Spinifex Press.

hooks, bell (1984) *Feminist Theory: From Margin to Center*, Boston, MA: South End Press.

Hubbard, Ruth (1985) 'Prenatal Diagnosis and Eugenic Ideology', *Women's Studies International Forum*, 8, 6, pp. 567–76.

Hughes, Donna (1999) 'The Internet and the Global Prostitution Industry', in Susan Hawthorne and Renate Klein (eds), *CyberFeminism. Connectivity, Critique and Creativity*, Melbourne: Spinifex Press, pp. 157–184.

Jeffreys, Sheila (1997) *The Idea of Prostitution*. Melbourne: Spinifex.

Klein, Renate (1989a) *The Exploitation of a Desire. Women's Experiences with in vitro Fertilisation. Women's Studies Summer Institute*, Geelong: Deakin University.

— (ed.) (1989b) *Infertility: Women Speak Out About Their Experiences of Reproductive Medicine*, London: Pandora.

— (1989c) *Das Geschäft mit der Hoffnung*, Berlin: Orlanda.

— (1992) *The Ultimate Colonisation: Reproductive and Genetic Engineering*, Dublin, Attic Press.

— (1995) 'Reflections on Cairo: Empowerment Rhetoric – but Who Will Pay the Price?', *Women's Studies International Forum*, 18, 4, 'Feminist Forum', pp. ii–v.

— (1996) '(Dead) Bodies Floating in Cyberspace. Post-modernism and the Dismemberment of Women', in Diane Bell and Renate Klein (eds), *Radically Speaking: Feminism Reclaimed*, Melbourne: Spinifex Press; London: Zed Books, pp. 346–58.

— (1999) 'The Politics of CyberFeminism: If I'm a Cyborg Rather than a Goddess Will Patriarchy Go Away?', in Susan Hawthorne and Renate Klein (eds), *CyberFeminism. Connectivity, Critique and Creativity*, Melbourne: Spinifex, pp. 185–212.

Klein, Renate and Robyn Rowland (1988) 'Women as Test-Sites for Fertility Drugs: Clomiphene Citrate and Hormonal Cocktails', *Reproductive and Genetic Engineering: Journal of International Feminist Analysis*, 1, 3, pp. 251–75.

Klein, Renate, Janice G. Raymond and Lynette J. Dumble (1991) *RU 486: Misconceptions, Myths and Morals*, Melbourne: Spinifex Press; Boston: Institute for Women and Technology.

Leeds Revolutionary Feminist Group (1981) *Love Your Enemy? The Debate Between Heterosexual Feminism and Political Lesbianism* [1979], London: Onlywomen Press.

Leidholdt, Dorchen and Janice G. Raymond (1990) *The Sexual Liberals and Their Attacks on Feminism*, New York: Athene Series, Pergamon Press.

Lippman, Abby (1993) 'Prenatal Genetic Testing and Geneticisation. Mothers Matter for All', *Fetal Diagnosis Therapy*, 8 (Suppl. 1), pp. 175–88.

Lorde, Audre (1981) 'The Master's Tools Will Never Dismantle the Master's House', in Cherrie Moraga and Gloria Anzaldúa (eds), *This Bridge Called My Back: Writings by Radical Women of Color*, New York: Kitchen Table Press.

Merchant, Carolyn (1980) *The Death of Nature. Women, Ecology and the Scientific Revolution*, San Francisco: Harper and Row.

Mies, Maria (1978) 'Methodischen Postulate zur Frauenforschung – dargestellt am Beispiel der Gewalt gegen Frauen', in *Beiträge zur Feministischen Theorie und Praxis*, 1, 1, pp. 41–63.

— (1983) 'Towards a Methodology for Feminist Research', in G. Bowles and R. Klein (eds), *Theories of Women's Studies*, London: Routledge, pp. 117–39.

— (1985) '"Why do we need all this?" A Call Against Genetic Engineering and Reproductive Technology', in *Women's Studies International Forum*, 8, 6, pp. 553–60.

— (1998) *Patriarchy and Accumulation on a World Scale: Women in the International Division of Labour* [1986], new edn, London: Zed Books; Melbourne: Spinifex Press.

Mies, Maria and Vandana Shiva (1993) *Ecofeminism*, New Delhi: Kali for Women; Melbourne: Spinifex Press.

Moravec, Hans (1988). *Mind Children. The Future of Robot and Human Intelligence*, Boston, MA: Harvard University Press.

— (1999) *Robot: Mere Machine to Transcendent Mind*, New York and Oxford: Oxford University Press.

Morgan, Robin (1978) *Going Too Far: The Personal Chronicle of a Feminist*, New York: Vintage Books.

— (ed.) (1970) *Sisterhood Is Powerful: An Anthology of Writings from the Women's Liberation Movement*, New York: Random House.

— (ed.) (1984) *Sisterhood Is Global: The International Women's Movement Anthology*, New York: Doubleday.

Raymond, Janice G (1994) *Women as Wombs: Reproductive Technologies and the Battle over Women's Freedom*, San Francisco, CA: HarperCollins; Melbourne: Spinifex Press.

— (2001) *A Passion for Friends: Toward a Philosophy of Female Affection* [1986], Boston, MA: Beacon Press; Melbourne: Spinifex Press.

Rich, Adrienne (1976) *Of Woman Born: Motherhood as Experience and Institution*, New York: W. W. Norton.

— (1979) *On Lies, Secrets, and Silence: Selected Prose 1966–78*, New York: W. W. Norton.

— (1980) 'Compulsory Heterosexuality and Lesbian Existence', *Signs*, 5, 4, 631–60.

Richter, Judith (1986) *Vaccination Against Pregnancy. Miracle or Menace?* London: Zed Books; Melbourne: Spinifex Press.

Rowland, Robyn (1992) *Living Laboratories. Women and the New Reproductive Technologies*, Sydney: Macmillan; Bloomington: Indiana University Press.

Schüssler, Marina and Kathrin Bode (1992) *Geprüfte Mädchen – Ganze Frauen. Zur Normierung der Mädchen in der Kindergynäkologie*, Zurich and Dortmund: eFeF Verlag.

Scully, Diana (1994) *Men Who Control Women's Health: The Miseducation of Obstetrician-Gynecologists* [1987], New York: Athene Series, Teachers College Press.

Scutt, Jocelynne (ed.) (1988) *The Baby Machine. Commercialisation of Motherhood*, Melbourne: McCulloch.

Spallone, Patricia (1989) *Beyond Conception. The New Politics of Reproduction*, London: Macmillan.

Spallone, Patricia and Deborah Steinberg (eds) (1987) *Made to Order. The Myth of Reproductive and Genetic Progress*, Oxford: Athene Series, Pergamon Press.

Stopczyk, Annegret (1998) *Sophias Leib: Entfesselung der Weisheit*, Heidelberg: Carl-Auer-Systeme Verlag.

Summers, Anne (1999) *Ducks on the Pond*, Ringwood, Australia: Penguin Books.

Wertheim, Margaret (1999) *The Pearly Gates of Cyberspace: A History of Space from Dante to the Internet*, Sydney: Doubleday.

Wittig, Monique (1992) *The Straight Mind and other Essays*, Boston, MA: Beacon Press.

8

'Women Never Surrendered': The Mau Mau and Globalization from Below in Kenya 1980–2000

Terisa E. Turner and Leigh S. Brownhill

Introduction: Gendered Class Analysis

In late 1999 an unprecedented alliance of diverse insurgent forces challenged the World Trade Organization in the now historic 'Battle of Seattle'. The corporate meeting on 'globalization from above' was shut down by an international alliance asserting 'globalization from below'. The main features of corporate globalization are well known.[1] The features of a people's world order, on the other hand, have been long evolving through countless sites of struggle.[2] One site of this contention is rural Kenya where the courage and creativity of peasant women stand for and defend a 'life economy' in place of the 'death economy' (McMurtry 1999: 171–8; Turner forthcoming).

Sir Roger Swynnerton was a colonial agricultural planner based in East Africa in the 1950s. In a 1985 interview he testified, from his imperial perspective, to the tenacity of this 'life economy' in Kenyan peasant women's insistence on growing food, not cash crops. According to Swynnerton:

> In Kenya twice a year we called our provincial agricultural officers together for a conference to discuss programmes [...] About the middle of the 1950s, one of our subjects of discussion was whether we should push for crop specialization in different areas of the country [...] leaving food crop areas to produce the subsistence requirements of the cash crop areas. One very experienced provincial agricultural officer said this just would not work. The African was so inured to securing his food supplies that when the first rain started pattering on the roof of his hut, the wife in her sleep would reach over on one side and pick up a hoe, the other side to pick up a bag of seed and in the middle of the night she would go out and start planting food. In no way would she stop doing that whatever the cash crop being grown. (Swynnerton, quoted in Bryceson 1985: 17)

One way to conceptualize capital's attempt to assert a 'new world order' and popular resistance to it is as a *'fight for fertility'*. The focus in the 'fight for fertility' is for control over the processes and results of fertility: the capacity to reproduce and sustain life in all its forms, principally people, their labour power and their food. Land and labour, as well as the knowledge, bodies and time of women, are central to the process of enacting or realizing fertility.[3] Much animal husbandry, agricultural production and food-processing is women's work. In Africa women do some 80 per cent of all farming. They give birth and nurture people world-wide. Women therefore have a special stake in exercising control over their own fertility. They contend for control with their own menfolk and with capital, foreign and local. The three parties to this struggle over control of the production of life are (1) women themselves, (2) their own menfolk and (3) local and international capitalists.

The *subsistence political economy* includes not only food production for local consumption and regional trade, but also a host of activities and sets of social networks whose main aim is to support and enhance human existence. Subsistence production, or what we alternatively refer to as the subsistence political economy, 'includes all work that is expended in the creation, re-creation and maintenance of immediate life and which has no other purpose' (Bennholdt-Thomsen and Mies 1999: 20).

Subsistence is life-supporting activity in which use values predominate. That is, people produce primarily for use and while they may trade items or services, the production is not primarily for exchange or for the appropriation of money demand. A subsistence way of life may be pre-capitalist or it may co-exist in the interstices of the capitalist political economy. Depending on the power relations which exist, the subsistence political economy may be more or less subsumed by the commodified political economy or autonomous from it. Those producing sustenance have an interest in working to make the society sustainable through conservation, restitution, relative regional autonomy and planning.

Capitalists operating nationally and internationally directly contribute to the destruction of the subsistence realm as they construct commodified social relations.[4] In the *commodified political economy*, life-sustaining activities are supplanted by profiteering and speculation – the turning of money demand into more money demand (McMurtry 1999). Commodification is central to capitalist industrialization from its outset. It is inherently global and enforces an ever more life-separative division of labour. It also structures and inflames divisions among labourers, for instance through constructing difference as divisive. Bennholdt-Thomsen and Mies (1999: 20–1) note that within the commodified political economy 'life is, so to speak, only a coincidental side-effect. It is typical of the capitalist industrial system that it declares everything that it wants to exploit free of charge to be part of nature, a natural resource. To this belongs the housework of women as well as the work of peasants in the Third World, but also the productivity of all of nature.'

In the fight for control over fertility, many men, and in particular kinsmen, act as intermediaries between women and capitalists. These peasant or waged men may enter into what we call '*male deals*' with capital. These intermediaries channel resources and women's labour into the commodified realm to make profits for capital and minor earnings for the (nevertheless exploited) men themselves. In contrast, some men break with the male deals and join women in '*gendered class alliances*' for the defence and elaboration of the subsistence political economy, against the incursion of capitalist commodified relations (Turner et al. 1997).

Bennholdt-Thomsen and Mies (1999: 11) define '*housewifization*' as the process by which 'women's work under capitalism is universally made invisible and can for that reason be exploited limitlessly'. This concept of the invisibility of women's work 'applies not only to "housewives" in the narrow sense in the industrial countries but also to the work of the women who do home work, to farm labourers, peasants, small traders, and factory workers', and increasingly, it also applies to 'men of the North' (Bennholdt-Thomsen and Mies 1999: 11–13).

Much work in the subsistence economy is exploited by capital which, for instance, depends on 'free' housework and food gardening for the daily reproduction of labourers. But capital also 'housewifizes' waged and contracted labour in the production of commodities. Profits in Kenya's coffee and tea-growing zones depend crucially on housewifization. First women were denied land titles in the process of 'decolonization' and land consolidation of the 1950s. Then, the men who got the titles took loans to grow coffee for export on their small farms. They paid back the loans with interest from harvest proceeds. Husbands expected wives to cultivate and weed the coffee. Wives expected to have a food garden. If prices fell, husbands could decide to put some of the wives' food plots under coffee.

Some men would simply keep the money gained from cash crop sales for themselves. Women's work was housewifized, in that their publicly recognized rights to land were curtailed. Two reductions in women's entitlements to land, introduced with colonial capitalist agriculture were, first, the suppression of the practice of widows marrying other women and thereby becoming 'husbands' with all the land rights of their deceased husbands (Mackenzie 1998: 34–6); and second, the failure or impossibility of husbands allocating to their wives plots of land on which to grow food crops. This second curtailment arose both because of land shortage as the rich accumulated huge tracts and because peasant land was being used for export and cash crops. The curtailment of women's land rights meant financial dependence on kinsmen and loss of autonomy. Women's work became 'invisible' and uncompensated.

In this chapter, we examine three moments in this fight for fertility in post-colonial Kenya. All three cases are struggles by some of the world's most exploited people against corporate globalization from above.[5] The first upsurge is Maragua women coffee farmers' rejection of coffee production from the mid-1980s to the mid-1990s. Those men who were able to disengage from the corporate agenda co-operated with their wives in gendered class alliances with the aim of replacing coffee with bananas and other food crops for consumption and trade.

The second insurgency is a 1992 hunger strike at Nairobi's 'Freedom Corner', carried out by mothers of political prisoners. These women fought for the liberty and rights of their children — the fruits of their own fertility. They confronted a state which was in the process of attacking urban and rural people and evicting them from their land. These land wars resulted in part from the World Bank sponsored privatization drive of the 1990s and the increasing resistance by subsistence producers to Kenya's neo-liberal structural adjustment programme (Brownhill et al. 1997; George 1999). The women at Freedom Corner were protected from police attack by male allies. Together the women and men secured the release of fifty-one political prisoners.

The third insurgency is the large-scale reappropriation of land by landless people across Kenya in the new millennium. Women, who lack secure access to land, have a tremendous stake in the outcome of this direct redistribution of the prerequisite to self-provisioning and social security. A key question is the extent to which women's subsistence interests will be served in this new battle in the ongoing fight for control over fertility in Kenya.

Why do we choose these three struggles to illustrate the fight for fertility? They build on each other in that the high point of the previous struggle is the starting point of the next (James 1992: 155–6).[6] That is, there is a strong historical continuity which, rather than being linear, manifests itself incrementally, gradually building with respect to the geographical scope, the political conceptions and the capabilities of the participants. The insurgencies illustrate some of the methods of fighting used by each of the three major contenders in the struggle to control women's reproductive, agricultural and domestic labour. The upsurges are at once intensely local and international. As such they provide insight into the interpenetration of global hierarchies and community democracies. The battles reveal some environmental consequences of profit-oriented versus subsistence agriculture. They reveal details about the gender relations which characterize struggles over the control of fertility. Finally, they suggest how international struggles 'circulate', stimulating more resistance elsewhere and consciously co-ordinating joint actions (Dyer-Witheford 1999: 68).[7] Grassroots 'globalization from below' is organized by and against corporate globalization from above.[8]

Historical Antecedents to the Fight for Fertility

The three instances of overt struggle for the fruits of women's labour examined here are all from Kenya's post-independence period. A brief note on the struggles of the colonial period is necessary to contextualize the case studies. Prior to independence in 1963 there were major upsurges in the fight for fertility in the 1920s and again in the 1940s leading to the Mau Mau war for 'land and freedom' (1952–60). In 1922 a Kikuyu woman, Mary Muthoni Nyanjiru, used a customary 'curse of nakedness' to lead a bid by several thousand Nairobi Africans to free a political detainee, Harry Thuku (Wipper in Turner forthcoming). This 'chief of women' was jailed for resisting the forced labour of African women on colonial agricultural estates and public works. The 1920s insurgency continued with the formation of an independent African church and school network. These institutions contributed to the organization of Mau Mau, which fought a war to expel the colonial occupiers in the 1950s (Brownhill 1994).

In the 1940s rural women repeatedly challenged the British efforts to cull cattle, seize land and restrict Africans to native reserves and 'settlement schemes' as debt peons. This challenge led directly to British counter-insurgency (Brownhill 1994). It escalated into the Mau Mau war during which the British, with 'male dealer' support from African 'home guards', crushed and dispossessed small peasants carrying out subsistence agriculture and trade. Then the British imposed capitalist farming. Many African men who were loyal to the British got title deeds to land. So did some Mau Mau men who surrendered. In contrast, Mau Mau women 'never surrendered' despite imprisonment and torture (First Woman, hereafter FW, 1 May 1994). After the war, many home guards and those male Mau Mau who surrendered used their title deeds as collateral for loans to invest in export crop farming. Their wives were forced to turn from food to export crop production and the husbands kept the cash income. In this process of 'housewifization', rural women lost much of their power to control land, crops, the labour process (which was collective), markets, surpluses of many kinds (including time), and community social relations. However, many engaged in holding actions such as funnelling coffee money, where possible, into strengthening the subsistence economy and into educating their children (Turner 1994: Ch. 2). When export crop income faltered in the late 1970s, they were well-positioned to reassert the subsistence economy. But this required that women confront tremendous opposition from husbands, the government coffee-buying co-operatives and the international firms backed by governmental organizations including the World Bank.

From Coffee to Bananas: Maragua Peasant Women Replace Export Crops With Local Food Crops[9]

In her study 'Gender and Command Over Property', Bina Agarwal came to the conclusion that dispossessed women need independent rights to land (Agarwal 1994: 1459–61). This is our starting point. How have women cultivators organized to gain rights over land? Are there lessons to be learned and applied elsewhere? We worked closely with women in Maragua, Kenya, throughout the 1990s and learned about their efforts to reclaim and reshape customary rights to land which had been appropriated by colonization and male deals.[10] Their struggle provides insight into the gendered character of the process of reclaiming land and social relations for subsistence.

'Every woman belongs to at least one woman's group,' Alexiah Kamene told us as if it were the most obvious fact of life. Kamene is a widow who lives in Maragua and grows bananas and vegetables on her 1-acre (0.4 ha) farm. She works part-time for a hotelier as a domestic servant and seasonally hires herself out with a group of other women to weed or harvest in the gardens of farmers with larger holdings. 'Banana money is better than coffee money. Men do still take the money from women. Single women manage better. You will find that banana traders are mainly divorced or widowed women.'

Kamene describes the situation in Maragua as she sees it. It is not a Utopia for landless women, but it is better than it was fifteen years ago when dutiful and unwaged women picked coffee which fetched incomes for their husbands, state officials and international merchants. Beginning in 1986, Maragua farming women have taken steps towards a new organization of society in which they, as producers, manage resources, outputs and incomes.

Maragua is a rural farming community in the area surrounding Mount Kenya. It lies in the middle of a coffee zone, about 80 km north-west of Nairobi, Kenya's capital. Maragua Location, a part of Kigumo Division, covers about 220 square miles. Some 100,000 people live there (Republic of Kenya 1993: 1, 12). Husbands own most of the small, 1–5-acre (0.4–2 ha) farms in Maragua. Technically and legally, their wives are landless. In practice, peasant women in central Kenya have customarily had the right to work on their husbands' farms and control the use of foodstuffs they themselves produced. Coffee production since the 1960s has slowly intruded into women's food gardens. This has been a source of conflict within families. Women cultivators have historically belonged to collective work groups which applied themselves to large tasks on each other's food plots. However, these groups never worked on men's cash crop plots since the income from cash crops was never allocated to women's needs. Wives worked individually, with children or with casual labourers, on husbands' cash crop plots, but did not control the yield. When women's food plots decreased in size, the time they had to work collectively with other women also diminished.

At independence the government lifted colonial restrictions on coffee-growing by Africans. In the 1960s and the first half of the 1970s, coffee production on smallholdings provided farmers with substantial incomes, and provided the state with more foreign exchange than any other commodity. In the last half of the 1970s coffee began to lose its attraction for producers. State corruption swallowed sales income, so producers were not paid fairly or promptly. Between 1980 and 1990 real international prices for Africa's coffee exports fell by 70 per cent (World Bank 1994).

By 1986 Kenyan farmers had faced ten years of declining income from coffee. Increasing numbers of women coffee cultivators received nothing from the coffee payments which the government remitted to male landowners. Oral testimony and direct experience confirm that more and more women threatened to stop caring for their husbands' coffee. Some men responded by declaring that if their wives would not work, they would chase the women away from the farms (FW, 2 January 1997). Government chiefs intervened to mediate between embattled wives and husbands. The chiefs sought to preserve both the marriages and the coffee production, and thereby safeguard the profits on which government revenues depended and on which were premised debt repayment and continued good relations with the International Monetary Fund and the Paris Club of donors.

By 1986 the contradiction between female coffee workers and male coffee farm owners contributed to a situation of declining overall production (Mgendi 1996b: 4; 1996a: I). In response to lower coffee export earnings the World Bank and International Monetary Fund provided funds to increase coffee production. The government raised coffee payments to encourage husbands to defend the industry by forcing recalcitrant wives back to work in coffee. The IMF introduced 'user pay' policies in health and education which created a greater need among producers for cash. This need constituted a coercive incentive to resume the production of cash crops. In effect, the IMF mounted formidable obstacles to women's efforts to refuse coffee production first by introducing incentives in the form of conditional loans to the state and second by requiring the state to pay higher coffee prices to men.

Despite the harsher discipline faced by women in their households, many of those who refused to produce coffee resolved to stay with their husbands and preserve their marriages. But the women planted beans between the coffee trees, contrary to restrictions against intercropping with coffee. They thus provided their families with food and began the tedious process of renourishing the chemically damaged soil. But this was not enough. Their husbands and state officials stood in the way of women's needs to produce food and secure cash income. Finally the women took decisive action. In Maragua and elsewhere in Kenya, women uprooted coffee trees and used them for firewood. The penalty for damaging a coffee tree was imprisonment for seven years. By late 1986 most women farmers in Maragua had planted bananas and vegetables for home consumption and local trade instead of coffee for export. This pattern was repeated with varying intensity through-out Kenya and the East and Central African regions as a whole.

By and large, in Maragua in 1986, the typical working man 'secured his food supplies' by participating in his wife's rejection of coffee. Husbands recognized that their wives' resistance contributed funds and organizational coherence which allowed men to hold on to their land in the midst of expanding and accelerating large-scale enclosures. Not only did Maragua women cultivators plant food, they also reinstated producer control over land. And they re-established and strengthened their collective women's work groups which form the basis for many activities such as savings and credit 'merry-go-rounds' (esusu in Ghana, susu in Trinidad and Tobago). In the merry-go-rounds, each woman in the group contributes a small sum of money into a 'pot' every week and every week, a different member receives the pot. She typically uses her share to pay school fees or to buy household utensils or a goat.

In 1996 the International Monetary Fund loaned 12 billion Kenyan shillings (US$ 218 million) to the government. In October of the same year, Kenyan president Moi launched an agriculture policy paper aimed at 'enabling the sector to run as a fully commercial enterprise' (Nation Reporter 1996: 1–2), with emphasis on export crops. Though Maragua farmers escaped the exploitation of the coffee market, the alternative they built exists within the framework of an increasingly privatized and com-modified society. The state and multinational corporations continue to regulate working women's labour by giving credit to (male) title deed holders to encourage commercial vegetable, fruit and flower horticulture. Foreign and local capitalists entice land-owning men in Maragua into labour-intensive and chemical-dependent export production. Husbands of women who have rejected coffee may view commercial horticulture as a means to reassert command over women's labour. Such is the temptation of the male deal. Meanwhile, the state upholds laws which favour men. Into the new millennium, the constitution of Kenya allows discrimination based on sex. This legal framework works in favour of the corporate agenda in that it limits women's subsistence choices.

The relations of production imposed upon producers by capital and the state have organized dispossessed women to resist. They began by refusing the discipline meted out by husbands who sought high returns on the crops women produce. While the IMF is stepping up pressure to privatize state assets, including coffee marketing bodies, women producers are creating an alternative to corporate takeover. Through reviving self-organized and autonomous customary work groups the women have begun to reconstruct subsistence society, up to and including the rebuilding of a regional trade system.

In sum, the women's dramatic attack on the coffee trees broke and restructured long-standing social relationships at three levels. First, the Maragua insurgents shifted effective control over resources from their husbands into their own hands. Second, they broke their relationships of debt peonage and subjection to the state coffee apparatus and established an alternative self-regulated banana trade. Third, the Maragua women extracted themselves from state-mediated relationships with foreign suppliers of agro-chemical inputs and a global coffee market which enriches non-subsistence traders and speculators at the expense of producers. In addition to these considerable achievements, the Maragua insurgency contributed in a significant way to forcing the single party state to legalize opposition parties.[11]

The 1992 'Freedom Corner' Hunger Strike by Mothers of Political Prisoners

Maragua women fought their husbands, the state and multinational corporations for land. At Freedom Corner, women fought the police, the state and their corporate sponsors for the release of their sons. Most Freedom Corner women had broken many of the relations of house-wifization. They were divorcees, widows and wives of the disappeared. These independent though poor women did not have kinsmen standing between them and the state. On the contrary, the state stood between the women and their sons. Most of these sons had been imprisoned for trying to 'set the country right'. Their mothers wanted them out of jail so that they could continue to secure land and take care of their ageing mothers (FW, 27 July 1997). In this upsurge in the fight for fertility, women fought to regain land and their children.

On 28 February 1992, eight African women met with Kenya's attorney general, Amos Wako, and presented him with an open letter protesting the 'continued incarceration by the Kenya Government of scores of political prisoners' (Nation Team 1992: 2.). Seven of the women were the elderly mothers of imprisoned men. The eighth was the prominent feminist and environmentalist, Dr Wangari Maathai. All were involved in a newly formed lobby group, Release Political Prisoners (RPP). At the end of the meeting, the attorney general took the matter of the political prisoners 'under advisement'. The eight women joined four others and marched a few blocks to Uhuru Park, across from the Parliament Buildings, in Nairobi's city centre. At 'Freedom Corner' the twelve women began a hunger strike to pressure the attorney general and the president to release all political prisoners in Kenyan jails. Within two days, thousands of people from across Kenyan society had come to Freedom Corner to contribute spiritual, material and physical support. On the fourth day, police and security officers beat the hunger strikers with clubs and dispersed their sympathizers with tear-gas, batons and guns (FW, 12 May 1996; 29 May 1996; 24 July 1996; 4 September 1996; 15 January 1997).

Hunger striker Ruth Wangari WaThungu, aged seventy, provided the following account of this harrowing attack:

> We were beaten with tear-gas, clubs, and the whole area was sealed off by policemen and security officials.
>
> But me, because of the experience I had in the forest during the Mau Mau war where we were beaten, gassed with tear-gas and faced with other problems, we learned how to defend ourselves.
>
> People fainted. Like Wangari WaMaathai and many other women. But me, when I saw that we were going to be beaten severely, I took a blanket and soaked it in water and covered my head plus some other young men who had not been affected by the tear-gas.
>
> When the effect of the tear-gas subsided and I took off the blanket, I only saw people lying down immobile – I saw Wangari WaMaathai was unconscious and was just throwing kicks and also WaGakonya and many other people in the same state and they looked like they were dead.
>
> After all this, I tried to think what I would do next. I then stripped off my clothes and remained stark naked and started fighting with the policemen, because I saw a young man called Kanene who was one of us and is one of us in RPP struggling with a policeman who wanted to shoot him. I came in between them and stripped off my clothes. When the young people saw me naked, they stopped fighting with the police and ran away.
>
> And we were left with only four policemen whom I know were Kalenjins and they were old men. We fought with them and God helped. At that time

the public members were in large numbers and there were many motorists who had a chance to pick up the unconscious people and rushed them to various hospitals. The people who managed to run away ran and I was left with the four policemen.

We stayed and at last calmness prevailed. And we now put on our clothes and stayed there even if [even though] they pulled down the tent and took it with them plus our other belongings. (FW, 29 May 1996)

The customary act of defiance that Ruth Wangari employed was *guturama n'gania*, (Gikuyu) or the 'curse of nakedness'. When women, especially old women or groups of women, expose their genitals to people who have offended or threatened them, they are saying, in effect, 'This is where your life has come from. I hereby revoke your life.' Those so cursed believe that they will lose their virility. They believe that their land will lose its fertility and they as individuals will be outcasts from society (Turner and Oshare 1993). The four policemen who did not run away were old men of another ethnic group who felt immune to Ruth Wangari's curse. But they did not shoot. They gathered up all of the women's belongings, including a tent which had been donated and erected at the site for the women by four Asian women and men. The police then arrested the women who remained at Freedom Corner and drove them back to their home villages. Within days, all had returned to Nairobi. They resumed their hunger strike in the basement of a church adjacent to Freedom Corner. A year later, having secured the release of fifty-one of the fifty-two men on their list, the women ended their vigil and remained linked through their group, Release Political Prisoners.

People's defence of the subsistence economy was given centre-stage by the mothers of Freedom Corner in 1992. The old women banished fear and broke the silence that had been imposed on all political discussions by the Kenyatta and Moi dictatorships. A public address system was donated anonymously. The old women defended this open mike. Through it, the most dispossessed and silenced people in the country were able to voice their diverse demands. The coalescence of this cross-section of subsistence defenders so threatened the state that police tear-gassed and beat the mothers on day four of the hunger strike. The beatings enraged the public. Ruth Wangari's employment of the *guturama n'gania* or the 'curse of nakedness' against the police marked a turning point in the fight for fertility. Peasant women in the remotest corners of East Africa were emboldened by their recognition that an old Mau Mau fighter was prepared to die for her cause. Wangari literally used her own reproductive power as a weapon in the struggle to control the life-and-death decisions of the police.

Thousands of people mobilized to support, defend, write for, speak to, pray with and urge on the mothers of Freedom Corner for a full year. This mobilization did not disappear when the women left the church. It coalesced into dozens of organizations with a multitude of specific demands. These groups expressed the resurgence of the 'civil commons'.[12] They came together to support one another in times of need. Release Political Prisoners defended Mungiki, a neo–Mau Mau mass movement, in 1994. Muungano wana Vijiji, an organization of squatters, enlisted the assistance of Release Political Prisoners when, on 5 May 1998, a forty-four-year-old woman, Salome Wacera Wainaina, was murdered by police while defending her land in Kamae, just outside Nairobi. The groups strengthened each other while simultaneously practising highly diverse styles of struggle in pursuit of prisoners' rights, women's rights, law reform, housing, culture and virtually every aspect of a humane existence. Each organization has a position on land redistribution (FW, 12 April 1997).

During and after the Freedom Corner insurgency, the state continued to wage war against subsistence advocates by supplying arms and transport for killers, rapists, arsonists and looters. These targeted the farms and families of specific women involved in the Freedom Corner action. Refugees from the land war streamed in to join the vigil. The women's success in liberating political prisoners established a foundation upon which refugees and other landless people formulated their demands for secure entitlements and a redistribution of life sustaining resources.

The New Millennium Land Invasions

The pent-up demands for land exploded early in the year 2000. In a fast-moving and well-organized campaign, various grassroots groups and communities reappropriated land, not only from white settlers but also from African landholders and the government. The following Kenya newspaper account conveys a sense of the furore:

In Laikipia East, MP Mwangi Kiunjuri threatened to lead squatters to occupy degazetted forest areas in his constituency if genuine cases are not considered first. And in Cherangany, MP Kipruto arap Kirwa told the Marakwet youths occupying a 14,500-acre Agricultural Development Corporation farm to defy the District Commissioner's order to vacate. [Two days earlier], armed Marakwet youths barred a surveyor and a chief from entering the ADC farm. The youths, who carried arrows, swords and machetes, confronted the deputy district surveyor, Mr Naphtali Kinoti, and Kaplamai chief Michael Arusei, who fled. The 400 youths surrounded the officer's vehicle and pushed it off the road, saying the two had been sent to parcel out the land to top government officials. (*Daily Nation*, 21 May 2000)

Barely a month after Zimbabwe's land invasions began in February 2000, certain Kenyan members of parliament were calling on the landless to take over property owned by multinational agribusiness.[13] In Kenya, as in Zimbabwe, the logic of the maxim 'willing buyer – willing seller' is being questioned by politicians for reasons of political expediency, and rejected outright by landless peasants who have engaged in a series of land invasions throughout both countries (Turner 2000: 13).

The occupations are a response to violent government efforts to impose capitalist social relations in the countryside. This Maragua-style resurgence of subsistence is linked to the Freedom Corner protest through the strengthening of women's autonomous trade and social networks. These bind together urban and rural squatters and peasants. Women's networking and their alliances with men willing to challenge housewifization were integral to the mobilization of land invasions by the landless in 2000. The state responded throughout the 1990s to the increasing presence of the subsistence political economy by mounting what it termed 'ethnic clashes',[14] beginning in 1991. These attacks amounted to eviction of rural subsistence farmers and the creation of a massive internal refugee population, which by 1998 exceeded 300,000 people, most of whom were women and children.

In the midst of a tremendous burst of organizational activity after 1992, much attention has been given to the proliferation of non-governmental organizations which supposedly replace the social service provision cut by the state under the imperatives of structural adjustment. Opposition political parties in the formal electoral arena have also received attention. But much more significant in the fight for fertility are the militant organizations of the dispossessed. These incorporate millions of members whose livelihoods have been attacked by the onslaught of commodification. Two such organizations are considered here.

Members of Muungano wana Vijiji (Kiswahili for Organization of Villagers) locate their struggle in the urban streets, slums and market stalls, where they persist in defending a sustenance market presence for African women and men against the highly commodified, globalized market in the region. This group arose when slum dwellers began to organize to defend themselves, their homes and businesses in the face of an onslaught of privatization-related slum and market demolitions, beginning with Nairobi's Muoroto village in March 1990. The multiethnic group, in which young and old, single, divorced and widowed women predominate, was bolstered in its earliest days by the Freedom Corner vigil, which some of them joined. Though focused on gaining secure communal title deeds to urban residential space, Muungano wana Vijiji also includes in its struggle care for orphaned children, battered women and prisoners and 'the liberation of people' (FW, 25 July 1998).

Mungiki (Gikuyu for Congress) is another of the most important organizations to expand dramatically after the Freedom Corner mobilization. Its members organized and defended victims of state-sponsored violence (the 'ethnic clashes') and vocally supported some of the land invasions of 2000 (*Daily Nation*, 19 April 2000). Mungiki claims to bind more than five million Kenyans into a disciplined multifaceted organization with the capacity to defend the subsistence economy. In early 2000 Mungiki carried out a daring attack on a police station to release some of its members from jail. Both Mungiki and Muungano are direct successors to the Mau Mau Land and Freedom Army of the 1950s in that members include large numbers of elderly Mau Mau fighters as well as their children and grandchildren. Further, both groups claim to be the inheritors of the Mau Mau legacy to defend entitlements to land and subsistence (FW, 23–25 July 1998).

Kenyan newspaper reports provide some indications of the scope of the millennial land 'jubilee', and its link to the Zimbabwe invasions. On 18 April 2000, anti-riot police dispersed thousands of squatters who had invaded Brooke Bond Kenya Limited land in Buret District. In Eldoret, Nandi leaders urged President Moi to follow the lead of his Zimbabwean counterpart Robert Mugabe by allowing them to invade East African Tanning and Extract Company land, which was up for sale. *The Daily Nation* reported that:

> Nandi community leaders, under Mzee Elisha arap Sang, 70, and Mr William K. Serem, said that, allowing the community to invade the farms which they believe formerly belonged to them, would help eradicate poverty. The group called on community members 'languishing in poverty in places like Tanzania, Uganda, Laikipia, Maasai, Pokot and even in Congo to claim their pieces of land from those who stole from them'. (*Daily Nation*, 19 April 2000)

Meanwhile, Attorney-General Amos Wako announced to the media that the constitution guaranteed the right of protection of private property, that land invasions violate the constitution and that such cases 'will be dealt with' (*Daily Nation*, 19 April 2000).

On 21 April 2000, MP Stephen Ndicho, described himself as 'a spokesman for those millions of Kenyans without land', and reiterated his call for the invasion of white-owned land. In an open letter to the attorney general, Ndicho invited prosecution: 'When I call on the white man to now leave these lands for repossession by native Africans, and you threaten to arrest and charge me with incitement, it goes down very badly as far as the millions of landless poor Kenyans are concerned.' Ndicho called for a new pan-Africanist movement aimed at reclaiming all the African land still under the ownership of whites on the continent 'because land ownership is not an exclusively Zimbabwean issue' (*Daily Nation*, 22 April 2000).

In May, Ndicho launched what he called the Pan-African Movement Over Ancestral Land (Pamoa), aimed at seizing farms from white settlers. Ndicho said that the president was trying to divert attention by saying that the call would amount to tribal clashes. The MP insisted: 'We are interested in white-owned land and not African' (*Daily Nation*, 8 May 2000).

Many of the large estates in Kenya are owned by wealthy black people. These large plantations have been invaded by the forces of popular repossession. The *Daily Nation* of 31 May 2000 reported: 'The latest wave of ranch invasions follows a series of incursions on farmland in the district between October last year and January. The President's Kabarak Farm at Laikipia's Segere Location was one of those affected. Other ranches invaded also belonged to prominent Kenyans' (*Daily Nation*, 31 May 2000).

More than 11,000 cattle died in May 2000 due to drought in Laikipia district where some 200,000 out of a total population of 300,000 people were said to be in urgent need of relief food. The invading pastoralists, who claimed that the ranches were part of their ancestral land, were reported to have told the district commissioner that they would 'rather die together with their livestock than leave the ranches before the rains came'. The Lokdong'oi ranch manager, Lance Tom Harrison, said he feared his 5000 beef cattle reared on the farm 'could die of starvation as about 8,000 cattle, which had moved onto his ranch with herders, would exhaust his pasture if not evicted within a week' (*Daily Nation*, 31 May 2000).

As tensions rose around the Zimbabwe land invasions, the British High Commissioner in Nairobi warned Kenyans that foreign investors were being scared off by the calls to take over white-owned land. However, he stated that 'British-Kenyans who own land here have no reason to panic at all' (*Daily Nation*, 17 May 2000). Foreign partisans and commentators have been virtually unanimous in declaring the supposed negative environmental impacts of small subsistence holdings and their alleged inability to provide sufficient food.[15] These prejudices ignore the ample evidence which demonstrates that Kenyan Africans' indigenous farming approach maintains substantial advantages over the monocropping and heavily input-dependent methods of commercial farmers and over the seed varieties the colonialists imported and popularized.[16] In Kenya's pre-colonial period, the 'rudimentary subsistence agricultural techniques' produced 'enormous quantities' and 'inexhaustible supplies' of 'sweet potatoes, yams, cassava, sugar cane, sorghum and millet' from Central Province, described by one traveller in the 1890s as 'the granary of a very extended district' (Thomson [1885] and von Hohnel [1897] cited in Mackenzie 1998: 20). In fact, those techniques created the vast surpluses noted by early European missionaries and explorers. Instead, the colonialists' and neo-colonialists' prioritization of export cash crops over provisioning of local communities has led to the large-scale conversion of African agriculture from millet to maize, from vegetables to coffee and tea and from cattle and sheep to wheat, pyrethrum and sisal. In addition, the colonialists' establishment of tribal reserves, which survive into the new millennium, has meant that far too many people are confined to far too small an area, leading to soil erosion and hunger. Outside the reserve, multinationals and local capitalists utilize enormous tracts of land for export crops, chemically damaging the soil and laying ruin to soil fertility. Environmental alarmists who believe that subsistence farmers who invade land will 'over-graze and under-utilize' that land, are stuck within the premises of the continued existence of the 'tribal reserve' where overcrowding results from fixed boundaries and gross inequality in the distribution of non-reserve land. Land may well be under-utilized from the perspective of profit-making while simultaneously be fully utilized in producing life-sustaining crops.

The Kenyan and the Zimbabwean land invasions of the new millennium differ from the Ugandan Idi Amin-style massacre and eviction of Asians in Uganda in the 1970s in three basic ways. First, the thousands of hectares of land being occupied by the landless are capable of directly sustaining thousands of people who will grow their own food and re-establish regional trade networks and social patterns of mutual support. This differs sharply from the expropriation of Asian firms and Amin's practice of handing them out to his cronies who quickly milked them dry.

Second, the land reappropriations in Kenya have so far shown that European-owned farms are not under special attack. In fact, all large landholdings are subject to invasion, whether owned by Del Monte, Brooke Bond, local white families or the president. Also subject to invasion are government farms which are in the process of being privatized, degazetted forest land and urban commons. The land invasions in Kenya (and quite probably in Zimbabwe)[17] are not motivated by a hatred for people of particular ethnicities or national origins. They are motivated by the extreme inequality in distribution of resources and incomes between the wealthy and the dispossessed. Africa's land invasions are class warfare.

Third, because the land invasions of the new millennium in Kenya are aimed at the dispossession of large landholders, they are distinctly set apart from state-sponsored violence in the land wars of the 1990s. In these, the government orchestrated the massacre and eviction of small-holding peasants. The beneficiaries were members of the African elite along with foreign firms in agribusiness or real estate speculation.

Conclusion

This chapter has analysed three instances of the rising resistance of Kenyan women to commodification, beginning with the smallholder coffee peasants of Maragua. In this first post-independence upsurge in the fight for fertility, women took direct action against their own housewifization by repudiating dependence on husbands for access to cash from coffee sales. In the second upsurge, the 1992 hunger strike by elderly Mau Mau women to free their imprisoned sons, the 'mothers of Freedom Corner' practised democracy and demanded its extension to all prisoners and landless Kenyans. The women, who could have access to land and subsistence only through their sons' entitlements, demanded and secured the men's release. In the face of a massive move to subsistence agriculture and open public defiance of single-party dictatorship, the government organized pogroms (Turner et al. 2001). The Moi regime misnamed the killings 'ethnic clashes' to divert attention from its own instigation and the struggle's gendered class character. State-sponsored terror was responsible for the loss of thousands of lives. Many of those who fled the violence joined other land-hungry Kenyans in the massive land invasions of the new millennium. The Kenyan land reappropriations were sparked by the takeovers of land in Zimbabwe which began in February 2000 (Turner 2000: 13).

How do these three successive moments in the fight for fertility build on each other, producing starting points for new tendencies? All were against privatization, structural adjustment and neo-liberalism in favour of a subsistence perspective; each laid the groundwork for the next upsurge. The land invasions of the new millennium find their organizational and philosophical groundings in the feminist actions in Maragua and Freedom Corner, which were aimed expressly at the elaboration and defence of subsistence economies and social relations. Maragua women demonstrated that a certain type of reappropriation of the means of production was possible, especially when men joined in women's plans to replace coffee with food crops. The reappropriation by peasants of subsistence production on the *land that they already owned* in Maragua foreshadowed the more difficult reappropriation by the dispossessed of *land owned by others*, notably transnational capital and the neo-liberal, privatizing state. The millennium invasions built on the explicit re-establishment by the women of Freedom Corner of open confrontation between the dispossessed and the corporate-sponsored state. This confrontation had been muted and pushed underground since the Mau Mau war ended in the 1960s.

How the three parties to the fight for control over fertility pursue their respective interests is particularly well illustrated in the 'bananas not coffee' insurgency. Three lessons that might be taken from the experience of women cultivators in Maragua are, first, that capital organizes women to break exploitative relationships with men and then to join with other women to pursue common class objectives which are shared by people of different ethnicities. The emphasis in structural adjustment programmes on increased coffee exports meant that husbands pressured women to divert more land and labour away from food production. Corrupt government officials and husbands appropriated most of the coffee money. As a result, very little reached the women producers, who were therefore unable to feed and educate their children. On the other hand, women and their families belonged to coffee co-operative societies. Women's affiliation in the co-ops laid a basis for the development of a common response to their exploitation. Together, women intercropped, refused to work on coffee and finally uprooted the trees. When women replaced coffee with bananas, they broke an individualized labour process organized by husbands and re-established a collective production process organized by their own work groups. Resistance to the coffee industry, as manifest in women's work groups in Maragua, cut across ethnic boundaries.

A second lesson relates to the fragility of men's alliances with state officials and international capital. When wives refused to produce coffee, the fragile 'male deal' between husbands, the state and capital, collapsed. The myth of the male breadwinner was exposed. The Maragua study suggests that working-class men's abdication of domination over women workers and wives not only extends the scope of all workers' initiatives to control resources, but also breaks hierarchical relationships which keep women and men producers hungry, enslaved to capital and repressed by dictatorship. In repudiating the 'male deal', peasant men positioned them-selves to work in a gendered class alliance with women in their common life interests.

A third lesson involves the movement of women cultivators into direct confrontation with international capital. Our analysis confirms the insight that neo-liberal government functionaries predicate their structural adjust-ment programmes on the effectiveness of husbands' discipline over wives' labour (Dalla Costa and Dalla Costa 1995). Those women who reject this discipline do so through a transformative process which starts by satisfying the needs of the dispossessed. This undercuts a crucial source of ethnic antagonisms: competition amongst factions of the exploited for resources which are dominated by capital. In repudiating gendered exploitation, women cultivators in Maragua, Kenya, go beyond neo-liberalism and the ethnicized violence through which it is imposed.

This review of the high points in Kenya's post-colonial fight for fertility suggests three general conclusions. First, housewifization simultaneously attenuates and necessitates resistance, because housewifization threatens the subsistence political economy. Second, gendered class alliances contributed to the success of the Maragua and Freedom Corner struggles. Third, globalization from below is advanced by land invasions but international co-ordination among the dispossessed seems required if the invaders are to hold the land in the long term and reinstitute a life economy. We have discussed the first two conclusions above. The third, however, requires more consideration.

What capacities do the invaders have to survive counter-insurgency on behalf of local and foreign capital? Colonial capitalists employed African accomplices or 'male dealers' in the alienation of Africans' land and in the virtual elimination of many ecologically and nutritionally beneficial in-digenous agricultural practices. These male dealers acted as home guards or armed defenders of British colonialism against the Mau Mau in the 1950s. Women and dispossessed men faced an independent African gov-ernment dominated by home guards after 1963. This 'home guard' state then organized armed attacks on subsistence defenders throughout the 1990s, which swelled the ranks of refugees and triggered the growth of organizations, such as Mungiki and Muungano wana Vijiji, to defend subsistence farmers and traders.

In 1998 the Kenyan government purchased riot control tanks from South Africa and used them on the streets against protesters. More generally, the threat of international intervention, overtly or covertly, through counter-insurgency strategies is heightened as multinational corporations and Euro-pean farmers are targeted for dispossession. In 1999 Susan George quoted 'the man who used to be charged with thinking about future warfare for the Pentagon' as stating: 'The de facto role of the U.S. armed forces will be to keep the world safe for our economy and open to our cultural assault. To those ends, we will do a fair amount of killing' (George 1999: 2).

How is the emergence of a people's world order advanced by the land invasions? As corporations compound the global range of their control, they impose increasingly similar conditions on more and more of humanity. In saying 'no' to corporate globalization, diverse social actors establish mutual awareness of one another's struggles and demands. These build on each other in the practical process of the circulation of struggles. Protesters in Seattle, in December 1999, and in Washington, DC, in April 2000, called for the reappropriation of what capital has alienated. In the year 2000, Zimbabweans and Kenyans actually dispossessed capital by appropriating land for life sustenance rather than foreign money profit. Like the banana-growing women of Maragua, the land occupiers, in effect, repudiated debt by refusing to allow the cultivation and export of luxury cash crops which deprive people of food in order to generate foreign exchange to service government loans. The anti-export crop farmers and land occupiers in

Kenya have advanced the intercontinental resistance to neo-liberalism by strengthening the organizational, spiritual and material foundations upon which further resurgence of the subsistence economy is being built.

We identify the growing internationalization of resistance, typified by the Zapatistas' employment of the internet to build support and defence, as a process of '*globalization from below*'. It attacks and replaces corporate globalization from above. Cross-border co-ordination of resistance has been elaborated in Africa through the internet as well as through personal contacts and many informal channels. Peoples in Zimbabwe and Kenya share similar histories of settler colonization by the British, armed anti-colonial struggles and neo-colonial 'willing seller – willing buyer' land policies instead of redistribution to small farmers at independence. Groups within both countries have now occupied land to resolve their impoverishment by local and multinational capital.

These reappropriations recall the massive and ongoing Brazilian land occupations of the Landless Workers' Movement (MST) and the struggles for subsistence of people on other continents. These struggles include the creation of local networks for self-sufficiency in food and social services; consumer boycotts of corporate coffee, beef, sugar, flowers and other export commodities which decrease the amount of land under subsistence food production; and campaigns demanding that taxpayers' money support sustenance food production and local trade, at home and abroad, as opposed to militarization, corporate food monopoly and export agriculture. This life-reclaiming process poses a range of challenges to corporate globalization from above. One challenge lies in its potential to link strikes by producers and boycotts by consumers of corporate commodities. Such a link squeezes the 'money sequencers' (McMurtry 1999: 102–13) from all sides. It constitutes an organizational framework for alternative 'fair trade' exchanges of self-valorized use values.

In this study we conceptualize the complex struggles between exploiters and exploited as a 'fight for fertility'. This radically reformulated viewpoint helps us move away from the constructed, false and disempowering image of the poor (and especially of poor women) as passive, incapacitated victims who accept being consigned to the category of what Susan George calls 'the outcasts, people who are not even worth exploiting' (1999: 1). In contrast, the 'fight for fertility' conceptualization provides us with analytical tools to render visible and to excavate the 'actually existing' alternatives to what McMurtry (1998b) calls the 'death economy'. The actually existing subsistence political economy in Kenya emerges as a strong node in an international array of more or less connected subsistence solutions to the problem of unbridled corporate drive for ever higher profits. The capacity of subsistence workers to withstand counter-insurgency (disguised as 'ethnic' conflict) depends on international solidarity, or the strengthening of globalization from below. A prominent motive in our documenting these three moments in the fight for fertility is, then, to invite solidarity with Kenya's women farmers whose creativity is a power for all peoples committed to local subsistence and its essential defence, the elaboration of a new international economic order through globalization from below.

Notes

An earlier version of this chapter was published as 'The Fight for Fertility in Africa: Kenyan Women, the Subsistence Economy and Globalization from Below', in Gordana Yovanovitch (ed.), *The New World Order: Agendas and Creative Spirits*, Toronto: Garamond, 2001.

1. Speaking in Seattle, at a forum on 'The WTO and the Global War System', during the build-up to the closing of the World Trade Organization on 28 November 1999, Susan George of Amsterdam's Transnational Institute identified three effects of globalization: 'One, it pushes money from the bottom to the top. Wealth moves upwards, towards those who already have wealth. All over the place inequalities are growing and wealth is moving towards the top. Two, globalization moves *power* from the bottom to the top, and concentrates it in the hands of very few people. In particular, it concentrates it at the international level where there's no democracy and no way for citizens to get a handle on what is happening. Three, globalization is creating a myriad of losers. It is creating a slice of people who are not useful to the global economy either as producers or consumers. We're creating through globalization a three-track society in which there will be the exploiters, the exploited and the outcasts, the people who are not even worth exploiting. This is clearly a scenario for tremendous instability' (George 1999).

2. Clarke 2000: 1, 6. The *CCPA Monitor* is published by the Canadian Centre for Policy Alternatives, 410–75 Albert Street, Ottawa, ON K1P 5E7, Canada. Email: ccpa@ policyalternatives.ca Website: Http://www.policyalternatives.ca

3. The 'new world order' is based on a 'new international division of labour' as capital flees the high-cost, militant labour sites of the North to the 'housewifized' South. According to Caffentzis and Federici, the global spread of female 'shadow work' represents capital's flight from 'the First World feminist revolt against reproductive labor work. The transnational explosion of the sex trade, pornography industry, mail-order-bride business, and baby adoption market all represent "enormous quotas of reproduction work which capital has exported in the same way that there has been a strategy of exporting part of the manufacturing process with the free enterprise zones" (Caffentzis and Federici 1994: 144, cited in Dyer-Witheford 1999: 135–6).

4. Against the social Darwinism of Rostow (1960) which poses ineluctable 'stages of growth' or 'catching-up development' from traditional (subsistence) to modern (industrial) societies we pose industrialization and technology as capitalist weaponry to break up not only worker solidarity but also peasant social relations of self-reliance and sustenance. In this vein Harry Cleaver argued that to combat communist insurgency in Asia, US development agencies sponsored new plant stocks and agricultural techniques aimed at breaking down the traditional village structures. This was intended to eliminate the communities within which 'guerrillas moved like fish in the sea', and to foster a proletariat for industry which could be fed from rural production. The Green Revolution,

argued Cleaver, 'provided agricultural technology as the civil side to counterinsurgency warfare' (Cleaver 1981: 276, cited in Dyer-Witheford 1999: 70).

5. Kenya has the world's second highest rich–poor gap, after Brazil. In the 1990s Amnesty International included Kenya in the list of ten most repressive, torture-ridden countries in the world. Torture and state-sponsored terror have persisted since the 1950s British war which quelled the Mau Mau Land and Freedom Army. The African men who fought on the side of British colonialists, through their home guard, people the ruling party and its forces of repression.

6. In this chapter we employ a feminist Marxist perspective which is grounded in C. L. R. James and Selma James's work on revolutionary insurgency, and the centrality of the 'invisible', 'housewifized' women to capitalist exploitation and to the process of social transformation. In 1947 C. L. R. James wrote of the movement of history, that 'At a certain stage a developing contradiction, so to speak, explodes, and both the elements of contradiction are thereby altered. In the history of society these explosions are known as revolutions. All the economic, social and political tendencies of the age find a point of completion which becomes the starting-point of the new tendencies' (James 1992: 155–6).

7. Dyer-Witheford outlines the conception that 'workers' struggles provide the dynamic of capitalist development' and capital seeks to free itself from the working class through imposing 'successively wider and deeper dimensions of control – toward the creation of a social factory' in which the reproduction of labour power plays a crucial but invisibilized role. Waged men command unpaid labour time outside the workplace in the form of housework. The social factory includes peasants and other unwaged people subject to capital's exaction. 'If capitalist production now requires an entire network of social relations, these constitute so many more points where its operations can be ruptured.' C.L.R. James pointed to the complexity of the exploited with each faction expressing specific demands and organizational forms. For Dyer-Witheford, recognition of this 'variety within labor' leads 'away from vanguardist, centralized organization, directed from above, toward a lateral, polycentric concept of anticapitalist alliances-in-diversity, connecting a plurality of agencies in a *circulation of struggles*' (Dyer-Witheford 1999: 68).

8. 'One capitalist always kills many. Hand in hand with this centralisation, or this expropriation of many capitalists by few, develop, on an ever-extending scale, the co-operative form of the labour-process, the conscious technical application of science, the methodical cultivation of the soil, the transformation of the instruments of labour into instruments of labour only usable in common, the economising of all means of production by their use as the means of production of combined, socialised labour, the entanglement of all peoples in the net of the world-market, and with this, the international character of the capitalistic regime. Along with the constantly diminishing number of the magnates of capital, who usurp and monopolise all advantages of this process of transformation, grows the mass of misery, oppression, slavery, degradation, exploitation; but with this too grows the revolt of the working-class, a class always increasing in numbers, and disciplined, united, organized by the very mechanism of the process of capitalist production itself' (Marx 1975: 763). For another discussion, see Dyer-Witheford 1999: Ch. 5.

9. A more detailed account is available in Brownhill et al. 1997. *Canadian Woman Studies/Les Cahiers de la Femme*, is published by York University, Ontario, Canada Email: cwscf@yorku.ca Website: Http://www.yorku.ca/org/cwscf/home.html.

10. We conducted interviews throughout the 1990s as part of a small international

group of participant researchers called First Woman (East and Southern Africa Women's Oral History and Indigenous Knowledge Network). All interviews are cited as 'FW' followed by the date.

11. In the town of Sagana, near Maragua town, small business women refused to deliver coffee to government buyers and simultaneously demanded that the KANU regime repeal section 2(A) of the Kenya constitution which outlawed opposition political parties. When the coffee industry collapsed, the Paris Club of donors, in 1991, ordered Kenya's President Moi to legalize multiparty democracy. He complied in 1992 (FW, 7 October 1996).

12. McMurtry (1998a) defines the 'civil commons' as any co-operative human construction and agency which facilitates the access of all members of a community to goods essential to life. The civil commons has innumerable expressions, from vernacular language itself to public health-care, regulated clean air and water, universal education, public art and architecture, open environmental spaces, nutritious food, adequate shelter and affective interaction.

13. Kenyan MP and member of the ruling Kanu party Mr Kipruto arap Kirwa said in parliament on 11 April 2000 that the 'Nandi MPs were serious in their claim that the East African Tanning and Extract Company land be returned to its original owners – the Nandi [...] He said the community would reclaim 24,000 hectares and another 30,000 hectares in the Nandi tea zones.' Around the same time, MP Stephen Ndicho began a vocal campaign of encouraging Kenyans to invade white-owned land. He called for the invasion of land owned by three multinationals in Central Province – Del Monte, Kakuzi and Socfinaf (*Daily Nation*, Nairobi, 13 April 2000). President Daniel arap Moi, however, demanded that Mr Ndicho 'stop advocating for the invasion of property owned by foreign companies and people of foreign origin' (Esipisu 2000: A10).

14. The so-called 'ethnic clashes' in Kenya are part of an international pattern of counter-insurgency against indigenous resistance to corporate takeover of local economies. First, the subsistence, mixed and national economy is destroyed by neo-liberal policies enforced by the World Bank and International Monetary Fund. Then resistance is crushed through state-sponsored terror, passed off to an international media audience as tribal atavism, and hence not worthy of the concern of, especially, western citizens. Michel Chossoduvsky has documented this pattern in eleven countries in *The Globalization of Poverty* (1998). The Peace Research Institute in Oslo, Norway, has found that of the ninety-eight major wars in the years 1990–98 there were five commonalities: (1) cash-poor agriculturally based economies; (2) high levels of land degradation, low fresh water availability and high population density; (3) a high rate of external debt; (4) a falling rate of export income from primary commodities; and (5) vigorous intervention in the economy by the International Monetary Fund. Most of these were wars taking place within the borders of a country. Susan George (1999) has argued that a high degree of mercenary intervention and covert operation by the United States military in escalating civil wars are established givens.

15. An indication of the threat that the subsistence economy poses to the commodified economy is provided by Fraser Thornburn (2000) who wrote: 'George Monbiot argues that land redistribution in Zimbabwe "would enable the poor to produce staple crops for the landless." It is precisely the severe population pressures in Zimbabwe that make productive commercial farms essential. Even without the current crisis, successful re-settlement would demand training and support, costing as much, perhaps, as the purchase of the land itself. Simply buying up the land and dividing it up among the poor would create new communal lands, over-grazed and under-utilized.' In a similar vein, a Kenyan

editorial about Zimbabwe's landless stated that, 'To the landless poor, neither the adverse economic implications of the subsequent land fragmentation, nor the threat of shrinkage in food production owing to envisaged employment of *rudimentary subsistence farming techniques*, make any difference. All they want is land and they want it now, not tomorrow. Half a loaf to them is a lot better than none, and it is big enough to kill for' (*Daily Nation*, 8 May 2000, emphasis added); www.nationaudio.com/News DailyNation

16. The advantages of indigenous crops and practices (MacKenzie 1998: 104–21) range from the nitrate-storing capacity of pigweed – which Kikuyu farmers did not weed out from their millet plots – to the high calcium, magnesium and protein content in indigenous millet; to the drought-, pest- and disease-resistance of indigenous millet which colonialists almost completely replaced with maize, of far lower nutritional quality and far higher negative impact on the environment. The indigenous practice of inter-cropping was found to provide more food than monocropping or any other system; protect soil from rain and sun; provide a constant insurance against locusts and produce fodder for cattle and goats. Indigenous methods of storing seed in wood ash are capable of preventing weevil damage for at least twelve months. These subsistence crops and techniques substantially enhanced women's control over production. In contrast, European capitalist market-focused agriculture has meant that the control over production and income has moved from women's to men's hands. Export-oriented agriculture has increased soil erosion through the enforcement of practices such as 'clean-weeding', which removes protective covering from around crops; terracing, which increases rain-drop erosion, 'deep-tilling', which disturbs the soil integrity and 'pure cropping', which exhausts the soil fertility and rules out the continuous ground cover effected through intercropping. 'Pure cropping' or monocropping leads to greater vulnerability to pests and disease (MacKenzie 1999:147–9).

17. See www.cosatu.org.za for a cautious and noncommittal statement from the Congress of South African Trade Unions on the Zimbabwe land invasions. In contrast to the South African President Thabo Mbeki's condemnation of the occupation of agri-industrial establishments in Zimbabwe and his call for a give-back, the powerful South African trade union confederation poses questions about land redistribution in Zimbabwe (COSATU, 25 April 2000). In South Africa land invasions have taken place since the Zimbabwe movement began. For instance, black African farmers in the eastern Cape have occupied land they long claimed as theirs, citing their impatience with the interminable delays of the virtually ineffective government land adjudication board.

References

Agarwal, B. (1994) 'Gender and Command Over Property: A Critical Gap in Economic Analysis and Policy in South Asia', *World Development*, 22, 10, pp. 1455–78.

Bennholdt-Thomsen, V. and M. Mies (1999) *The Subsistence Perspective: Beyond the Globalized Economy*, London: Zed Books.

Brownhill, L. S. (1994) 'Struggle for the Soil: Mau Mau and the British War Against Women 1939–1956', unpublished paper, Master of Arts Programme, Department of Sociology and Anthropology, Guelph: University of Guelph.

Brownhill, L. S., W. M. Kaara and T. E. Turner (1997) 'Gender Relations and Sustainable Agriculture: Rural Women's Resistance to Structural Adjustment in Kenya', *Canadian Woman Studies/Les Cahiers de la Femme*, 17, 2 (Spring), pp. 40–4.

Bryceson, D. F. (1995) 'African Women Hoe Cultivators: Speculative Origins and Current

Enigmas', in D. F. Bryceson (ed.), *Women Wielding the Hoe: Lessons for Feminist Theory and Development Practice*, Oxford: Berg, pp. 2–20.

Caffentzis, G. and S. Federici (1994) 'Modern Land Wars and the Myth of the High-tech Economy', in Cindy Duffy and Craig Benjamin (eds), *The World Transformed: Gender, Labour and International Solidarity in the Era of Free Trade, Structural Adjustment and GATT*, Guelph, Ontario: RhiZone.

Chossoduvsky, M. (1997) *The Globalization of Poverty*, London: Zed Books.

Clarke, T. (2000) 'How to Take Advantage of the WTO's "Crisis of Legitimacy"', *CCPA Monitor* (Reporting on Business, Labour and the Environment), 7, 2, (June), pp. 1, 6.

Cleaver, H. (1981) 'Technology as Political Weaponry', in Robert Anderson (ed.), *Science, Politics and the Agricultural Revolution in Asia*, Boulder, CO: Westview Press, 261–76.

Dalla Costa, M. and G. F. Dalla Costa (eds) (1995) *Paying the Price: Women and the Politics of International Economic Strategy*, NJ: Zed Books.

Dauda, C. L. (1992) *'Yan Tatsine and the Male Deal: Islam, Gender and Class Struggle in Northern Nigeria*, unpublished MA thesis, Department of Political Studies, University of Guelph, Ontario.

Dyer-Witheford, N. (1999) *Cyber-Marx: Cycles and Circuits of Struggle in High-Technology Capitalism*, Urbana and Chicago: University of Illinois Press.

Esipisu, M. (2000) 'Mugabe Foe Threatens Retaliation for Deaths', *Globe and Mail*, Toronto, Canada, 27 April, p. A10.

First Woman (FW), interview, name withheld, Nairobi, 1 May 1994; Wahu Kaara, Maragua, 12 May 1996; Ruth Wangari WaThungu, Nairobi, 29 May 1996; Ruth Wangari WaThungu, Nairobi, 24 July 1996; Wanjiru Kahiga, Nairobi, 4 September 1996; Zawadi Women's Group, Sagana, 7 October 1996; Revd Samwel Theuri, Tumu-tumu, 2 January 1997; Elizabeth Wanjiru WaGatenjo, Nairobi, 15 January 1997; Dennis Akumu, Nairobi, 12 April 1997; Wahu Kaara, Nairobi, 24 April 1997; Beldina Adhiambo, Nairobi, 27 July 1997; Women of Mungiki, Nairobi, 23 July 1998; Men of Mungiki, Nairobi, 23 July 1998; Women elders of Mungiki, Nairobi, 24 July 1998; Muungano wana Vijiji members, Nairobi, 25 July 1998.

George, S. (1999) 'The Corporate Utopian Dream', in Estelle Taylor (ed.), *The WTO and the Global War System*, Vancouver: International Network on Disarmament and Globalization (405–825 Granville St., Vancouver, BC V6Z 1K9; tel. 604-687-3223; www.indg.org), pp. 1–2.

James, C. L. R. (1992) 'Dialectical Materialism and the Fate of Humanity' [1947], in Anna Grimshaw (ed.), *The C. L. R. James Reader*, Oxford: Blackwell, pp. 153–81.

Kaona, B. (1996) 'Oyugi's Widows Sue Their Sons', *East African Standard*, Nairobi, 22 November, pp. 1–2.

King, A. (1980) 'The Functionary in Kenya's Colonial System', in B. E. Kipkorir (ed.), *Imperialism and Collaboration in Colonial Kenya*, Nairobi: Kenya Literature Bureau.

MacKenzie, A. F. D. (1998) *Land, Ecology and Resistance in Kenya, 1880–1952*, Ports-mouth, NH: Heinemann.

— (1991) 'Political Economy of the Environment, Gender, and Resistance Under Col-onialism: Murang'a District, Kenya, 1910–1950', *Canadian Journal of African Studies*, 22, 4, pp. 226–56.

McMurtry, J. (1998a) *Unequal Freedoms: The Global Market as an Ethical System*, Tor-onto: Garamond Press; Westport, CN: Kumarian.

— (1998b) 'The Economics of Life and Death', unpublished paper presented at the World Congress of Philosophers Conference, Boston, MA, August.

— (1999) *The Cancer Stage of Capitalism*, London: Pluto Press.

Mamdani, M. (1996) *Citizen and Subject: Contemporary Africa and the Legacy of Late Colonialism*, Princeton, NJ: Princeton University Press.

Marx, K. (1975) *Capital: A Critique of Political Economy* [1867] Vol. I, New York: International Publishers.

Mbilinyi, M. and A. Mosha (1995) 'A Gender Perspective on Environmental Policy', paper presented to Gender and Development Seminar Series of the Tanzania Gender Networking Programme (TGNP), Dar es Salaam, 22 February (TGNP, PO Box 8921, Dar es Salaam, Tanzania).

Mgendi, C. (1996a) 'Reasons for Decline in Agricultural Production', *Daily Nation*, Nairobi, 3 October, p. 1.

— (1996b) 'Sector Records Negative Growth Rates', *Daily Nation*, Nairobi, 13 December, p. 4.

Mies, M. (1982) *The Lacemakers of Narsapur: Indian Housewives Produce for the World Market*, London: Zed Books.

— (1986) *Patriarchy and Accumulation on a World Scale: Women in the International Division of Labour*, London: Zed Books.

Nation Correspondent, (1996) 'Widows: Chief Has Taken Our Land', *Daily Nation*, Nairobi, 4 November, p. 16.

Nation Reporter (1996) 'Government Plans Fundamental Reforms for Agriculture', *Daily Nation*, Nairobi, 3 October, pp. 1–2.

Nation Team (1992) *Daily Nation*, 28 February, p. 2.

Okello, R. (1993) 'Women, the Dispossessed Land Tillers', *Daily Nation*, Nairobi, 4 November, p. II, supplement.

Republic of Kenya (1993) *Murang'a District Development Plan, 1994–1996*, Rural Planning Department, Office of the Vice President and Ministry of Planning and National Development.

Rostow, W. W. (1960) *The Stages of Economic Growth: A Non-Communist Manifesto*, Cambridge: Cambridge University Press.

Thornburn, F. (2000) 'Laying Claim to Zimbabwe's Land', *Guardian Weekly*, 11 May, (gwsubna@time.ca or http://guardianweekly.com), p. 13.

Turner, T. E. (1994) 'Rastafari and the New Society: East African and Caribbean Feminist roots of a Popular Movement to Reclaim the Earthly Commons', in Terisa E. Turner (ed.) with B. Ferguson, *Arise Ye Mighty People! Gender, Class and Race in Popular Struggles*, Trenton, NJ: Africa World Press, pp. 9–58.

Turner, T. E. (2000) 'Land to Make a Living', *Guardian Weekly*, 8–14 June (gwsubna@time.ca http://guardianweekly.com), p. 13.

Turner, T. E. (forthcoming) *Counterplanning from the Commons: Gendered Class Analysis and Globalization From Below*, Elizabethville, NJ: Africa World Press.

Turner, T. E. and C. S. Benjamin (1995) 'Not in our Nature: The Male Deal and Corporate Solutions to the Debt-nature Crisis', *Review: Journal of the Fernand Braudel Center*, XVIII, 2 (Spring), pp. 209–58.

Turner, T. E. (ed.), with B. Ferguson (1994) *Arise Ye Mighty People! Gender, Class and Race in Popular Struggles*, Trenton, NJ: Africa World Press.

Turner, T. E. and M. O. Oshare (1993) 'Women's Uprisings Against the Nigerian Oil Industry in the 1980s', *Canadian Journal of Development Studies*, XIV, 3, pp. 329–57.

Turner, T. E., L. S. Brownhill and W. M. Kaara (2001) 'Gender, Food Security and Foreign Policy Toward Africa: Women Farmers and the Sustenance Economy in Kenya', in Rosalind Irwin (ed.), *Ethics and Security in Canadian Foreign Policy*, Vancouver: University of British Columbia Press, pp. 145–76.

Turner, T. E., W. M. Kaara and L. S. Brownhill (1997) 'Social Reconstruction in Rural Africa: A Gendered Class Analysis of Women's Resistance to Cash Crop Production in Kenya', *Canadian Journal of Development Studies*, XVIII, 2, pp. 213–38.

Wipper, A. (forthcoming) 'Kikuyu Women and the Harry Thuku Disturbances: Some Uniformities of Female Militancy', in T. E. Turner (ed.), *Mau Mau Women: Their Mothers, Their Daughters, A Century of Popular Struggle in Kenya*.

Wood, E. (1986) *The Retreat from Class: A New 'True' Socialism*, London: Verso.

World Bank (1994) *Adjustment in Africa: Reforms, Results and the Road Ahead*, Washington, DC: World Bank.

9

War, Globalization and Reproduction

Silvia Federici

First came the foreign bankers eager to lend at extortionate rates; then the financial controllers to see that the interest was paid; then the thousands of foreign advisors taking their cut. Finally, when the country was bankrupt and helpless, it was time for the foreign troops to 'rescue' the ruler from his 'rebellious' people. One last gulp and the country had gone. (Pakenham 1991: 126)

> You who hunger, who shall feed you?
> Come to us, we too are starving.
> Only hungry ones can feed you.
>
> (B. Brecht, 'All or Nothing')

As Maria Mies has shown (1986; Bennholdt-Thomsen and Mies 1999), a key aspect of the present phase of globalization is the ongoing destruction of subsistence economies and, in particular, subsistence agriculture, the primary means of sustenance for much of the world's population. As we know, the structural adjustment programmes imposed by the World Bank and the International Monetary Fund (IMF) on the countries of the 'Third World' have this as one of their most basic objectives. What needs to be stressed, however, is the key role that war plays in this process.

In what follows I argue that the destruction of subsistence economies is one of the main reasons behind the proliferation of conflicts in Africa, Asia and Latin America, and the zest of the USA for military intervention throughout the 1980s and 1990s.[1] More broadly, I argue that war is on the global agenda precisely because the new phase of capitalist expansionism requires the destruction of any economic activity not subordinated to the logic of accumulation, and this is necessarily a violent process. Corporate capital cannot extend its reach over the planet's resources – from the fields to the seas and forests to people's labour, and our very genetic pools – without generating an intense resistance world-wide. Moreover, it is in the nature of the present capitalist crisis that no mediations are possible, and that development planning in the Third World gives way to war.[2]

That the connection between integration into the global economy, the destruction of subsistence economies and warfare is not generally recognized is due to the fact that globalization today, while in essence continuing the late-nineteenth-century colonial project, presents itself primarily as an economic programme. Its first and most visible weapons (as already mentioned) are structural adjustment programmes, trade liberalization, privatization and intellectual property rights. All these policies are responsible for an immense transfer of wealth from the Third World to the metropoles, and the expropriation of Third World assets and resources by the multinational corporations, but they do not require territorial conquest, and thus are assumed to work by purely peaceful means.[3]

Military intervention too is taking new forms, often appearing under the guise of benevolent initiatives, such as 'food aid' and 'humanitarian relief', or, in Latin America, the 'war against drugs'. A further reason why the marriage between war and globalization – the form that imperialism takes today – is not more evident is that most of the new 'globalization wars' have been fought on the African continent, whose current history is systematically distorted by the media which blame every crisis on the Africans' alleged 'backwardness', 'tribalism' and incapacity to achieve democratic institutions.

Africa, War and Structural Adjustment

In reality, the situation in Africa shows the coincidence between the implementation of the structural adjustment programmes (SAPs) introduced in the 1980s by the World Bank and the International Monetary Fund (IMF) to facilitate the advance of multinational capital in the region, and the development of a state of constant warfare. It shows that structural adjustment generates war, and war, in turn, completes the work of structural adjustment, as it makes the countries affected dependent on international capital, and the powers that represent it, beginning with the USA, the European Union (EU) and the UN. In other words, to paraphrase Clausewitz, '*structural adjustment is war by other means*'.

There are many ways in which structural adjustment promotes war. This type of programme was imposed by the World Bank and the IMF on most African countries starting in the early 1980s, presumably to spur economic recovery and help the African governments pay for the debts which they had contracted during the previous decade in order to finance development projects. Among the reforms it prescribes are land privatization (beginning with the abolition of communal land tenure), trade liberalization (the elimination of tariffs on imported goods), the deregulation of currency transactions, the downsizing of the public sector, the defunding of social services, and a system of controls that effectively transfers economic planning from the African governments to the World Bank and non-governmental organizations (NGOs).[4]

This economic restructuring was presumably intended to boost productivity, eliminate inefficiency and increase Africa's 'competitive edge' in the global market. But the opposite has occurred. More than a decade after its adoption, local economies have collapsed, foreign investment has not materialized, and the only productive activities in place in most African countries are once again, as in the colonial period, mineral extraction and export-oriented agriculture that contributes to the gluts in the global market, while Africans do not have enough food to eat.

In this context of generalized economic bankruptcy, violent rivalries have exploded everywhere among different factions of the African ruling class who, unable to enrich themselves through the exploitation of labour, are now fighting for access to state power as the key condition for the accumulation of wealth. State power, in fact, is the key to the appropriation and sale on the international market of either the national assets and resources (land, gold, diamonds, oil, timber), or the assets possessed by rival or weaker groups.[5] Thus, war has become the necessary underbelly of a new mercantile economy, or (according to some) an 'economy of plunder' (Bayart et al. 1999), thriving with the complicity of foreign companies and international agencies which (for all their complaints about 'corruption') benefit from it.

As in Russia, the World Bank's insistence that everything be privatized has weakened the state and accelerated this process. In the same way, the deregulation of banking activities and currency transactions (also demanded by the World Bank) has helped the spread of the drug trade which, since the 1980s, has been playing a major role in Africa's political economy, contributing to the formation of private armies (Bayart et al. 1999; Williams 1998).

A further source of warfare in Africa has been the brutal impoverishment into which structural adjustment has plunged the majority of the population. While intensifying social protest, this, over the years, has torn the social fabric as millions of people have been forced to leave their villages and go abroad in search of new sources of livelihood; and the struggle for survival has laid the ground-work for the fomenting and manipulation of local antagonisms and the recruitment of the unemployed (particularly the youth) by warring parties. Many 'tribal' and religious conflicts in Africa (no less than the 'ethnic' conflicts in Yugoslavia) have been rooted in these processes. From the mass expulsions of immigrants and religious riots in Nigeria in the early and mid-1980s, to the 'clan' wars in Somalia in the early 1990s (Chossudovsky 1998), to the bloody wars between the state and the fundamentalists in Algeria (Stone 1997), in the background of most contemporary African conflicts there have been the World Bank's and the IMF's 'conditionalities' that have wrecked peoples' lives and undermined the conditions for social solidarity.

There is no doubt, for instance, that the youths who have been fighting the numerous African wars of recent years are the same who two decades ago could have been in school, and could have hoped to make a living through trade or a job in the public sector, and could have looked to the future with the hope of being able to contribute to their families' well-being. Similarly, the appearance of child-soldiers in the 1980s and 1990s would never have been possible if, in many countries, the extended family had not been undermined by financial hardships, and millions of children were not without a place to go except for the street and had someone to provide for their needs (Human Rights Watch 1995).

War has not only been a consequence of economic change; it has also been a means to produce it. Two objectives stand out when we consider the prevailing patterns of war in Africa, and the way in which warfare intersects with globalization. First, war forces people off the land, i.e. it separates the producers from the means of production, a condition for the expansion of the global labour market. War also reclaims the land for capitalist use, boosting the production of cash crops and export-oriented agriculture. Particularly in Africa, where communal land tenure is still widespread, this has been a major goal of the World Bank, whose *raison d'être* as an institution has been the capitalization of agriculture.[6] Thus, it is hard today to see millions of refugees or famine victims fleeing their localities without thinking of the satisfaction this must bring to World Bank officers as well as agribusiness companies, who surely see the hand of progress working through it.

War also undermines people's opposition to 'market reforms' by re-shaping the territory and disrupting the social networks that provide the basis for resistance. Significant here is the correlation – frequent in contemporary Africa – between anti-IMF protest and conflict (Federici 1992). This is most visible perhaps in Algeria where the rise of anti-government Islamic fundamentalism dates from the anti-IMF uprising of 1988, when thousands of young people took over the streets of the capital for several days in the most intense and widespread protest since the heyday of the anti-colonial struggle.[7]

External intervention – often seizing local struggles and turning them into global conflicts – has played a major role in this context. This can be seen even in the case of military interventions by the USA that are usually read through the prism of 'geo-politics' and the Cold War, such as the support given by the Reagan administration to the governments of Sudan and Somalia, and to UNITA in Angola. Both in the Sudan and Somalia SAPs had been under way since the early 1980s when both countries were among the major recipients of US military aid. In the Sudan, US military assistance strengthened the Neimeri regime's hand against the coalition of forces that were opposing the cuts demanded by the IMF; even though, in the end, it could not stem the uprising that in 1985 was to depose him. In Somalia, US military aid helped Siad Barre's attack on the Isaaks, an episode in the ongoing war waged by national and international agencies over the last decade against Africa's pastoralist groups (Africa Watch 1990).[8]

In Angola, too, US military aid to UNITA served to force the government not just to renounce socialism and the help of Cuban troops, but to negotiate with the IMF, and it undoubtedly strengthened the bargaining power of the oil companies operating in the country (Sogge 1994: 105).

Food Aid as Stealth Warfare

In many cases, what arms could not accomplish was achieved through 'food aid' provided by the USA, the UN and various NGOs to the refugees and the victims of the famines which the wars had produced. Often delivered to both sides of the conflict (as in the Sudan, Ethiopia and Angola), food aid has become a major component of the contemporary neo-colonial war-machine, and the war-economy generated by it. First, it has entitled international organizations other than the Red Cross to claim the right to intervene in areas of conflict in the name of providing relief (in 1988 the UN passed a resolution asserting the right of donors to deliver aid) (Macrae and Zwi 1994a: 11–12).[9] It is on this basis that the US/UN military intervention in Somalia in 1992–93 (Operation Restore Hope) was justified.

Even when it is not accompanied by troops, the delivery of food aid in a conflict situation is always a form of political and military intervention as it prolongs the war by feeding the contending armies (often more than the civilian population), it shapes military strategy, and it helps the stronger party – the one best equipped to take advantage of food distribution – to win (Duffield 1994: 60–3). This is exactly what took place in the Sudan and Ethiopia in the 1980s where, by providing food aid, the USA, the UN and NGOs such as CARE became major protagonists in the wars fought in these countries.[10]

In addition, food aid contributes to the displacement and the relocation of rural communities, by setting up feeding centres organized around the needs of the NGOs; it undermines local agriculture by causing the prices of locally marketed produce to collapse; and it introduces a new source of warfare, since the prospect of appropriating the large food supplies and selling them locally or internationally provides a new motive for conflict, indeed, the creation of a war-economy, especially in countries that have been radically impoverished (Duffield 1994).

So questionable has food assistance been in its effects, so dubious its ability to guarantee people's livelihood (which would have been better served by the distribution of agricultural tools and seeds and, first of all, by the end of hostilities), that one has to ask whether the true purpose of this initiative was not the phasing out of subsistence farming, and the creation of a long-term dependence on imported food – both centrepieces of World Bank reform, and conditions for the integration of African countries into the global economy. This question is all the more legitimate considering that the negative effects of food aid have been well known since the 1960s, when it became the object of much protest and research throughout the Third World. Since then, it has been almost an axiom that 'you don't help people by giving them food, but by giving them the tools to feed themselves', and that, even under famine conditions, what people need most to survive is to preserve their ability to farm. How the UN and the World Bank could have forgotten this lesson is indeed inexplicable, unless we presume that the appearance of food aid in contemporary war-related operations in Africa has had as one of its major objectives the commercialization of land and agriculture and the takeover of the African food markets by international agribusiness.

It must be added that 'relief operations' relying on the intervention of foreign NGOs and aid organizations have further marginalized the victims of conflicts and famines, who have been denied the right to control the relief activities while being portrayed in the international media by the same NGOs as helpless beings unable to care for themselves. Indeed, as Macrae and Zwi point out, the only right that has been recognized has been the right of the 'donors' to deliver assistance, which, as we have seen, has been used (in Somalia in 1992–93) to call for military intervention (Macrae and Zwi 1994a).

Mozambique: A Paradigm Case of Contemporary War

How war, first, and then humanitarian relief can be used to recolonize a country, bring it to the market and break its resistance to economic and political dependence is best seen in the case of Mozambique (Hanlon 1991; 1996). Indeed, the war that the Mozambique National Resistance or Renamo (a proxy of apartheid South Africa and the USA) waged against this country for almost a decade (1981–90) contains all the key elements of today's new globalization wars:

1. *The destruction of the country's physical and social (re)productive infrastructure to provoke a reproduction crisis and enforce economic and political subordination.* This Renamo achieved through (a) the use of systematic terror against the population (massacres, enslavement, the infliction of horrendous mutilations) that forced people off their land, and turned them into refugees (more than one million people were killed in this war); (b) the demolition of roads, bridges, hospitals, schools and, above all, the destruction of all agricultural activities and assets – the basic means of subsistence for a population of farmers. (The case of Mozambique shows the strategic significance of 'low-intensity warfare', beginning with the use of land-mines as a means to prevent people from going out to farm, and thereby creating a famine situation requiring external help.)

2. *The use of 'food aid' delivered to displaced people and victims of famine to ensure compliance with economic conditionalities, create long-term food dependency, and undermine a country's ability to control its economic and political future.* It must not be forgotten that food aid is a great boost to US agribusiness, which profits from it twice, first by being relieved of its huge surpluses and, later, by profiting from the helped country's dependence on imported food.

3. *The transfer of decision-making from the state to international organizations and NGOs.* So thorough was the attack on Mozambican sovereignty that, once it was forced to ask for aid, Mozambique had to accept that the NGOs be given the green light in the management of relief operations, including the right to enter any part of its territory, and distribute food directly to the population at places of their choice. As Joseph Hanlon has shown in *Mozambique: Who Calls the Shots?*, the government was hard put to protest the NGOs' politics, even in the case of right-wing NGOs such as World Vision that used the relief distributions for political and religious propaganda; or NGOs such as CARE that were suspected of collaborating with the CIA.

4. *The imposition of impossible peace conditions*, such as 'reconciliation' and power-sharing with Renamo (the Mozambican government's and population's most irreconcilable enemy, responsible for many atrocities and the massacre of more than one million people) which created the potential for permanent destabilization. This 'reconciliation' policy, now cynically and widely imposed, from Haiti to South Africa, as a 'peace-condition' – the political equivalent of the practice of feeding both parties in a conflict context – is one of the most telling expressions of the present recolonization drive, as it proclaims that people in the Third World should never have the right to have peace, and to protect themselves from proven enemies. It also proclaims that not every country has the same rights, since the USA, or any country of the EU, would never dream of accepting such a foul proposition.

Conclusion: from Africa to Yugoslavia and Beyond

The case of Mozambique is not unique. Not only are most African countries practically run by US-supported agencies and NGOs; the sequence – destruction of infrastructure, imposition of market reforms, forced reconciliation with murderous, 'irreconcilable' enemies, destabilization – is found, in different degrees and combinations, everywhere in Africa today, to such a point that several countries, like Angola and Sudan, are in a state of permanent emergency and their viability as political entities is now in question.

It is through this combination of financial and military warfare that the African people's resistance against globalization has so far been held in check, in the same way as it has in Central America (El Salvador, Nicaragua, Guatemala, Panama) where throughout the 1980s open US military intervention was the rule.

The difference is that, in Africa, the right of the USA/UN to send troops has generally been justified in the name of 'peace-keeping', 'peace-making' and 'humanitarian intervention', possibly because under any other condition, a landing of the marines (of the type we have seen in Panama and Grenada) would not have been internationally accepted. These interventions, however, are the new faces of colonialism, and not in Africa alone. This is a colonialism that aims at controlling policies and resources rather than gaining territorial possession, in political terms, a 'philanthropic', 'humanitarian', 'foot-loose' colonialism that aims at 'governance' rather than 'government', for the latter involves a commitment to a specific institutional and economic set-up, whereas modern-day free enterprise imperialism wants to maintain its freedom always to choose the institutional set-up, the economic forms and the locations best suited to its needs.[11] However, as in the colonialism of old, soldiers and merchants are not far apart, as the marriage of food-aid distributions and military intervention today again demonstrates.

What is the significance of this scenario for the anti-war movement, and the claim made by this chapter that war is still on the global agenda?

First, that we can expect the situation that has developed in post-adjustment Africa – with its mixture of economic and military warfare and the sequence of structural adjustment–conflict–intervention – to be reproduced over and over in the coming years throughout the Third World. We can also expect to see more wars develop in the former socialist countries, for the institutions and forces that are pushing the globalization process find state-owned industry and other remnants of socialism as much of an obstacle to 'free enterprise' as African communalism.

In this sense, NATO's war against Yugoslavia is likely to be the first example (after that of Bosnia) of what is to come, as the end of state-socialism is being replaced by liberalization and the free market, NATO's advance to the East providing 'the security framework'. So close is the relation between NATO's 'humanitarian intervention' in Yugoslavia and 'humanitarian intervention' in Africa that relief workers – the ground troops of the contemporary war-machine – were brought from Africa to Kosovo, where they have already had the opportunity to assess the relative value of African and European lives in the eyes of international organizations, measured by the quality and quantity of the resources provided to the refugees.

We should also see that the situation we confront is very different from the imperialism of the late nineteenth and early twentieth centuries. For the imperialist powers of those days were tied to, and responsible for, specific and territorially-defined social, political and infrastructural arrangements. Thus, in the imperialist era of the gun-boat and the machine-gun, which could kill thousands of people from afar, responsibility for massacres, famines and other forms of mass killing could always be identified. We know, for instance, that it was King Leopold of Belgium who had a personal responsibility for the killing of millions of people in the Congo (Hochschild 1998). By contrast, today, millions of Africans are dying every year because of the consequences of structural adjustment, but no one is held responsible for it. On the contrary, the social causes of death in Africa are increasingly becoming as invisible as the invisible hand of the capitalist market (Walton and Seddon 1994).

Finally, we have to realize that we cannot mobilize against the bombings alone, nor demand that bombing stops and call that 'peace'. We know from the post-war scenario in Iraq that the destruction of a country's infrastructure produces more deaths than the bombs themselves. What we need to learn is that death, hunger, disease and destruction are presently a daily reality for most people across the planet. More than that, structural adjustment – the most universal programme in the Third World today, the one that, in all its forms (including the African Growth and Opportunity Act), represents the contemporary face of capitalism and colonialism – is war. Thus, the programme of the anti-war movement must include the elimination of structural adjustment in all of its many forms if war, and the imperialistic project it embodies, is to finally come to an end.

Notes

1. By a recent count there were seventy-five countries experiencing some form of war in 1999 (Effe 1999); thirty-three of them are to be found in Africa's forty-three continental nations. This is the 'Fourth World War' against the world's poor that Sub-comandante Marcos often writes about.

2. For a description of this new phase of capitalism that emphasizes the disappearance of interclass mediations see Federici (1999) and Midnight Notes Collective (1992). The phrase 'new enclosures' is used in these articles to indicate that the thrust of contemporary capitalism is to annihilate any guarantees of subsistence that were recognized by socialist, post-colonial or Keynesian states in the 1950s and 1960s. This process must be violent in order to succeed.

3. The immense existing literature on structural adjustment, globalization and neo-liberalism has amply described this transfer of wealth. See: Brecher and Costello 1994; Bello 1994; Barnet and Cavanagh 1994; and Federici 1999.

4. The literature on structural adjustment in Africa is also immense. Since the mid-1980s, NGOs (both international and domestic) have become essential to the implementation of structural adjustment programmes, as they have taken over the areas of social reproduction that the state is forced to defund when it is structurally adjusted. As Alex de Waal writes: 'the combination of neo-liberalism and advocacy of a "human face" has created a new role for international NGOs as subcontractors in the large-scale delivery of basic services such as health, agricultural extension and food rations [...] Often, the larger service-delivery NGOs (CARE, Catholic Relief Services, Save the Children Fund) have been drawn in when there has been a crisis such as famine or institutional collapse, and have stayed on afterwards. In other cases, NGOs have placed advisers in ministries (health is the favourite) and occasionally they have even taken over responsibility for entire services. The basic drug supply for clinics in the capital of Sudan, primary health care in rural Uganda and almost all TB and leprosy programmes in Tanzania are just three of the "national" health programmes largely directed by international NGOs using funds from Euro-American institutional donors' (de Waal 1997: 53).

5. A good example of this plundering of weaker groups is to be found in the Sudan, where, in the late 1980s, the Sudanese government gave the Murahaliin militia, drawn from the Baggara Arabs, the right to plunder the cattle wealth of the Dinka. 'Their raids were frequent, widespread and devastating. The raiders stole livestock, destroyed villages, poisoned wells and killed indiscriminately. They were also implicated in enslaving captives. Displaced survivors fled to garrison towns, where they were forced to sell their cattle and other assets cheaply' (de Waal 1997: 94). For more on this process see Duffield (1994: 54–7).

6. For an analysis of World Bank policies promoting the capitalization of agriculture in Africa, see Caffentzis (1995).

7. The actual warfare between the government and the Islamic fundamentalists began with the government's refusal to recognize the electoral gains of the fundamentalists in early 1992. The roots of the conflict, though, are to be found in the government's harsh response to the 1988 anti-IMF riots. (See Stone 1997.)

8. In 1987, Oxfam reported that a European Commission official responded to its request to aid pastoralists in southern Sudan with a self-fulfilling prophecy: 'In his view, pastoralism was, in any case, non-viable and in decline all over the region.' Oxfam went on to comment: 'It is important to note that USAID, UNICEF, and EEC have all recently expressed similar views concerning pastoralism in the South; that it is on the way out and in twenty years would have disappeared anyway' (Keen and Wilson 1994: 214).

9. As de Waal writes: 'the first negotiated agreement on access to a war zone [was] Operation Lifeline in Sudan April 1989 [... this was] followed in 1991–2 with the concept of "cross-mandate" operations, for example in eastern Ethiopia, where UNHCR, UNICEF and WFP assisted refugees, displaced people and impoverished residents with-

out discrimination. The cross-mandate approach was further developed in the former Yugoslavia' (de Waal 1997: 69).

10. One of the most egregious examples of this transformation of aid providers into military protagonists is the assistance given by the USA and the UN in the Ethiopian government's war against the Eritrean People's Liberation Front (EPLF) and the Tigray People's Liberation Front (TPLF) in the 1980s. The famous 'We are the Children' famine of 1984–85 was not caused by drought, overpopulation, or improper land use as claimed at the time; its true cause was the Ethiopian government's many offensives against the EPLF and TPLF as well as its resettlement programme which forcibly moved hundreds of thousands of people from the north to the south of the country (during which 50,000 people died). Food relief provided by the USA, the UN and various NGOs (which totalled almost $3 billion between 1985 and 1988) was essential for the continuation of the Ethiopian government's war effort as well as its resettlement scheme. So thorough was the co-operation and complicity between the USA, the UN and NGO personnel with the Ethiopian government that they hid the causes of the famine; they hid the diversion of food aid to the military (at most 15 per cent of the aid went to civilians, the rest went to the army), they hid the human costs of the resettlement scheme, they accompanied the Ethiopian Army 'to gain access to the famine areas' and, on top of it, they loudly complained that their humanitarian efforts were being hindered when the EPLF or the TPLF recaptured territory! Alex de Waal, a co-director of African Rights, has provided us with an in-depth, eye-opening account of this travesty (de Waal 1997: 115–27) which is especially valuable since he was directly involved in the events he reports on.

11. This is similar to the 'new slavery' discussed in Bales (1999) where contemporary slave-owners in Thailand and Brazil avoid responsibility for their slaves who are then 'disposable' when they become unprofitable.

References

Africa Watch Report (1990) *Somalia. A Government at War with Its People*, New York: Human Rights Watch.

Allen, Chris (1998) 'The Machinery of External Control', *Review of African Political Economy*, 76, 25 (March).

Association of Concerned Africa Scholars (ACAS) (1996) 'The Aid Debate', *ACAS Bulletin*, 47 (Fall).

Bales, Kevin (1999) *Disposable People: New Slavery in the Global Economy*, Berkeley: University of California Press.

Barnet, Richard J. and John Cavanagh (1994) *Global Dreams: Imperial Corporations and the New World Order*, New York: Simon and Schuster.

Bayart, Jean-François et al. (1999) *The Criminalization of the State in Africa*, Oxford: The International African Institute in Association with James Currey.

Bello, Walden (1994) *Dark Victory: The United States, Structural Adjustment and Global Poverty*, London: Pluto Press.

Bennholdt-Thomsen, V. and M. Mies (1999) *The Subsistence Perspective: Beyond the Globalized Economy*, London: Zed Books; Melbourne: Spinifex.

Brecher, Jeremy and Tim Costello (1994) *Global Village or Global Pillage: Economic Reconstruction from the Bottom Up*, Boston: South End Press.

Caffentzis, George (1995) 'The Fundamental Implications of the Debt Crisis for Social Reproduction in Africa', in M. R. Dalla Costa and G. Dalla Costa (eds), *Paying the Price*, London: Zed Books.

Chossudovsky, Michel (1998) *The Globalization of Poverty. Impacts of the IMF and World Bank Reforms*, London: Zed Books.

Ciment, James (1997) *Algeria. The Fundamentalist Challenge*, New York: Facts on File.

Clough, Michael (1992) *Free at Last? U.S. Policy Toward Africa at the End of the Cold War*, New York: Council of Foreign Relations.

Current History, 'Africa's Wars', *Current History*, May 1999.

Dalla Costa, Maria Rosa and Giovanna Dalla Costa (eds) (1995) *Paying the Price*, London: Zed Books.

— (eds) (1999) *Women, Development and the Labor of Reproduction*, Trenton, NJ: Africa World Press.

de Waal, Alex (1997) *Famine Crimes. Politics and the Disaster Relief Industry in Africa*, Oxford: African Rights and the International African Institute in association with James Currey.

Duffield, Mark (1994) 'The Political Economy of Internal War: Asset Transfer, Complex Emergencies, and International Aid', in J. Macrae and A. Zwi (eds), *War and Hunger. Rethinking International Responses to Complex Emergencies*, London: Zed Books.

Effe (1999) *Effe: La Rivista delle Librerie Feltrinelli*, 13.

Federici, Silvia (1992) 'The Debt Crisis, Africa and the New Enclosures', in Midnight Notes Collective (eds), *Midnight Oil: Work, Energy, War, 1973–1992*, New York: Autonomedia.

— (1999) 'Reproduction and Feminist Struggle in the New International Division of Labor', in M. R. Dalla Costa and G. Dalla Costa (eds), *Women, Development and the Labor of Reproduction*, Trenton, NJ: Africa World Press.

Ghai, Dharam (1991) *The IMF and the South*, London: Zed Books.

Hanlon, Joseph (1991) *Mozambique: Who Calls the Shots?*, Oxford: James Currey.

— (1996) *Peace Without Profit. How the IMF Blocks Rebuilding in Mozambique*, Oxford: James Currey.

Hochschild, Adam (1998) *King Leopold's Ghost*, Boston: Houghton Mifflin.

Human Rights Watch/Africa (1994) *Child Soldiers in Liberia*, New York: Human Rights Watch.

— (1995) *Slaves, Street Children and Child Soldiers*, New York: Human Rights Watch.

Keen, David and Ken Wilson (1994) 'Engaging with Violence: A Reassessment of Relief in Wartime', in J. Macrae and A. Zwi (eds), *War and Hunger. Rethinking International Responses to Complex Emergencies*, London: Zed Books, pp. 209–21.

Macrae, J. and Anthony Zwi (1994a). 'Famine, Complex Emergencies and International Policy in Africa: An Overview', in J. Macrae and A. Zwi (eds), *War and Hunger. Rethinking International Responses to Complex Emergencies*, London: Zed Books.

— (eds) (1994b) *War and Hunger. Rethinking International Responses to Complex Emergencies*, London: Zed Books.

Midnight Notes Collective (eds) (1992) *Midnight Oil: Work, Energy, War, 1973–1992*, New York: Autonomedia.

Mies, M. (1986) *Patriarchy and Accumulation on a World Scale. Women in the International Division of Labour*, London: Zed Books

Nzongola-Ntalaja (ed.) (1986) *The Crisis in Zaire: Myths and Realities*, Trenton, NJ: Africa World Press.

Outram, Quentin (1997). '"It's Terminal Either Way": An Analysis of Armed Conflict in Liberia, 1989–1996', *Review of African Political Economy*, 73, 24 (September).

Pakenham, Thomas (1991) *The Scramble for Africa: White Man's Conquest of the Dark Continent from 1876 to 1912*, New York: Avon Books.

Prunier, Gerard (1995) *The Rwanda Crisis. History of a Genocide*, New York: Columbia University Press.

Rau, Bill (1991) *From Feast to Famine: Official Cures and Grassroots Remedies in Africa's Food Crisis*, London: Zed Books.

Sogge, David (1994) 'Angola: Surviving against Rollback and Petrodollars', in J. Macrae and A. Zwi (eds), *War and Hunger. Rethinking International Responses to Complex Emergencies*, London: Zed Books.

Stone, Martin (1997) *The Agony of Algeria*, New York: Columbia University Press.

Tanner, Victor (1998) 'Liberia Railroading Peace', *Review of African Political Economy*, 75, 25 (March).

Walton, J. and D. Seddon (1994) *Free Markets and Food Riots*, Oxford: Blackwell.

Williams, Phil (1998) 'The Nature of Drug-Trafficking Networks', *Current History*, April.

10

Seattle: A Convergence of Globalization and Militarization

Theresa J. Wolfwood

Seattle, 2 December 1999

At a meeting of Diverse Women for Diversity, on the Tuesday after the big demonstration against the World Trade Organization (WTO) in Seattle, I spoke about the connection between trade agreements and militarization, using Chiapas as an example. The peasants of Chiapas understood that the North America Free Trade Agreement (NAFTA) would destroy their communal land-ownership and their self-sufficient agriculture when they rose up in armed rebellion. I described to the audience a day in 1997 when I was hiking in the hills of La Selva in Chiapas with the community leader of the village where I was a human rights observer; as we talked, Mexican military helicopters buzzed us, helicopters made in the United States of America, with engines made in Canada. Just as I was explaining this connection between trade and militarization, a woman rushed into the hall, ran up to the stage, grabbed the microphone and announced, 'Martial law has been declared in Seattle'.

America Had Come Home

America came home to its own, educated, mainly white young people who were demonstrating non-violently against the WTO in the Seattle streets while the world watched. Police, National Guard, hundreds of plainclothes police and special military *agents provocateurs* turned on courageous, self-disciplined people who peacefully opposed the dictatorship of corporate-ruled secretive and powerful international alliances, the WTO, the International Monetary Fund (IMF) and the World Bank. I witnessed the vandalizing of Niketown while the police stood by and watched. The few who committed acts of property damage, probably including paid *provocateurs*, were not arrested.

For decades, people the world over have been victims of the military might of the USA and other Minority World bullies. From Cuba to Angola, from the Mayan jungles to the streets of Jakarta, from Iraq to Columbia, people have been the object of the brutal force of US power, the bomb and the buck working together. Now we know a little of what happens to those who challenge the global hegemony of corporate power. Governments and their media talk about 'democracy', but when the people demand it, out come the guns, the tear-gas, the bombs and the poison.

The analysis and experience of Majority World workers for peace and social justice also came home to America. In Seattle it was not only the lessons of corporate rule. We learned from people who have risked their lives and freedom to resist military and corporate domination in the last fifty years. We learned to form small democratic groups with solid bases in communities, rather than big hierarchical groups that lose touch with the grassroots and soon become co-opted and charmed by the corporate elite who manipulate them and call them 'responsible'. As our social movements grow in numbers, sophistication, efficiency of communication and effectiveness of action, we will have to anticipate the attempts to weaken us. We can expect campaigns against us based on denial, smear tactics, infiltration, 'divide and conquer' strategies, lies, co-option, flattery and pay-offs amounting to no more than a few crumbs from the corporate tables. In Seattle the 'good non-governmental organizations (NGOs)' were given official observer status, while grassroots groups met and demonstrated in public.

This new strength of citizen groups from around the globe was richly evident not only in the streets, but in the dozens of packed meetings taking place in churches and halls for a week in Seattle while the WTO itself faltered and failed to make new agreements. Majority World delegates to the WTO, usually ignored and dismissed by the big players (USA, European Union, Japan and Canada), were united in their opposition to new rules that would destroy local economies; they were heartened by the support of all those thousands who converged on Seattle to tell the world: 'The WTO has got to go, the people came and stole the show.' Placards such as 'Turtles and Teamsters, United At Last' showed how many groups are connecting and reaching a new common awareness and sharing strategies for future actions.

Agriculture and the WTO

Opposition to WTO agriculture policy is an important part of international resistance. Corporate control is the major threat to global food security. Market women in the villages of Cameroon ordered their representative to tell the WTO that 'We have our own food, our own voice and our own agriculture policy', and that they do not want large companies controlling their agriculture. Mexicans told us that the average income of Mexicans had declined by 40 per cent since NAFTA came into effect (see how prophetic the Zapatistas were?) and that Mexico's small farmers go broke as cheap US-grown corn is dumped there. Beautiful banners told us 'GMO [Genetically Modified Organisms] corn kills Monarch butterflies' that travel annually from Canada to Mexico. Genetic modification and patent laws are destroying the subsistence agriculture that feeds over half the world's people.

At the 'Food and Agriculture Day' of forums, workshops and another major demonstration, Nettie Weibe of Carlyle, Saskatchewan, spoke movingly of the destruction of the Canadian family farm. As farms are forced into monoculture with seeds, fertilizers and herbicides, processing and marketing controlled by a few global corporations, family farms and culture are being eroded like our topsoil. She said that the Canadian government is not a victim, but a major global power in agribusiness dominated by giant transnational corporations (TNCs). Her words were echoed by Monica Opole of Kenya who said that corporate agriculture there leached not only the soil of Africa but the culture of communities.

We were inspired by the 'Cremate Monsanto' movement in India, democracy movements in Indonesia and Guatemala, and the peasants of Central America and the Philippines who fight for their land, save their seeds and practise traditional ecological farming. We learned of new studies that show that large single-crop farming is not as productive as small-scale mixed farming. Corporate chemical monoculture does not feed the world. When we listened to activists from the Majority World we sensed their power and determination – giving the lie to the criticism that Minority World groups impose their values on others!

All the big chemical and mechanized farms are sudsidized in the USA and the European Union, their food crops are dumped internationally, driving small farmers off their land and into cities as their farms are seized by banks and big corporations.

Miltarization and World Trade

It is not only big agriculture that is subsidized and protected; the military industry has a special status in every trade agreement. In NAFTA the military corporations are exempt from any rules that forbid special national treatment of industries. The governments of Canada the USA continue to subsidize and promote military production. The former has just started a new $30 million programme to help arms sales abroad. Canada continues to subsidize companies that contribute handsomely to political parties, such as Bombardier, a major donor to the Liberal Party. It has become almost impossible for any level of government in Canada to encourage local development and fund local employment, except in military industries. NAFTA exemptions for military industries were built into the Multinational Agreement on Investment (MAI) and military industries have been excluded from WTO regulations for 'free market trade'. Military equipment made in Canada ends up in Mexico, Indonesia, Chile and many other countries directly and indirectly through the export of parts and equipment to the USA. In too many cases, Canadian-manufactured armaments are used against our friends who are struggling for dignity and independence.

We must unplug all nuclear power and related war and toxic industries. We can support new renewable energy technologies and conservation and we must disempower the military. Nuclear energy has always been the benign, respectable front for nuclear weaponry, but the two are inseparable. We have to stop all nuclear development. As we continue to be threatened by nuclear war preparations, we have to integrate our work for the environment and peace. War preparations bleed our social programmes, allow our governments to shirk major responsibilities to citizens and to divert our resources to death industries. If our land and water are contaminated by nuclear poison, organic foods won't save us.

While the 1999 Christmas season was upon us, the Canadian government signed another ten-year contract with the USA military for the use of Nanoose Bay as a maritime weapons testing range. So American nuclear-armed and -powered ships will continue to use Canadian waters and threaten lives. The government claims the agreement is necessary for defence and security, but it also sold off the Canadian National Railway to a US corporation. It would seem that having the major transport system in the power of a foreign company is not a threat to security.

We know that Canada is a society that worships consumerism, but what about its love affair with violence and militarism? It is not just biased trade agreements but the forces of globalization and our immersion in a culture of war that we must confront and change.

While social services are slashed and hiring is frozen, the armoury in downtown Victoria, Canada, has a permanent 'Now Hiring' sign. As rural peoples in the Majority World are driven from their land because of failing cash crops, cheap imports and landlords who convert to mechanized farming, women are forced to support their families in globalized employment in sweatshops, domestic servitude and the sex trade. Young men, unemployed and angry, are ripe for militarization. Modern warfare is based on the greed of the increasingly rich defending their privileges from the poor who are becoming more numerous and more impoverished every day as complicit governments support corporate rule. When national governments attack their neighbours or their own people who demand justice, it is this growing disposable population of desperate young men who are brainwashed and forced into the killing business. They do the dying and the dirty work for the elites, in exchange for status and pay. So-called 'rogue states' are not oppressive dictatorships such as Burma and Indonesia, but countries that will not obey global corporations. These states, like Serbia and Cuba, are punished by embargoes and military intervention. Watch Colombia and Venezuela, where indigenous people's land claims threaten oil companies.

Globalization and militarization are inseparable. The North Atlantic Treaty Organization (NATO) bombed Yugoslavia so that multinational corporations can have access to state-owned mines and oil pipelines, and so that foreign-armed thugs can use Yugoslavian territory for the international drug trade, one of the top ten commodities traded globally. After a war that destroyed Iraq's social infrastructure and killed thousands of civilians, nine years of economic sanctions have killed a million and a half people, mainly children. Many are suffering the results of poisoning by depleted uranium used in bombs and missiles. Canada enforces a trade embargo that prevents its farmers from selling grain to Iraq, once a major customer.

We live in a constant state of war preparedness, and Canada now supports the USA in new dangerous space-wars plans. That $6.6 billion that Canada has committed to Arctic war projects would go a long way in its education system. Then maybe Canadian professors would not need to accept US and Canadian military research contracts. Imagine if the universities were so well funded that dispensing machines on campuses sold local fruit juice as well as (or instead of) one brand of sticky sweet brown syrup? What professor defends freedom of choice and expression when it comes to the corporate buy-in, not only of dispensing machines, but of classrooms, of teaching materials, research and industry 'chairs' of teaching? University groups can publicize corporate takeovers in education while campaigning for proper public funding.

Canada needs more agriculture for the local market and urban links with rural producers, like the 'brown box' programmes of regular, pre-ordered seasonal food. The greater the local organic non-GM sales, the less power the TNCs have. Monsanto (the company that gave Vietnam Agent Orange, and now its cousin, Roundup) is slipping on the stock market; people's rejection of Bovine Growth Hormone, GMOs and the 'Terminator' seed (now supposedly abandoned) have damaged their sales and image. But look what's coming! With government support, Monsanto is now getting into GM trees. Just because people don't eat forests does not mean the environment and lives will not be damaged.

Knowing is Not Enough, Act for Peace ad Justice!

We must act now to save our land, water and forests for future generations.

Activist groups, inspired by Seattle, are starting a GMO-free Canada campaign. There are lists of GM foods to boycott and to talk to retailers about – mainly soy, canola and corn products. The University of Victoria has developed a GM potato. GM apples are also being developed in British Columbia. UK activists stopped the sale of GM foods in their supermarkets; we can too.

The WTO and its buddies like NATO and the Organization of Economic Co-operation and Development (OECD) won't go away after even a week of spectacular demonstrations and speeches in Seattle. What these events do is alert the world to the dangers of globalization while the bureaucrats and executives retreat to their fortresses to plan their next assaults on our freedoms. As we saw the failed MAI incorporated into the WTO, the failed WTO plans will be incorporated into the newest scheme, the Transatlantic Economic Partnership. This agreement will combine NAFTA, the EU and the Free Trade of the Americas Agreement into a new form of corporate rule. So we must bring home that inspiration and knowledge we gained in Seattle and start working against all secret elite trade agreements.

More than anything we need to create a culture of peace and justice at home in solidarity with those who struggle in much worse conditions than are faced in Canada. Plan an action! As the posters in Seattle said, 'We need Clean, Green Fair Trade, not "Free Trade"' and 'Carry on the spirit of Seattle'. The real civil society cannot be bought off with bits of funding and fancy lunches, while the government complains we have no leaders. We are all leaders! Strategy workshops at Seattle showed us how to stop the World Bank and IMF in their impoverishment of the Majority World; British activists shared their success in making supermarkets go GM-free. There is no lack of direction for social activists to follow.

We need to root out the culture of violence in our own society. Let's stop the glamorization of violence in the media, entertainment, toys and video games. We can stop the takeover of education, starting at the elementary level, by corporations who present a bland, passive, consumption-orientated version of teaching and learning. The United Nations declared 2000 the International Year for the Culture of Peace – why don't we respect our UN commitments as much as we adhere to trade agreements? Let's expose the Canadian government's complicity in war preparations and corporate domination. We can take over governments, starting at the local level. We have to see that creating a culture of peace, justice, ecology and co-operation is our real work as we resist globalization and militarization. Seattle was a milestone. There can be no turning back and we cannot rest on the laurels of one success.

As the Zapatistas say, ' We Want a World with Room for Many Worlds'. *La Lucha Continua*!

Part III

On Resistance to Globalization II: Subsistence in Practice

11

Mexico: Creating Your Own Path at the Grassroots

Gustavo Esteva

'On the night of 2 July [2000] Mexico finally became a democracy.' This statement, in *Time*, expressed the view of the media pundits celebrating the outcome of the elections in Mexico as another step forwards in the implementation of the neo-liberal agenda.

At the grassroots, in Mexico, the people were also celebrating, but for very different reasons. They had no illusions about the implications of the elections. 'For us', said an indigenous leader on 3 July, 'the system is like a snake; what happened last night is that it shed its skin and now has a different colour.' What they perceived was not a victory of neo-liberalism and democracy, but the funeral of the oldest authoritarian regime in the world, to which they had courageously contributed. They evaluated the elections in the frame of their struggle to transform their resistance into liberation. Strengthened by what they interpreted as their own success, they thus celebrated the opportunity to promote further the creation of what they came to call a 'convivial society', in which radical pluralism and ecological endurance would be an expression of their art of living and dying, through the practice of subsistence.

This chapter recounts the story of a grassroots initiative that illustrates how the people's analysis of this juncture in the history of Mexico has been translated into reality.

The Background to the Elections

For seventy years, the Mexican political system could be best characterized as a peculiar form of monarchy. Every six years, the 'king' was replaced by another member of the 'revolutionary family': the group in power since the revolution of 1910. In 1982, another 'family' took its place. Instead of 'revolutionary' ancestors, they had Harvard or Yale credentials, and a pedigree certified by the World Bank, the IMF or the US government. They used all the authoritarian tools of the old regime to dismantle it and to impose the neo-liberal catechism. In order to avoid Gorbachev's mistakes, they put off most of the political reforms demanded by the people and the political opposition. They declared that economic reforms should be concluded first.

In December 1993 they were celebrating their success. The neo-liberal orientation of the economy was firmly established; they were receiving universal applause and support; to consolidate their reforms, they were planning to stay in power for the next twenty-five years.

At midnight on 1 January 1994, the North American Free Trade Agreement (NAFTA) between Mexico, the USA and Canada came into force. Barely two hours later, thousands of indigenous people armed with clubs, machetes and a few guns occupied four of the main towns in Chiapas, a province on Mexico's southern border with Guatemala, and declared war on the Mexican government. The rebels, calling themselves Ejército Zapatista de Liberación Nacional or Zapatistas, appealed for an end to 500 years of oppression and forty of 'development'. They expressed the hope that a new political regime would allow the indigenous peoples to reclaim their commons and to regenerate their own forms of governance and their art of living and dying. It was time to say '¡Basta ya! Enough!'

The Zapatistas created a political option rapidly adopted by a broad and vast array of popular coalitions of the discontented. Observing that millions of people supported their cause but not their means, the Zapatistas became the champions of non-violence. As many Mexicans, they saw in globalization a dangerous threat and explicitly proposed an alternative. Fully aware of the limitations of representative democracy – in which the citizen-subjects freely elect their oppressors – they saw it merely as a political umbrella for the transition to radical democracy. Fully aware that the nation-state is a regime of domination, a straitjacket dissolving or preventing cultural diversity, they saw it as a provisional framework to advance towards a new political regime.

The uprising changed the balance of forces. In the first months of 1994 the political opposition obtained more concessions from the government than in the previous fifty years. The mutation of civil society further undermined the regime and paved the way for a political transition.

After the 2000 elections, many who had struggled for years for democracy were puzzled, if not frustrated or depressed. Instead of an opportunity for public debate and citizen participation, as they had hoped, the political campaigns became a media circus. The polling process on election day was clean and peaceful as never before, but the process leading up to it was as dirty as in the past. And instead of a popular government which they had hoped would stop the neo-liberal onslaught, the elections put power into the hands of a rich businessman, the former president of

Coca-Cola in Mexico, who wants to advance the project of corporate globalization.

These concerns have a good foundation in reality. The highly un-democratic institutions as well as most of the uncertainties that existed under the former regime persist. The aggression against the communities in Chiapas, what the experts call a 'low-intensity war', continues. The waves of violence in both the cities and the countryside which have become part and parcel of the implementation of the neo-liberal agenda are likely to increase in the coming years, as the mafia-like interest groups of the old regime attempt to occupy the spaces left by its death. Nobody can anticipate the evolution of the power structure after the political quake of 2 July.

Perhaps the best analogy to the current situation is to be found in France at the end of the eighteenth century. Like the French revolu-tionaries, the Mexicans need to clean up the mess left by the *ancien régime* and to forge new institutions. But their challenge is not to organize a more democratic nation-state, designed better to accommodate the logic of capital in the era of globalization, as the dominant view holds; rather, they need to escape from the grip of the dominant discourses and promote the first social revolution of the twenty-first century. The Mexican people need to advocate a form of localization that rejects both globalization and localism in order to affirm themselves in the 'places' that belong to them and to which they belong. Instead of enclosing themselves within these spaces, as they have often done in the past, they must reach out to join forces with others who are also struggling to reclaim and regenerate their commons, the places where they practice subsistence.

Opciones Conviviales de Mexico

A group of organizations and networks from civil society in Mexico began to meet informally in 1997 to examine the current situation and prospects. They shared the conviction that the political classes would not be able to deal with the problems of the majority of the people of Mexico. They also recognized that their main asset, the heterogeneity and autonomy of people's organizations, was also their main weakness: dispersion. They thus organized an exercise of reflection in action, to co-ordinate their efforts and to articulate a shared agenda. This agenda would not be con-ceived as the catechism of a new sect or an enlightened vanguard, but as the rigorous and disciplined articulation of people's experience and hopes, taking into account their diversity and pluralism.

In 1998, they created groups to reflect, discuss, and elaborate the new agenda. These groups began at once (1) to organize seminars, lectures and fora for public debate; (2) to identify, document and examine community-based praxis and alternatives; (3) to promote reciprocal visits of people involved in such alternative projects; (4) to formulate perspectives on the situation in Mexico from different regions and groups; (5) to disseminate information and proposals through existing networks and the media; and (6) to interact with groups involved with similar initiatives in Mexico and elsewhere. Opciones Conviviales de Mexico, an informal association of persons, organizations and networks from civil society, was thus born.

To accomplish these and other tasks, a group of some twenty to forty people came together for at least ten hours during every week from October 1998 to October 1999. More than 200 experts, intellectuals and political or social leaders were invited to participate in this process, and their ideas were examined in seminars and workshops and discussed in individual groups and organizations.

As a result of this process, the participants put together a draft agenda for civil society in Mexico. Since January 2000, this agenda has been disseminated throughout the country for discussion in small groups. The participants also began to edit documents giving empirical and theoretical foundation to the agenda and specifying its proposals. At the same time, a directory of all the organizations that might support the implementation of the agenda began to be prepared.

Most of the proposals included in the agenda are based on specific experiences at the grassroots level. The implementation of the agenda, which has already started, basically consists in the extension and co-ordination of those experiences.

Social Ideals

The agenda examines how the ideals for which many Mexicans gave their lives or at least their souls were perverted or distorted by the old regime. All of these ideals have essentially been reduced to one: the goal of economic growth. Reaching that goal, the elite continually declared, would bring justice, peace, sovereignty, independence, liberty, democracy and well-being for all. To put the economy at the centre of social and political life and to make it grow would achieve national integration and the prosperous and happy unity of all Mexicans.

A prime objective of the agenda is the dismantling of this illusion. It reveals that the growth of the formal economy lacks sense as a social goal. Focusing all social efforts on economic growth conceals what is really being pursued: prosperity for the few at the cost of misery for the many and the destruction of the environment and the commons. Instead of involving the entire population in the articulation of a sensible vision for Mexico, a blank cheque is handed to the ringleaders of government and the market so that they promote their interests in the name of a social well-being that never arrives and which, by this path, never will.

The agenda urges the people of Mexico to abandon this folly and to advocate growth in all areas that are in their common interest and a decrease in areas that favour a privileged few. People's abilities to sustain themselves, their vital autonomy, should be a major growth area. Places and ways in which people can exert their freedom and their initiative should flourish. Opportunities and favourable conditions for the good life should multiply, according to how each person and each culture defines the good life. And to make all this possible, the importance given to growth in the formal economy, and of everything that is contrary to the good life for all or destroys nature, should be denied.

The agenda advocates the recovery of our sense of proportion, which is only another form of common sense, of what is held in common in a community. Contrary to the society of waste, of throwaway, and of continuous destruction, it reaffirms the value of sensible and responsible doing without.

Neither the proclamation of new social ideals nor the rehabilitation of old ones is attempted by the agenda. There are words that seem to bring everyone together such as peace, freedom, justice – but after examining what these words mean to each individual, a plurality of views becomes evident. These words express different things for different people. Most people have a hard time understanding (and rightly so) exactly what could be meant by a concept such as 'freedom' when it is applied to trade and markets. For the great majority, what the courts administer isn't justice. Nor can many people see as 'peace' the turbulence that dooms their daily life to economic upheaval and even less is it the institutionalized war that the companies, the government, the police and the army impose on them.

The agenda identifies certain principles that most people still apply in their own 'places' and is absent in the shapeless spaces created by the market or the state. In neighbourhoods and villages, in work centres or places where people meet, certain principles still prevail, in spite of how much has threatened them and continues to undermine them. They are not abstract definitions or distant rules, but living ideals rooted in daily life.

The agenda seeks to defend and extend radical pluralism: to transform existing plurality into a political position. To be a pluralist means to recognize and respect differences – in gender, beliefs, colour of skin, sexual preferences, dreams or hopes – and make oneself their safeguard. It means radically to reject all pretence of homogeneity that, in the name of an illusory equality making some more equal than others, attempts to suppress those differences, equalizing the social majorities in oppression, in inequality. It means to accept hospitably the radical otherness of the other, the different.

Pluralism means to celebrate these differences, to affirm oneself in them, creating with them new forms of relationships. It seeks to create a *we* which is open, supportive and fully inclusive, that leaves behind forever all exclusions, eliminating them in the fiesta of convivial diversity. Following the example of the Zapatistas, the agenda proposes to create a Mexico in which many Mexicos can fit, the many Mexicos who the Mexican people really are and want to continue being.

The agenda also seeks to contribute to the endurance of the natural and social realities that form the basis of our collective survival and struggle. That land, forests, water, soil and air, endure. That cultures, social structures and people's initiatives endure. That the destructiveness that comes from outside or from inside be stopped. Mexico can be an enduring society only if the natural environment that sustains it also lasts. This is contingent upon rebuilding people's relationship with the land, on recognizing the common roots of all peoples and cultures in the soil, in harmony with all the beings who populate the cosmos in which they are immersed.

The agenda affirms a convivial society. Machines, tools and technologies have more capabilities than ever. But they have made real men and women less and less capable. People are plugged into them in a way that increases their workload, thus throwing more and more people into unemployment. The real value of wages paid for a day of hard work is now half of what it was fifty years ago. Instead of reducing daily toil and helping them to overcome their restrictions, tools and technology serve today to subjugate people and to concentrate in the hands of a few the fruits of the efforts of all.

In a convivial society technology is at the service of people's creative ability and their harmonious living together. The institutions, the tools, and the material or social instruments increase the abilities of all as each one defines what s/he understands as the good life and can dedicate him/herself to create it, so that these instruments are not used to separate people and subject them to their control.

In a convivial society, personal freedom is realized in mutual interdependence with others. Life itself is a creative and autonomous relationship with other people and with the environment, thus liberating the people from the conditioned responses of the isolated and alienated individual to demands that others or the environment impose.

In such a society, physical and social safety do not depend on the financial powers, the bureaucrats or the police, but rather on the type of relationships among men and women, on their communities, on social and political institutions based on co-operation rather than competition, on solidarity rather than envy, on community rather than individualism, and on harmony rather than confrontation. In a pluralistic, enduring and convivial society, there will be security created by everyone, and not damaged by police and armies, as well as confidence in a future.

The agenda invites everyone and all to join together joyfully to celebrate their awareness that they can remake life today in the shape of tomorrow. It aims at the transformation of resistance to whatever has tried to convert anyone to something s/he is not into a liberating action directed by the people themselves. It invites us all, in Gandhi's words, to 'be the change [that] we wish for the world'. Instead of surrendering our will for change to alienating ideologies, the agenda urges us to make of the present a creation of the time to come.

Regenerating Political Life

The agenda deplores the fact that the democracy which continues to be presented as a model is a form of government in which the power of the people is constantly transferred to state institutions. The dominant political mythology acknowledges that people are the source of all legitimate power; but affirms that they can have it but not maintain and exercise it. The parties and the media have sequestered democracy everywhere. Not only do they manipulate the voters, giving them the illusion of suffrage, but they severely limit the range of choices available to electors. In this system, a minority of the people decides which party will be in charge of the government, and a very small group writes and promulgates the laws and takes all the important decisions. The political power of the people comes down then to the capacity to transfer it to the few, whom they cannot control.

In the societies called democracies, the state operates like a conglomeration of limited liability corporations, each one of which is dedicated to promoting its own benefit and serving its own interests. The whole produces 'well-being' for some, in the form of education, health, employment, entertainment, and so on. From time to time, the political parties bring together all the stakeholders to choose a board of directors. And these stakeholders are not only the private national or transnational corporations, but also the professional unions in their service or in the service of the state. While defending their own interests, those organizations strengthen the system from which they derive dignity and income, but which keeps them subordinate and under control.

To struggle for democracy today, the agenda affirms, implies confronting the authoritarianism of the market or the state; not to surrender to a formal illusion, but to widen, strengthen and deepen the spaces in which the people still can exert their own power. The majority of those who constitute 'the people' are not affiliated to a political party nor do they want to be actors or spectators in the multi-ring circus into which political activity has been converted. For them, democracy is a matter of common sense: that ordinary people govern their own lives. It does not allude to a class or type of government, but to its end. The people do not associate the word democracy with a collection of institutions, but with an historical project created with the power of the people.

The agenda rejects the myth that one man – a leader constructed with publicity tricks – can lead and control all the political forces and actors. It also rejects the ruse that pretends to put in his place a party platform or a technocratic group. As democracy will exist only when real men and women govern their own lives, according to the style of governance that has been practised in thousands of their 'places', it affirms radical democracy, democracy in its essential meaning, in its root.

The agenda describes a society in which the power is in the hands of the people for the very exercise of power, not only in the moment of electing representatives. It advocates living in a state of democracy; to maintain this open and concrete condition in daily life. And this condition exists when the people provide themselves with political bodies in which they can exercise their power.

Many Mexicans already suffer the alienation of modern mass societies: they do not belong to a place, to a community. That is how they have been stripped of their power. As rootless masses they lose the ability to mobilize. The economic illusion of the sovereignty of the consumer, which attributes to the mass of buyers' control of the market, as in politics, which attributes to the electoral mass the control of political power, only hides the true state of things, which is that people are continually being stripped of their economic or political power as specific and real persons.

In communities the unity of politics and place is restored. In them, the people do not surrender their power to the state. In the community, the social order is based on mutual, common obligations, which give a true foundation to the exercise of power. Instead of abstract individuals formally endowed with rights, real men and women, knots of nets of real, specific relationships, follow their own initiatives, not those coming from an order or law formulated above and outside them. They can thus create the place to which they belong and which belongs to them. Although this form of existence has its highest expression in indigenous communities, it extends broadly, in the most diverse forms, among the urban and rural majorities. The agenda urges us not to give up these community experiences of real self-governance for an individualistic and statistical democracy manipulated by political parties and the media.

Democracy, the agenda reiterates, depends on place, on the local areas in which the people live. Democracy does not mean transferring power to another place.

The current crisis no longer derives from economic cycles but from the present scale of economic activity. It is necessary to restore a human scale to political bodies; to replace the enormous dimensions of globalized integration with a dike system of interconnected but highly self-sufficient local markets and small political bodies, in which economic fluctuations can be controlled because they are never out of proportion; the ripples of a pond, however animated, can never assume the size of the huge swells passing through the united water masses of the open seas. There is a need to dismantle inefficient and corrupt bureaucracies, but instead of privatizing the functions of the state, as neo-liberals are doing, the idea is to socialize them: to leave them in the hands of the people, reducing the size of political bodies to human dimensions. In a new political design, it will be possible to reserve some general functions, well delimited, for political bodies that adopt the real democratic style of the communities, where the authorities apply the principle of command by obeying, on the scale of the whole society.

The agenda considers that the time is right for this reinvention of governance. In the era of globalization, the main function heretofore given to the state, that is the administration of the national economy, is rapidly disappearing together with sovereignty, as national economic frontiers collapse. The process of transferring economic and political functions to macro-national structures and international institutions now coincides with a process whereby regions and communities are reclaiming their autonomy. The social and political tensions now coming to the surface will make feasible the effort to give a new form to all political bodies, including those of nation-states. The continuation of the current structures which attempt to govern the entire world by force and with the market, can yield only apocalyptic results. Replacing these structures, on the other hand, opens all kinds of options.

In Mexico, the crossroads is clear: a growing authoritarianism, in which the 'democratic' state will assume a more naked form of power, a police state which protects capital from its own excesses and maintains control over the whole population; or else, a society structured around people's power. To prevent the authoritarian prospect it is not enough to consolidate and deepen democracy at the grassroots; it is necessary, at the same time, to reclaim the use of political and juridical procedures, which are fitted one into the other and together constitute the structure of freedom. It is freedom, above all, that the real struggle for democracy deals with, not well-being. The concept of public law maintains all its force even when society reserves access to the legal machinery for a privileged few; even when it systematically mocks justice and dresses despotism with the cloak of fake courts. In resorting to juridical procedures, an effective articulation of the demands of the popular movements can validate the power of the people without handing it over and, on the contrary, broaden spaces for its exercise, thereby progressively limiting the power of the state.

Neither the political parties nor the structures of power seem to have noticed the true character of the current situation. People are not in the mood for a popular revolt, but for political rebellion, peaceful insurgency. They are not preparing a civil war, but a transforming peace. And they do not want to weaken or stop their mobilization, nor settle for cosmetic changes. They intend to profoundly change Mexican society through the progressive creation of political spaces in which they can effectively govern themselves, in a society which is authentically democratic.

The paradox which defines the transitional nature of the current situation is described by the agenda. There will be an effort to deepen formal democracy, but at the same time it will be transformed into something else, into radical democracy. The nation-state will be strengthened, playing by its rules, but at the same time its substitution by another form of social organization will be prepared. To resolve this paradox, the agenda advocates resorting to juridical and constitutional procedures, in order to broaden and consolidate the formal democratic elements in society, and, at the same time, to make entirely evident and give public legitimacy to what the majority of Mexicans suspect: that the ideologies and the party platforms cannot express the diversity of people's interests. Simultaneously, the inability of elections and the activities of political parties to achieve people's goals on the one hand, and more viable alternative means to achieve people's goals on the other, should become clearly evident in a form comprehensible to everyone.

The agenda will therefore rely on ordinary language and formal structure, until reaching the point at which it will be possible to resort to the constitutional process. Radical democracy will be fully established only when a new formal and real constitution exists. The transition only defines a process of re-creation of political spaces, in which the people can freely exert their power and articulate their initiatives, while the dominant political mythology breaks apart. Along the way, persons and initiatives that restore self-confidence will emerge from people's organizations. New governing procedures and laws that recognize the legitimacy of the conflict of interests, appreciate the value of precedents, and are formulated by ordinary people recognized by their communities as their representatives, will be adopted in the process. A new constitution will make it possible to resort to juridical procedures, within a spirit of continuous opposition to the state or professional bureaucracies, bringing to fruition the institutional transformation that is required. Among other things, the organization of work could be modified in this way, to create convivial alternatives to the industrial mode of production.

According to the agenda, nothing is more offensive, or antithetical to an authentic state of law, than the sexist or patriarchal regime now prevailing. As much as legislation and institutions, a large part of social behaviour perpetuates a male chauvinist bias. It advocates constant struggle to revamp the whole rubric of gender as we know it, so that the asymmetrical complementarity of men and women can flow in harmony without falling into the discrimination and oppression of the current regime, nor into the destructive homogenization that pretends to remedy it. It demands an unrelenting defence of women's liberty, so that they can exercise it fully in all aspects of their lives.

Subsistence and Good Life

The main content of the agenda, which cannot be fully explored here, is focused on subsistence as the basis of good living: in the creation and maintenance of life in the here and now.

The proposals for the regeneration of both the cities and the countryside are classified in accordance with people's daily activities. The agenda redefines people's needs: instead of the *nouns* which establish a fundamental dependence on the market, professionals and institutions – education, health, employment – it utilizes common *verbs* that describe the real action taken by people in the creation of their own lives: eat, learn and study, heal, settle, exchange.

All the specific proposals of the agenda – the ways and means freely to create people's lives in the here and now – are based on succesful experiences at the grassroots level. The agenda presents them as a source of inspiration, not as a model, as it articulates its different components.

The ongoing implementation of the agenda is in fact the extension and deepening of these grassroots initiatives. It does not lead to a manifesto or a platform, orchestrating people's efforts from the top down, like politicians, governments, political parties or churches usually do. It delineates a common ground, the shape and limits of a territory of meaning and action (a new horizon of intelligibility) based on experiences to be shared.

The Proposal

The agenda ends with the following words: Radical hope is the essence of popular movements. It spread among us when the universal reign of formal democracy and economic globalization, with its trail of disasters for common people, appeared like an inevitable destiny in Mexico and in the world.

Private hope and public despair form the breeding ground for the collective manipulation of the masses in modern democracies. Their leaders ceaselessly attribute the daily disasters to all kinds of phantoms, while at the same time they encourage individual expectations and the struggle of every man for himself. Our proposal seeks to renew the social fabric and co-ordinate personal hopes with collective hopes. Instead of new promises of development and well-being, it tries to recover the original sense of the term prosperity, from the Latin *pro spere*: in accordance with hope.

Instead of illusory and alienated futures formulated in the name of bankrupt ideologies, we propose the construction of a *por-venir* (the time to come) defined and determined by the people, by real men and women, in all their plurality and diversity.

Instead of the carpetbagging and administration of the people's hopes, which defines the political activity of the government and the political parties, we intend to renovate authentically democratic politics in which the art of the possible consists in extending it: the art of creating the possible from the impossible. The Mexico that we are going to create will not have a single, uniform definition. It will be a common space, shared in harmony by all men and women, by all of the peoples and cultures who have been, are, and want to continue being Mexicans.

12

Resisting 'Technology' and Defending Subsistence in Bangladesh: Nayakrishi Andolon and the Movement for a Happy Life

Farida Akhter

To challenge and critique the masculine/patriarchal foundations of knowledge systems in order to open up possibilities for both alternative analysis as well as the rebuilding of social movements for the emergence of new communities is not an easy task. Maria Mies has inspired many women (and men) to take up that challenge. The purpose of this chapter is to acknowledge the fact that she has inspired and influenced her friends and colleagues in many different ways. I will deal here particularly with my work in the peasant-based movement for ecological agriculture in Bangladesh known as Nayakrishi Andolon. Professor Mies's interaction with us at various points in time has triggered critical reflection and innovative social practice, and her writings have been a source of constant inspiration. I personally have benefited particularly from her friendship and the intimate exchange of ideas between us. Since the inception of Nayakrishi Andolon, when the idea was just forming, Professor Mies has always taken a keen interest in the movement and shared her ideas whenever she felt it necessary.

Nayakrishi Andolon

Nayakrishi Andolon (New Agricultural Movement) is both a collective as well as an individual initiative by over 60,000 farming households in Bangladesh who are practising ecological agriculture. In the quantitative sense, it is an interesting and successful farmers' movement in terms of innovative ecological practice as well as in terms of its ability to mobilize communities. From the economic point of view, it is indeed interesting to note that Nayakrishi ecological farming methods are more viable and productive than conventional agriculture. While these are very significant achievements, they do not differentiate Nayakrishi Andolon from other communities and movements in the region or in the world who practise ecological agriculture. The most significant and important features of Nayakrishi Andolon are qualitative rather than quantitative, and reveal a much more ambitious and far-reaching agenda than the membership numbers or the more abundant harvests might suggest.

The distinctive features of this unique new agricultural movement should be understood at three levels. The first is the culture of resistance of the farmers against the processes of privatization and colonization of 'body' and 'mind'. Nayakrishi Andolon is not a mere technological inter-vention to encourage the practice of sustainable agriculture; rather it is a cultural movement based on a new paradigm. Second, the constitutive practice of rebuilding community is at the level of production, without being trapped into the metaphysics of 'production'. The reason is that the goal of Nayakrishi Andolon is not to produce more food for consumers, but to create life, diversity and '*ananda*' (to live a happy life). It is not satisfied with despiritualized material achievements; but instead demands an authentic life of joyful existence within the community (UBINIG 1995). Third, Nayakrishi believes that new types of organizations, institutions and community power should be built to confront the logic of profit and the neo-colonial processes of globalization, but that this should be achieved through politico-organizational strategies that do not necessarily presuppose a violent power struggle.

Nayakrishi Andolon refuses to be trapped in a conflict-based model in its organizational strategy. The transformation of power relations is con-ceptualized as the result of a transformation in the material relations of life, livelihood and the cultural perception of '*ananda*' or happy life. Life is primarily conceived as joyful through diverse and multiple non-antagon-istic interactions with the living environment and the members of human communities, local or global. The political task to defend this joy triggers the ideas, needs and ethical justification to transform the industrial model of culture and the colonizing paradigm of egocentricity defined by the profit-based system.

Masculinity, Intellectual Liberalism and Strategic Dogmatism

We share many of our perceptions of these distinguishing features of Nayakrishi Andolon with the subsistence perspective and other insights developed by Maria Mies and her colleagues. The resistance against privatization and colonization of 'body' and 'mind' should be understood concretely, in tangible terms. The body includes both the earth and the female body, or for that matter any 'object' to be hunted and colonized by agents or self-conscious subjects. Privatization is the process of exclusion, the enclosure by which the privatizing subject excludes or terminates other subjects or entities from the enclosed environment. The notion of private property is not enough to designate this process. This colonization is the process by which the agent or the self-conscious subject treats earth, women or human knowledge systems either as a means of production or as the source of raw materials. Privatization and colonization can take place because the agent or the subject consciously constructs a Nature external to Man or Man external to Nature, or reduces one to the status of the product of the other. As a result of this process, a person remains eternally outside of what is an integral part of his or her body or self. The construction of such relations and forms of life and activities which are based on such a permanent division, are referred to as 'masculine' in this work and the relations such masculine agents or subjects establish are referred to as patriarchal.

Once we understand masculinity in this context we can better appreciate the feminine and anti-patriarchal nature of Nayakrishi Andolon. The movement does not divide the world into Man and Nature, Body and Soul, Matter and Mind, and so on. It is true that the farmers do not use pesticide in the fields, as in any form of organic or ecological agriculture, but it is not because they a have a better biological technique of pest management compared to the chemical poisons. Instead, poisons are avoided because the farmers see the earth as the extension of their own bodies and minds. If chemical poisons are not to be used, what justification is there to use biological poisons? If earth is my body I can not poison it either with chemicals or with biological agents. This is not an intellectual construction on the part of the farmers. The whole movement started when farmer women began resisting the use of pesticides, arguing that it destroys their '*deha*'. The Bengali word '*deha*' literally means 'body', but these women were using it in a more profound way to include the earth, to include their homesteads and agricultural fields as well. Here '*deha*' means whatever we sensuously perceive as our dwelling place. For these reasons, people who have only a superficial understanding of Nayakrishi Andolon sometimes wonder why Nayakrishi farmers are not interested in using biological pesticides.

Maria Mies's analysis of capitalist patriarchy (1986) departs from the classical political economy of Karl Marx, but retains the revolutionary potential of his analysis and insight. As our group has its roots in the radical social movements of Bangladesh, this new analysis has not always been easy for us to accept. Marx was and still is our primary source of inspiration. What we have learnt from Maria is to rid ourselves of ideological dogmatism in the area of intellectual creativity but to remain firm on political 'dogmatism' in the area of direct social/ecological and political action and practice. She helped us not to fall into the trap of liberalism in the name of confronting ideological dogmatism. Implicitly or explicitly, she has always insisted on an exit from intellectualism in favour of social practice, just as Marx insisted on the exit from philosophy. This particular aspect of her work is very important to mention here since we have noticed that well-intentioned academics and other intellectuals often find her 'dogmatic' when they engage with her in determining the strategic position she might take on a particular issue. This difficulty often arises because she does not confuse practice with intellectual analysis.

Intellectual analysis can be constructed or deconstructed in many different ways in a playful manner for the sake of better understanding truth or meaning, but in historical time and context there can be only one practice. We can discuss endlessly how we could or should eat a mango. But if we are at all interested in the mango we must ultimately decide on only one way to ingest it. Unfortunately once we have eaten the mango, we cannot repeat the same action with the same mango. This obvious truth is not always recognized by intellectual liberals. If we are not careful to maintain the difference between the activities of intellectual representation and material action, we may find Professor Mies quite 'dogmatic' and it is too early to assess how much her writings have shaped or will influence debates in the academic world. But there is no doubt that Maria Mies is among the few who have influenced grassroots movements in the South quite directly. What has attracted us and many others in the Majority World to her analysis and activism is this strategic 'dogmatism' and this common-sense materialism of social practice, without which no social movement can be built and no social action is possible.

Resisting Technologies

Initial experiences with reproductive and genetic engineering all over the world show that these technologies are aggravating the deteriorating position of women in society and intensifying the existing differences among people in terms of race, class, caste, sex and religion. These technologies also contribute to the further destabilizing of the already critical ecological situation (*Declaration of Comilla* 1991).

It was this recognition of ourselves, our own human integrity being at stake, I believe, which opened our eyes to the fact that the great hope, that technological progress would liberate us, was a dangerous lie (Mies 1989).

I first came to know Maria Mies in 1985 at the Women's Emergency Conference held in Sweden. The conference was on new reproductive technologies. At this conference the Feminist International Network on New Reproductive Technologies (FINNRET) was transformed into the

Feminist International Network of Resistance to Reproductive and Genetic Engineering (FINRRAGE). FINRRAGE soon coalesced into an active network, whose members were critically concerned with the development of so-called reproductive and genetic engineering technologies and their effects on women. The works of FINRRAGE members such as Renate Klein, Jalna Hanmer, Janice Raymond, Gena Corea and others have shown that these technologies establish and reinforce a variety of different forms of reproductive control and coercion over women.

The change from FINNRET to FINRRAGE was not a change in the paradigm of our analysis of technology or the content or focus of our intellectual interests. Instead it flagged a concrete social position of practice, the strategic need to 'resist' new reproductive technologies in the North and all other coercive reproductive technologies in the South. It was a profound shift from our role as intellectual analysts to social activists. Maria was quite vocal on taking this strategic position and I supported her with many of my other colleagues in insisting that the word 'resistance' be included in the name of our group. As a South Asian, and particularly as a Bangladeshi working with grassroots women affected by racist population policies and harmful contraceptives, what other position could I take from a common-sense, materialist point of view?

All empirical evidence proves that intra-uterine devices (IUDs), Depo-Provera, other hormonal contraceptives and coercive sterilization are an assault against women, not only against their bodies but also against their integrity as persons. Women have been treated like rats breeding children, and, just as in the case of pest control, the goal of birth control has been the termination of women's reproductive power. The mirror image of the same attitudes and strategies is evident in the technologies of *in vitro* fertilization, artificial insemination, sex determination, genetic engineering, and so on which force women to breed. As a social practice, 'resistance' is the key to confronting this masculine intervention into the bodies of women.

FINRRAGE was criticized by both friends and foes for adopting a position of resistance against technologies. The origin of such criticism is the failure of hegemonic intellectual liberalism to make the distinction between reflection and action, representation and practice, etcetera. From the position of the intellectual liberal, we may be eager to keep the question of technology open for critical reflection, and to go only as far as to represent the realities of the lives of women and how they are affected by technologies. None of us in FINRRAGE who were determined to adopt a strategic position of resistance against 'technology' was against maintaining such spaces for intellectual reflection about technology, if necessary. But our common-sense materialism dictated that we must take an unequivocal and clear strategic position not only to resist technologies, but also to resist the realities that produce sanitized categories such as 'technology'.

We cannot talk about women, we cannot discuss human beings, nature and knowledge systems without fundamentally questioning the origin of the patriarchal notions of instrumentality, intervention and coercion. What is a technology? It is an instrument used to affect a body external to the agent who is using it. This notion of technology is based on the predatory, patriarchal or colonizing paradigm that must not only be resisted, but also exposed as a smokescreen that conceals deeper intellectual, social, economic and political relations. This patriarchal paradigm has its source far back in history but in the capitalist era it has undergone a sanitizing mutation. Specific capitalist relations of production that led to the development of contraceptives and especially of the new reproductive technologies (NRTs) now hide behind a sanitized neutrality that mystifies the processes by which the illusion and ideology about technology is constantly generated. In the era of capitalism or in so-called 'civilization', which is masculine, predatory and based on colonialism and racism, resistance against 'technology' is a political issue. This resistance has as its purpose not merely to put a stop to certain technological developments, but rather to open up new possibilities of life and relationships. Technology in its material form and cultural formulation encapsulates the mystery of the capitalist-patriarchal world in a concentrated bubble. Only by bursting this bubble can we create alternative possibilities to re-create the world according to feminine principles of care and non-antagonism.

Once the predatory, colonizing and patriarchal nature of technology is grasped, the objections of intellectual liberals become spurious. Assertions such as, 'It is not true that technologies are bad in themselves, it is only a question of how they are used' or, 'There are good technologies and bad technologies, we should choose the good ones', or, 'We demand safe technologies', are revealed to be just so many capitulations to the patriarchal paradigm.

'Technology will bring emancipation to women' has been a theoretical paradigm for the feminists of the northern countries since the early 1930s and 1940s. Feminists in the northern countries did not deal much with the question of technologies in the sphere of industrial production, but the birth control pill was interpreted as the main historic step to further women's liberation. Gradually this issue became part of the question of women's rights; women wanted to liberate themselves from the burden of pregnancy by using technologies including the pill, IUDs, injectables and many other contraceptive technologies. Eventually the birth control movement in the North faded in importance, as women became part of the workforce and gained easy access to contraceptives. In the meantime, the demographic scenario changed, with the fertility rate declining and the infertility rate emerging as a problem among women in the North. Contraceptive technologies, which were once part of a demand for emancipation on the part of northern women, became an important tool for the coercive and racist population control programmes implemented without the knowledge and consent of women in the South. The technology rejected by northern women was transferred to the South. Meanwhile in the North, corporate science has shifted its focus from anti-fertility technologies to pro-fertility technologies such as *in vitro* fertilization (IVF), pre-natal diagnosis and genetic engineering.

FINRRAGE, as a network of northern and southern women activists, maintain that technology cannot be a solution to more fundamental social questions. In a patriarchal society women are embodied with the responsibility to reproduce. This is true in northern as well as in southern societies. Feminists around the world have taken a short cut to deal with the issue, and resorted to technological fixes to fight patriarchy. They claimed to have taken control of the womb by using technological devices. For human history to continue, human beings must reproduce the species and produce the necessities of life. That means that men and women must relate with one another in some way. Until now, this history has been one of patriarchy and privatization of nature and the means of production. Social forms of these relationships, relations of reproduction in particular, are embodied in the institutions of marriage and the laws of inheritance. These relationships are based on patriarchy, giving men command over the sphere of social reproduction. When we fail to confront these forces of domination at the social level we tend to seek 'solutions' at the personal level, where technology becomes an 'easy answer'.

FINRRAGE was the first international network of northern and southern women to challenge and resist technologies, not technologies as such, but technologies that are being produced at this phase of history when patriarchal relations are the dominant mode of relations in reproduction. By resisting technologies, we are actually resisting patriarchy.

Reclaiming Life

Our resistance to technology was a strategy to reclaim life from predators and colonizers. This strategy towards technology deepened our understanding of the 'green revolution' in agriculture beyond the conventional radical critique. Despite our strong solidarity with it, we soon became aware of the contradictions and limitations of the radical critique of green revolution technology. If modernization of agriculture and technological progress are inherently emancipating, how do we explain the increasing misery of farming communities in the Third World? Can it be fully explained only in economic terms, within the paradigm of political economy as understood by the conventional radical position influenced by Marx? In the early years of organizing Nayakrishi Andolon, we felt that this sort of explanation was not enough. We also realized that Marx's conception of technology is often at odds with many popular left movements that claim technology or tools to be synonymous with progress. In Bangladesh it was very difficult to propose an alternative practice.

We felt that any reading of technology in Marx must be subsumed under his conception of relations of production and needed further qualification in connection with what the farmer women of Bangladesh call '*deha*' (see above).

Modern agriculture was introduced to Bangladesh in the mid-1960s as a package consisting of high yield variety (HYV) seeds, chemicals, poisons and machines to extract water from the ground. The immediate effect was the poisoning of the environment, including both the surface and groundwater. The proponents of this sort of agriculture claimed that it had produced more 'food' by calculating only rice or wheat production. Suddenly 'food' had been reduced to a staple crop that is responsive to fertilizers and requires poisons for pest management. There are no baseline data available on the actual availability of food before the introduction of the green revolution and the claims of increased food production if not outright lies, are at best contestable. The pollution of the environment has had a negative impact on other food sources. Fish stocks, for example, which are the major source of food for the people of Bangladesh, have been drastically reduced, largely as the immediate effect of the pollution of surface water.

The spread of deep tube wells for irrigation has caused an unmitigated disaster for Bangladesh in the form of arsenic poisoning. In fact, it became increasingly difficult for us to find empirical evidence for any positive effects resulting from new technologies. As we began to question the value of technologies in a deeper way, Maria Mies and her colleagues Veronika Bennholt-Thomsen and Claudia von Werlhof were developing their ideas on the subsistence perspective (Bennholdt-Thomsen and Mies 1999) and their strategy of resistance to technology, which eventually provided us with the intellectual framework we needed in our work with farming communities.

We were impressed by Professor Mies's insistence on finding common links between women in Germany and women in Bangladesh. First, she realized that both of these groups of women are subsistence producers. By 'subsistence' we do not mean that they are engaged in hopelessly outdated production or a backward lifestyle in any sense, but instead that they are directly concerned with the production of food and life rather than with the acquisition of money to buy food to live. Second, she found that the products of their subsistence labour are taken away from them free of cost or for very little money. The conclusion she drew from these common realities of the housewife in an industrialized country and the peasant woman of Bangladesh is that the nature of capitalism is qualitatively different from how it has so far been understood both by Marxists and by liberals. Capitalist exploitation of wage labour is qualitatively different from its exploitation of subsistence work, due to the latter's life-creating and life-maintaining character. Capitalism not only exploits subsistence production, it also destroys it.

While we had heard about the destructive role of capital in relation to subsistence production from Marx and the Marxists before, the demand to include subsistence production as a life-creating activity in the analysis of capitalism resounded with our own experiences in the farming communities of Bangladesh. The liberal ideas that the commodification of life-creating activities is the path to progress and that the farmers of Bangladesh sooner or later will catch up and be at the same level in terms of 'global development' as the people of the industrialized countries sounded more and more ridiculous to us. Nayakrishi Andolon members and activists began to feel far more strongly that the defence of the life-creating activities of farming communities is their only hope for survival.

While we were becoming familiar with Maria Mies's ideas, Nayakrishi Andolon was just taking shape in one or two villages. We discussed these ideas with the farmers, particularly farmer women. They could easily see the links between their situation and that of the women of the North who were producing by their work the labour needed for the factories and offices of profit-making companies. While these farmers were eager to learn about new methods of mixed cropping, to find more intelligent ways to produce composts for their field, and to think more creatively about raising and caring for their scavenger chickens and domestic animals, they were equally interested in discussing political issues. They felt strongly that defending subsistence activities is not the same as defending poverty. Life-producing activities cannot be reduced to a sector of economic production. They must be grasped and analysed differently.

As Nayakrishi Andolon has grown in strength it has further incorporated the ideas of the subsistence perspective into its biodiversity-based life activities. These activities are designed to create not only life, but also the conditions of life. The generation and regeneration of biodiversity has become part of the central foundation of the movement.

In Bangladesh, women always conserve seeds. This is perhaps a general phenomenon found in all agrarian communities. Despite all the technological interventions and efforts to accelerate a commercial seed sector in Bangladesh, seed preservation still continues to be an important activity carried out by women. Women continue to keep the seeds of paddy (rice), vegetables, fruits, and many other crops. It is ironic that new laboratory-made varieties of paddy have been introduced to Bangladesh despite the fact that the country was already enjoying at least 15,000 varieties of paddy. Seed not only re-creates life but symbolizes subsistence in a profound way that reveals the contours of the cultural life of rural Bangladesh. The subsistence perspective as the appreciation of life-creating activities has evolved into a strong movement to conserve seed and genetic resources by the Nayakrishi Andolon (Mazhar 1999).

The central approach of Nayakrishi initiatives now squarely lies in the conservation, management and use of local seed and genetic resources as well as in adopting and improving regeneration activities suited to farmers' seed. Thus hundreds of local varieties of rice, vegetables, fruit and timber crops have been reintroduced within a short period of time. For example, farmers in Nayakrishi areas now cultivate at least 200 varieties of rice, and the number is increasing. The Nayakrishi farmers, especially the women, have developed formal relationships among themselves as members of seed networks through which they share and exchange seeds, thus enhancing the genetic resource bases of their communities and creating bonds of mutual support which can be called upon when a flood or some other disaster occurs.

The success of Nayakrishi Andolon is directly related to the commitment of the movement to start with local and indigenous knowledge systems and then critically integrating the insights of modern science where necessary. Nayakrishi Andolon strongly believes in the capacity of the farmers as authentic knowledge producers, no matter how they articulate this knowledge, orally or otherwise.

Incorporating the ideas of the subsistence perspective, Nayakrishi farming practice first conceived of itself as a 'biodiversity-based production system'. As Nayakrishi Andolon has grown in strength, it has developed clarity of thought and singularity of purpose and practice. This has brought about the rejection of economic categories and thus the reconceptualization of this biodiversity-based production system as 'biodiversity-based life activities' (Mazhar 2000). This evolution in thinking reflects Nayakrishi Andolon's constant search for a completely new foundation for social relations based on care, love and responsibility as manifested in '*ananda*' or joy of life activities.

In conclusion, let me tell a story. In 1994, Maria Mies visited the Nayakrishi farmers in a village in Tangail. They talked to each other despite the language barriers. She sang and danced with them, which made them very happy. They invited Maria to become a member of the Nayakrishi group by paying 2 taka (US$10 = 50 taka) as a symbolic membership fee and as a gesture of her willingness to belong to the group. They also asked her to deposit savings every week. With the accumulated savings money they would purchase land to grow crops. When Maria told them it is not possible for her to attend the weekly meetings in Bangladesh as Germany is quite far, the Nayakrishi farmers said, 'It does not matter, you deposit it in your own village!'

References

Bennholdt-Thomsen, V. and M. Mies (1999) *The Subsistence Perspective: Beyond the Globalized Economy*, London: Zed Books; Melbourne: Spinifex Press.

Declaration of Comilla (1991) Proceedings of FINRRAGE-UBINIG International Conference, 1989, Dhaka: UBINIG.

Mies, M. (1986) *Patriarchy and Accumulation on a World Scale: Women in the International Division of Labour*, London: Zed Books.

— (1989) *'What Unites Us, What Divides Women from the South and from the North in the Field of Reproductive Technologies'*, contribution to the FINRRAGE-UBINIG Conference, Dhaka.

Mazhar, F. (1999) *Seed and Genetic Resource Conservation: Experience of Nayakrishi Seed Network*, Dhaka.

— (2000) *Biodiversity-based Rural Strategy for 'Poverty Alleviation'. Insights from the experience of Nayakrishi Andolon (New Agricultural Movement) of Bangladesh*, UBINIG, presented at the Workshop on Biodiversity for Poverty Alleviation on the Occasion of Sharing the Benefits from Biodiversity, 15th Session of the Global Biodiversity Forum, 12–14 May 2000 at UNEP, Gigiri, Nairobi, Kenya.

UBINIG (1995) *Shahaj Way to Ananda*, Reflections on UBINIG works on environment and development, Narigrantha Prabartana, Dhaka.

13

Local Lifeline: Rejecting Globalization – Embracing Localization

Helena Norberg-Hodge

Why is it that everything we hold dear seems threatened? Why do we feel insecure in our working lives, in our neighbourhoods and streets, even within our own homes? Why, in spite of massive public awareness campaigns and educational efforts, does the environment continue to deteriorate from year to year? Why are communities and families fragmenting, while ethnic conflict, poverty, violence and crime are continuing to grow? Why are millions leaving the land to crowd into urban slums? Why is democracy slipping away?

If each of these problems is considered to be separate and unconnected, solving all of them can easily seem impossible. When they are viewed systemically, on the other hand, the potential for solutions expands enormously. Such a systemic analysis reveals that the many disparate symptoms of breakdown stem from the same root cause: a massive and centralized system of production and distribution – one that transforms unique individuals into mass consumers, homogenizes diverse cultural traditions, and destroys wilderness and biodiversity, all in the name of growth and efficiency. In the process it is dividing us from each other and from the natural world on which we ultimately depend.

The South has subsidized the growth of this system for the past 500 years, at great expense to its culture, its land and its economy. In fact, the western industrial system that now dominates the world could not have arisen without access to the South's raw materials, labour and markets. This exploitative process continues today, with 'development', 'structural adjust-ment' and 'free trade' treaties taking the place of conquest and outright colonialism. In its present phase – economic globalization – this system is reaching into the farthest corners of the planet in an attempt to absorb every local, regional and national economy into a single centrally managed world economy. As more and more areas of life are colonized, it is becoming increasingly clear that this process really benefits no one, not even the populations of the North.

These same economic policies have led to the growth of huge multi-national corporations which now dominate world trade. Many of these corporations have grown so large they outstrip governments in size and power: fifty of the 100 largest economies in the world are, in fact, not countries, but corporations. Accountable to no electorate, these bodies wield enormous economic power. Five hundred corporations now control 70 per cent of total world trade. Just six of them control 100 per cent of world trade in the staple grains of rice, wheat and maize.

Thanks to 'free trade' treaties like the General Agreement on Tariffs and Trade (GATT) and the North American Free Trade Agreement (NAFTA), corporations can easily move their operations to countries where taxes and labour costs are low and environmental regulations weak. Corporations are often lured away – or induced to remain – with free land, tax breaks, capital outlays and other forms of government assistance. Publicly funded communications networks enable corporations to wield central control over widely dispersed corporate activities, and to conduct advertising campaigns that reach hundreds of millions of potential customers. Their sheer size and financial power allows them to extract price breaks from suppliers and lending institutions. On such an uneven playing field, how can the local grocer possibly hope to compete against a large supermarket chain? Is it any surprise that with each year the number of small businesses, shopkeepers and independent farmers continues to plummet?

Globalization is often portrayed as the natural result of economic 'efficiency' or as an inevitable evolutionary trend. But it is far from a natural process: it is occurring because governments are actively promoting it and subsidizing the framework necessary to support it. Of course, trade between peoples and nations is nothing new – it is a phenomenon which has existed for millennia. But in the past trade was always a secondary concern, while the primary economic goal was how best to meet people's needs and wants using the resources available within relatively short distances. Only once essential needs had been met locally did questions of trading surplus production with outsiders arise.

Today, however, trade has come to be pursued as an end in itself. Justification for this modern emphasis comes from an 1817 theory proposed by David Ricardo, which holds that all nations are better off if they specialize their production in areas of 'comparative advantage', and then trade the surplus in order to obtain desired imports. The theory implicitly equates a country's prosperity with its reliance on trade and the scale of its imports. Even though modern industrial economies bear little resemblance to the economies of the early nineteenth century, 'comparative advantage' still guides government planning and decision-making today, and is at the heart of the dogma of 'free trade'.

In thrall to an outdated economic theory, governments are scuttling national laws and regulations that protect local businesses, jobs and resources, all in an effort to encourage more trade. Politicians, economists and business leaders often speak of the need for improvements in 'infrastructure'; what is almost never acknowledged is that this is a particular kind of infrastructure, suitable to a particular kind of society and economy: one that is large scale and centralized, and that encompasses huge markets. What's more, there is no recognition that other viable forms of infrastructure, suitable to other forms of society and economy, even exist.

Economic globalization is affecting us all, as individuals, as families, as communities, and it is putting the biosphere itself under increasing strain. More specifically, globalization is leading to:

Erosion of democracy. Even in nominally democratic countries, the influence of the individual is shrinking as decision-making becomes centralized in (often unelected) supra-national bodies like the United Nations, the World Trade Organization and the European Commission. The problem is compounded as these centralized political institutions adopt policy measures influenced by and reflecting the wishes of corporate economic interests. In this situation, it is becoming virtually impossible even for nation-states, let alone local communities or individuals, to retain control over their own destinies.

Global dependence. Tied to a complex system of imports and exports, countries are becoming ever more tightly linked to a volatile global economy over which they possess little or no control. National self-reliance, even in such elementary concerns as food production, is thus severely compromised. Natural disasters, wars and economic slumps in one corner of the world can have a direct impact on countries many thousands of miles away.

Loss of government autonomy. Governments in the South (and increasingly in the North) are encouraged to undertake structural adjustment programmes to enhance international 'competitiveness'. This means cutting social spending back, while increasing funding for the infrastructures needed for the expansion of industry and trade. World Bank/International Monetary Fund (IMF) lending to southern countries is typically made conditional on such programmes. Loan repayments not only constrain government fiscal policy (at the expense of welfare, education, health and so on), but also reinforce dependence on the global economy.

Artificial scarcity. People's everyday needs and wants (for food, clothing, housing and luxuries) are becoming homogenized to meet the requirements of an economic system premised on standardized mass-production. As people everywhere abandon abundant local resources in favour of the narrow range of resources required by the industrial system, the result is artificial scarcity and heightened competition.

Urbanization. The globalization of the economy is leading to a massive population shift from rural areas to the cities. Although today the majority of the world's population still lives on the land, it has been estimated that by 2025 over 60 per cent will live in urban centres. Urbanization, particularly in the South, is synonymous with a host of problems: overcrowded slums, unemployment, poverty, poor sanitation and pollution. Even in the North, large-scale urbanization is directly related to the loss of real community, with indirect consequences that range from alienation and suicide to crime, violence and drug abuse. If the urbanization of the world's population continues at present rates, it will raise these problems to unprecedented levels, with potentially catastrophic results.

Undermining food security. Not only are the populations of the world becoming urbanized, but also values and ideals are increasingly based on an urban, western model. In the South, agriculture and fishing are consistently portrayed as 'backward' and 'primitive', while the urban consumer lifestyle is held up as the ideal to emulate. Global commodity market structures and subsidies, meanwhile, operate to minimize returns to small farmers and other primary producers while maximizing profits for corporate intermediaries. Farmers and fishermen are left with little incentive to continue. The exodus from food production raises a fundamental question: where will our food come from in the future? By way of example, food production in the Confederation of Independent States (former USSR) has fallen by approximately 30 per cent since the introduction of economic liberalization policies in the early 1990s. This trend is reflected in other countries, and is extremely disturbing.

Growing gap between the 'haves' and the 'have-nots'. Economic globalization is leading to a widening gap between rich and poor – both between the countries of the North and the South, and within individual countries themselves. Industrial production is increasingly dependent on large-scale computerized and automated processes, thereby marginalizing human labour. The mobility of multinational corporations also operates to drive down wages. If the world's people are to continue to leave their farms for the cities in search of scarce jobs in the industrial sector, how will the majority survive, jobless and with little prospect of future employment? Widespread poverty is inevitable. Indeed, the 'jobless growth' scenario, if it continues much longer, could lead to the general breakdown of social stability and order, and ultimately to war between the haves and have-nots. Already the wealth of 350 billionaires equals the annual income of the poorest 45 per cent of the world's population. And the inequity continues to grow.

Environmental breakdown. Globalization will intensify the already serious ecological consequences of industrialization. In addition to polluted air and water and growing piles of toxic waste and nuclear debris, we face the danger of climate change from deforestation, ozone depletion and global warming. If present trends continue, this assault on the biosphere will only worsen. In fact, the ecological impact of massive urbanization and industrialization in China and other parts of the world would be catastrophic.

Loss of cultural diversity. Globalization is replacing the earth's cultural diversity with a uniform western monoculture. People around the world are being bombarded by media and advertising images that present the modern, western consumer lifestyle as the ideal, while implicitly denigrating indigenous traditions. The ensuing psychological pressure to live up to an impossible ideal is creating a profound sense of insecurity, especially among the many millions of people who do not fit the 'blonde hair, blue eyes' stereotype. This sense of inferiority and self-rejection is to blame for much of today's ethnic conflict and violence, particularly in the South.

In this global economic system, there are ultimately no winners. Workers are left either unemployed or in low-paying jobs with minimal safety conditions and little job security. Large corporations are driving primary producers and shopkeepers out of business. Small farmers are devalued and financially destroyed, and are drawn off to the mega-cities, leaving behind villages and small towns devoid of economic and cultural vitality. The environment is becoming increasingly polluted and destabilized in the pursuit of short-term profits. But even the wealthy few, ultimately, cannot escape the growing problems; they too must survive on an ecologically degraded planet, and must deal with social breakdown in the form of crime, violence and ethnic friction.

Still worse is that locally adapted forms of infrastructure are being systematically destroyed (wherever they still exist) to serve the needs of these corporations. In recent years, most of this destruction has occurred in the Third World, where localized economies are reshaped to industrial contours in a process described as 'development'.

Even though smaller-scale options would cost far less than building according to the corporate blueprint, governments have systematically ignored them. Like most important choices, decisions about the kind of infrastructure a society invests in are inherently political. Real debate on this issue is extremely rare, even in countries described as democratic. What little debate there is generally focuses on the margins: whose backyard will the motorway run through? What safeguards will be in place at the nuclear power plant? How can the communications tower be built without ruining the aesthetic appeal of the mountain? Meanwhile, small-scale infrastructure options that provide for people's needs, not the needs of giant corporations, are ignored or dismissed out of hand. The result is a self-fulfilling prophecy: if public monies are continually invested in the infrastructural needs of a large-scale, global economy, no one should be surprised if that is the sort of economy that 'evolves'.

Ever more rapid and globalized communications networks, long-distance transportation and centralized energy systems are prerequisites for corporate expansion. Without heavy government investment, transnational corporations could not have become as large and as powerful as they are today. The supposed 'efficiencies of scale' that they benefit from have been possible only because of hidden subsidies.

Another example of government support to corporations is in research and development (R&D). Global growth depends upon a steady stream of technological innovations. These provide corporations with better access to geographically dispersed markets and resources, and expand the range of products they sell. Large companies rely heavily on publicly funded research for these technologies. The governments of industrialized countries are the biggest sources of funds for research and development. Among them, the US, Japan, Germany, France, Britain, Italy and Canada provided more than $170 billion for research annually in the early 1990s (Renner 1997: 112–13.) More than a third of that total went towards military spending, with spin-offs that eventually reach industry in general. Little of this spending generates anything of fundamental use to small-scale producers or locally based economies, but instead adds to the technological treadmill that undermines local and regional economies.

In agriculture and health, much research funding is being poured into bio-technology. The UK's Department of Trade and Industry (DTI) provided businesses with £7.5 million in bio-technology R&D grants in 1994 alone. This research went hand-in-hand with DTI's Biotechnology Means Business programme, which 'promotes the use of modern bio-technology by companies which have not previously used it within their operations' (*United Kingdom Report to the Commission on Sustainable Development, 1995*: section 2).

Europe's corporate planners are aware that globalized markets and expanded trade also require still faster and more extensive transport networks, and they have used their influence to place transportation high on the agendas of the European Commission and individual European governments. Much of this corporate lobbying has been undertaken by the European Roundtable of Industrialists (ERT), composed of chief executive officers (CEOs) and other executives from Europe's most powerful corporations: Volvo, Fiat, Olivetti, Philips, Bosch, Siemens, ICI, Unilever, Renault, BSN, Nestlé, Ciba-Geigy and others (Cowles 1995: 506).

At its initial meeting in 1983, this group was described by the *Financial Times* as a 'Who's Who of European industrial heavyweights' (Cowles

1995: 505). The group has since grown, and now includes representatives from forty-five of Europe's largest transnational corporations. For the European Round Table (ERT), the goal is a single European market of 360 million people, larger than that of either North America or Japan, giving European corporations an edge in global competition. The means to that end include a greatly expanded transport and communications network, along with the political and monetary changes needed to eliminate all trade barriers between European nations. The latter steps are already well under way.

One result of this framework of subsidies and other support is that the prices of mass-produced goods transported halfway around the world are artificially 'cheap' compared with local goods. This has been particularly true in food production. In 1997, the UK imported 115,000 tonnes of butter, 51,000 tonnes of which came from outside the EU, and exported 67,000 tonnes of butter, 27,000 tonnes of which were exported outside the EU. In 1996, the UK imported 434,000 tonnes of apples, 202,000 tonnes of which came from outside the EU. Over 60 per cent of UK apple orchards have been lost since 1970. In 1997, the UK imported 105,000 tonnes of pears, 72,000 tonnes of which came from outside the EU (Sustain 1999: 7).

What are the benefits of transporting basic foods thousands of miles, when they can be (and indeed for centuries have been) produced locally? And once all the hidden public subsidies are taken into account, how can these arrangements be described as economically 'efficient'? Economic globalization is no natural or evolutionary occurrence, it is a process of specific and planned change, supported by taxpayers' money.

Cutting the Middleman Down to Size – Local Initiatives

Around the world more and more citizen groups are waking up to the social and environmental impact of this heavily subsidized global economy. They are realizing that it is the prime culprit behind ecological crises such as global warming and food shortages in the South and food scares like those caused by 'Mad Cow' disease (BSE), salmonella and genetically modified organisms (GMOs) in the North. Increasingly, the public is pressing for major policy changes at the national and international levels. Among other things they are demanding that governments take control of the global financial markets that are systematically subordinating human and environmental well-being to profit. They are also working to strengthen local economies.

Many forms of economic localization are emerging across the world. Local money systems are an important way of promoting economic self-reliance by enabling a community to reduce its reliance on the national (and international) economy. Local exchange trading systems (LETS), for example, allow goods and services to be marketed without the need for money. The most successful LETS scheme is in the small American town of Ithaca, New York, where hundreds of thousands of 'Ithaca Hours' have been traded by more than 3000 participants. The currency is accepted by more than 250 local businesses. There are also now more than 400 LETS schemes in the UK.

Of all the movements promoting localization, the most successful is the local food movement. For virtually the whole of human history people have relied on local food produced on relatively small, diversified farms. The logic is unassailable: locally grown food is fresher, and therefore tastier and more nutritious than food transported over long distances.

Contrary to common belief, local small-scale diversified food production is also more efficient than large-scale monocropping. The orthodox view of agricultural development holds that industrial agriculture – with its consolidation of land, mechanization and use of chemicals – has vastly increased agricultural productivity. In fact, however, the superior productivity of industrial agriculture is largely a myth, propagated for years by proponents and beneficiaries of this type of agriculture. Study after study, carried out in diverse locations all over the world, shows that small-scale, diversified agricultural systems almost always have a higher total output per unit of land than large-scale monocultures (see Douthwaite 1996: 251–332).

A variety of local marketing methods are currently being promoted as part of the rapidly growing local food movement. Many of these systems are revitalizing traditional practices while updating them to suit contemporary needs. The number of farmers already selling direct to consumers varies from country to country. In the UK, about 5 per cent of farmers sell directly, accounting for about 9 per cent of fresh produce sales. In Germany and the USA, the figure stands at 15 per cent; in France and Japan, it is 25 per cent. But in all these cases, the volume of produce sold is low – only 5 per cent in the USA and 14 per cent in France (Festing 1997: 409–21). This is a result of the fact that most direct selling is the preserve of small farmers who account for a small proportion of overall agricultural output in industrialized countries. Nevertheless, the potential for local trade is clearly huge, and many countries are currently experiencing a rapid increase in this type of marketing. Farmers' markets were once common throughout the world, but experienced a major decline when subsidized large-scale monocultural production and long-distance transport marginalized local marketing. Now, however, these markets are resurgent. In the UK, the first new farmers' market, in the city of Bath, opened its doors to producers based within a 30–40-mile radius. Public interest in the Bath market has been extraordinary, and such markets are now being set up all over the country. Between the mid-1990s and the end of the decade, the numbers of UK farmers' markets rose from zero to 270 (Norberg-Hodge 2000: 12). The 1998 United States Department of Agriculture (USDA) farmers' market directory listed 2675 farmers' markets in the USA, up from 1755 in 1994 (USDA 1998).

Farmers' markets offer a range of in-season fresh produce, often harvested that same day. Many also have vendors selling a variety of meats and dairy products, most of which are free of the hormones and antibiotics found in goods that come from large supermarkets. Some farmers' markets even feature live music, and all of these markets promote a sense of community, both through the friendly, relaxed atmosphere, and through the fact that money spent there supports local enterprises, and remains within the community.

Community Supported Agriculture systems (CSAs) are another emerging local food initiative and are the next best thing to growing your own food. The basic model is simple: consumers provide support for growers by agreeing to pay for a share of the total produce, and growers provide a weekly share of food of a guaranteed quality and quantity. Every week, boxes of produce are delivered, either to the subscribers' homes or to a central pick-up point.

In the UK, box schemes have grown rapidly from just two in 1992 to more than 400 in 1997, supplying over 50,000 households a week with fresh, healthy produce. Most schemes are certified organic and most are working at full capacity, the problem being lack of supply, not of demand (Soil Association 1999: 17).

Customers often come to highly appreciate both the relationship with the farmer and the extremely fresh produce, which is offered through the box schemes. Many build on this relationship so that customers keep in

---

Goosemoorganics Box Scheme

Goosemoorganics was established by Arnold Warneken and Alex Marsh in 1993 on Goosemoore, Wetherby. Alex and Arnold bought the two and a half-acre field opposite their house and grow organic vegetables. The business began with thirty vegeboxes but now supplies 1500 boxes per week. The majority of boxes go to house-holders who act as co-ordinators for a group of customers. (Soil Association 1999: 18)

touch with news from the farm, are invited to celebrations, or can even do some work on the farm in return for produce (Soil Association 1999: 18). Members know where their food originates, and farmers benefit from receiving payment at the beginning of the season. In this way, a community shares the risks and responsibilities of farming. Selling to a local market also means that it is in the economic interest of farmers to grow a greater variety of produce.

These local food systems are not a dream; they are a reality, now, and their success is proving that they can be replicated across the world. They do not need to grow bigger; the farmer does not need to produce more and more to flourish, does not need to sell at ever greater distances. These systems are proliferating, showing that the global juggernaut can be resisted and even reversed.

However, if these local initiatives are genuinely to flourish and prosper in more of our communities, changes at the policy level are clearly necessary. Current economic policies across the world are artificially lowering the prices of industrially produced foods by shifting the costs of production on to the community. If groups campaigning for sustainable farming, wildlife issues and better food do not take these hidden subsidies into account, and do not challenge the economic basis of our current monocultural, export-based food system, they risk falling into the trap of arguing that consumers should pay more for better food – when, as farmers' markets and other initiatives show, they can actually pay less. This approach marginalizes the poor and opens campaigners to charges of elitism. Furthermore, to overlook hidden subsidies is to miss a fantastic opportunity: if these resources were

---

Flaxland Farm CSA

Flaxland Farm was started in 1995 by Jon Taylor and some friends and now grows for seventy members over thirty-four weeks, on only 2 acres. They grow seventy different varieties of crops, and members pay a subscription of £195 over the year. Flaxland delivers largely to the Canterbury area, including a drop-off at a health-food shop. Some members also pick up from the farm; the members at a nearby village take turns collecting all the boxes for the community. Many members also help on the farm in return for produce. Flaxland is also involved in a local exchange and trading system (LETS). An annual Pumpkin Festival attracts many members and friends to celebrate and helps build the community. (Soil Association 1999: 20)

diverted towards decent agriculture and local retailing, society would pro-duce better food at no extra cost at all.

Recognizing the global consequences of the economic system also gives agricultural and environmental groups common cause with those cam-paigning for social justice and human rights internationally. These diverse bodies are now beginning to join hands to demand a different set of economic priorities, and the redrawing of the global economic map.

We do have the power to change things. There is nothing inevitable or evolutionary about the global economic system. It can exist only as long as we are prepared to accept and subsidize it. We can reject it. And we can start by enjoying the wealth of benefits from re-linking farmers and con-sumers. Fresh, local food for all may be one of the most rewarding – and certainly the most delicious – ways to save the planet.

References

Cowles, M. G. (1995) 'Setting the Agenda for a New Europe: The ERT and EC 1992', *Journal of Common Market Studies*, 33, 4.

Douthwaite, R. (1996) *Short Circuit: Strengthening Local Economies for Security in an Unstable World*, Devon, UK: Green Books.

Festing, H. (1997) 'The Potential for Direct Marketing by Small Farms in the UK', *Farm Management*, 9, 8.

Norberg-Hodge, H., T. Merrifield and S. Gorelick. (2000) *Bringing the Food Economy Home*, Devon, UK: ISEC.

Renner, M. (1997) 'R&D Spending Levels Off', *Vital Signs*, New York: W. W. Norton.

Soil Association. (1999) *Local Food for Local People*, Bristol, UK: Soil Association.

Sustain (the alliance for better food and farming) (1999) *Food Miles – Still on the Road to Ruin?*, London: Sustain.

USDA. (1998) *National Directory of Farmers Markets*, Washington, DC: USDA, Agri-cultural Marketing Service.

United Kingdom Report to the Commission on Sustainable Development,1995 (1995).

14

Women in the International Gardens: How Subsistence Production Leads to New Forms of Intercultural Communication

Christa Müller

Integration versus parallel societies, assimilation versus ethnicization? These polarizations have increasingly dominated recent debate on migration to Germany.[1] Indeed, it has to be asked whether popular ideas of 'integration' adequately reflect the true diversity of intercultural processes that already characterize German social reality. If, instead of focusing on outer attributes such as the number of headscarves or muezzin calls, we look at everyday subsistence strategies, at the ways migrant women, children and men live their daily lives, it becomes evident that transnational and transcultural spaces have in fact long since been established. This is where new forms of ethnic and multiethnic identities are being invented and lived out.

The Refugee Women Felt That They Needed to be Doing More Than Simply Drinking Tea and Making Table Decorations

One example of this kind of new social space is the International Gardens association in Göttingen (Lower Saxony, Germany), a self-organized grassroots project run by migrants and Germans. The idea of having a garden originated with Bosnian women refugees in the Women's Café in the Göttingen Refugee Advice Centre. The women felt that, in the long run, they needed to be doing more than simply drinking tea and making table decorations. They were eager to get out of institutions run by social workers, and take their everyday lives into their own hands again. The women themselves clearly pinpointed the importance of self-reliance and working for their own subsistence in order to lead what they perceived as a tolerable life in exile: 'At home we had our gardens. That's what we missed the most. We so much wanted to have gardens in Germany as well.'

That was in 1995. One year later the International Gardens project leased its first piece of land. Starting with a gardening project for Bosnian women, the concept of the International Gardens developed gradually from praxis. Today, 220 women, children and men from fourteen nations use four gardens with a total area of approximately 12,000 square metres to produce organically grown fruit, vegetables and herbs.[2]

The significance of the gardens lies in the fact that they provide impulses for ways in which migrants could 'put down roots' in future, as well as for an enriching cultural variety in Germany as a country of immigration. At the same time, the activities of this grassroots project demonstrate that subsistence production[3] – embedded in the context of exile – not only encourages new forms of community-creating processes, but also sets the necessary conditions for renegotiating gender relations. The combination of economic, ecological and socio-cultural elements in the International Gardens, the variety of methods of cultivation and of subsistence-oriented techniques and skills used, together with the emergence of new forms of intercultural communication that arise through working together, the public showing and practising of the cultures of origin – as opposed to their being hidden or forgotten – have a whole range of effects, both inner and outer, which transform the way migrants in Germany perceive themselves, and the way they are perceived. Simultaneously, these new forms of multiethnic identities lay the foundations for future lifestyles in which less dominant social groups such as migrants, and especially the women among them, become the path-breakers and decision-makers instead of occupying more familiar marginal positions.

The question posed somewhat dualistically in classical migration research – whether immigration tends to lead to integration, or instead to the formation of ethnic ghettos – is shown to be inadequate when migration processes are additionally analysed from the perspectives of economic and environmental sociology, as represented in the approach used in subsistence research. The thematization of gender relations in particular shows how many different forms of social networking arise from the ways women arrange and use the spaces available to them in everyday life. In other words, I am attempting to link the constructs 'self' and 'other' with the social conditions of the production of survival, since I assume that being in command of one's situation plays a vital role in being able to recognize the self in the other and the other in the self, the necessary preconditions for intercultural communication. And to be in command of the situation people need autonomy in the way they live their lives. Although the feeling of being in control is differently conveyed according to the respective culture, focusing on work which is essential to sustaining life highlights the significance of women in both material and socio-cultural subsistence production.

Understanding Oneself as the 'Other' is not Just a Task for the Host Society, But Also One for the Migrants Themselves

Self-determination in the organization and conduct of their lives is something frequently denied to people in exile. There is no provision for their active participation in socially relevant activities; many feel they have been immobilized, and their lives are being managed for them. Treating migrants this way also conveys the message that the 'majority' in the society has nothing to learn from them. The loss is thus a double one: exiles lose the power to organize their own lives, and the host society passes over the opportunity to be inspired by other cultures and ways of life. The most important condition for a different kind of treatment of migration and migrants would be to develop a different perspective, as Elisabeth Bronfen emphasizes:

> The attitude that would seem appropriate to the modern phenomena of mass migration and the global circulation of signs is not so much one of regarding the 'others' who suddenly appear in 'our' midst as a problem which has to be dealt with for better or for worse, as one of understanding oneself as the other from the outset. (Bronfen et al. 1997: 6)

Understanding oneself as the 'other' is not just a task for the host society, but also one for the migrants themselves. The International Gardens in Göttingen are based on individual migrations, not on the activities of more or less established, homogeneous ethnic communities. The actors in this case are refugees, whose future is often uncertain, and who have to react with great flexibility to the situation in exile. Understanding themselves as the 'other' affords migrants the chance to recognize what is 'self' in the supposedly 'other', and to discover their own experiences and emotional states in others. Subsistence-oriented strategies of the kind on which the praxis of the International Gardens is based are ideally suited to self-recognition processes of this nature. At the same time they enable the migrants to take their lives in their own hands once more. People from places where subsistence gardening still plays a major role in everyday life frequently find it degrading to sit at home, unable to support themselves in any way. Jamila Alidousti, a forty-four-year-old Persian woman, stresses how significant a person's own work is for her or his sense of self-worth.

> We are unemployed. That is not good. It is always better to have something to do. I come from Iran, I'm from a good family. Before the revolution, we had a large farm. And here I am like someone living on social security. That's life, sometimes it's good for me, sometimes bad. But just because I don't have any money, I don't want to think I'm not worth anything.

In the garden, the migrants plant what they are familiar with from home. Whether the seedlings take or not, how the plants grow, what they need and how they look later on; all this gives the refugees information about the soil on which they now live, and about the people settled here.

The experiments that the gardeners undertake with plants and seeds are thus always also social experiments. If Persian seeds are not able to germinate in heavy Lower Saxon loam or Kurdish coriander is drowned by the watering-can, this also means the migrants are having interactive experiences with their new home.

Work in the gardens can be a way to transcend cultural differences and bind people together, not least in their shared contact with elemental things like earth and plants. By carrying on the daily agrarian pursuits of their culture of origin, the gardeners are establishing a link between the place they have left and the one they now live in. The familiar appearance of the plants gives substance to their own histories. Like the plants, the people gradually start to put down roots in the gardens, in Göttingen, in Germany.

One woman 'garden-activist' described how, walking in the forest in Göttingen, she had discovered a herb which she previously assumed to grow only in Kurdistan: 'We tried it, and it was delicious. Soon everyone got to hear of it. Now other Kurds phone me, and we all go into the forest and look for these herbs. We collect lots of them and freeze them, so we can eat them in winter too.'

Not only do the migrants appreciate the processes of exchange that arise from the work connected with the gardens; they also value the produce. Ms Abid, a forty-six-year-old founding member of the project, explained how important access to good-quality food is in order to lead a dignified life in exile:

> At home, everything was organic, everything was fresh. Here, unfortunately, it isn't. Here there is a lot of poison in the food. In Baghdad, there are markets everywhere, and everything is brought in fresh every morning. The chickens are still alive on the market. Here, organic food is very expensive. I can't afford it. When my parents bought bread, they first chose the kind of wheat, and if the bread didn't taste good, we took the bread back and it was exchanged. Some Germans think we were poor, but we were not poor. Here we are poor. We cannot afford decent food.

The International Gardens project sees itself as a forum where new forms of communication can arise from many different languages, ways of working, skills and experiences of life (Shimeles 2000). Work is the most familiar form of community, and subsistence-oriented work plays a decisive role in developing new ways of being and living together. All the participants like it best when they grow, cook or show what they know from their culture of origin; and thus experience is exchanged and broadened among the migrants themselves. Ms Abid elucidates:

> When one woman has baked something, she brings it along; someone else brings tea, someone else coffee, home-made juices. We swap recipes. When there is a festivity, everyone cooks their own specialities, everyone brings their own music along. We show each other our dances, but also seeds, plants, herbs and fruit. We have seen a lot from the Bosnians in particular. They have shown us a lot in the garden, for example about digging, or how deep beans need to be planted.

In the winter months, the gardening activities in the International Gardens are more closely combined with other crafts and skills. Since 1999, a self-built middle-European-style brick oven has stood in one of the four gardens. In spring 2000 the project women built an oriental oven of clay and straw. Tassew Shimeles, an immigrant from Ethiopia who is the project co-ordinator and agricultural adviser, views bread-baking from an intercultural perspective: 'Almost all peoples have their own bread, and the way it is baked says something about that culture.'

The project demonstrates different aspects of bread baking in practice. Another dimension of the work done in the International Gardens becomes apparent here: it does not present museum-like tableaux of 'different cultures'; instead, things are actually done, and in this straightforward way the transfer or reinvention of cultural features is effected, mixing earth and culture, sense experience and economic necessity (the bread is eaten), and here too a piece of the culture of origin is created anew and linked with other cultures.

Women Quite Clearly Dominate in the New Transcultural Spaces

Practising and publicly demonstrating baking in ovens built by the participants themselves also means confronting the political history and economy of bread, providing tangible evidence of how the 'lack of bread' can lead to wars, flight and migration – and providing an explanation for the fragmentation of the refugees' own biographies. Simultaneously, the refugees, who are often people from 'simple' backgrounds, develop an interest in world affairs: 'I didn't know anything about Sri Lanka before. Now, thanks to the Tamils here with us in the garden, I've learnt a lot about world politics,' said one gardener. Getting to know the world from a variety of ethnic, religious and political perspectives compensates perhaps to some degree for being uprooted from their own countries of origin. The involuntary journey to new worlds, often involving the trauma of a dramatic flight, can thus be reconstructed and understood in retrospect; the globalization of the migrants' lives and the enormous personal challenges they face become manageable through communal forms of production and exchange.

In these transcultural spaces, women quite clearly dominate. It is striking that the International Gardens are not politicized in the sense of a power-oriented strategy, as is the case in many male-dominated refugee groups, associations or resistance movements. On the contrary, conflicts between Kurds and Turks or Croats and Serbs, for example, are successfully set aside. Although social praxis in the garden, like migration, is deliberately placed in a political context, the central focus of the activities is not the attempt to gain control over people and resources, but rather ensuring the continuity of material, social and cultural self-sufficiency. Against the background of the dominant division of labour between men and women, however, a subsistence orientation will inevitably also be women-centred. In the gardens, women from all social strata become aware that subsistence labour is valuable work, and that they are the ones who uphold and create that social reciprocity which everyone holds so dear and which is often so painfully missed in exile.

The strength of the women is reflected in the culturally highly valued goods they produce; goods based on subsistence and not commodity pro-duction, and which, in exile, do not appear 'on their own' through the often 'invisible' labour of women, but have to be fought for and won over and over again. The exceptional situation of migration makes it clearer than perhaps any other that women are the ones who create the daily conditions upon which life is based, and make these available to the community.

Self-provision by Taking Control of One's Life Conditions Includes the Reciprocal Provision for One Another's Needs

Related to the production of that which is necessary to life is the concept of self-determined work for one's own needs (*Eigenarbeit*), which has emerged together with the idea of an 'alternative economy'. *Eigenarbeit* implies satisfying one's own needs through one's own deeds; acting on one's own initiative, either alone or with others, to make, repair or organize something. *Eigenarbeit* includes manual work as well as social and cultural activities. A central principle is that it should improve quality of life as well as heightening the autonomy of the individual. The aim is to achieve as great as possible an emancipation from consumption, not by means of abstinence and sacrifice, but rather the opposite: by contributing to a self-determined life through what one does oneself (Mittelsten Scheid 1999).

What is practised, for example in the *Eigenarbeit* house in Munich, shows that this concept allows forms of communication which cannot be arbitrarily or artificially created, but have a material basis. When people who are working together meet, they share a common topic. Here, the production of goods whose meaning is related to their use value is embedded in social relations; in consequence, new forms of reciprocity can also be practised. Doing one's own work also promotes social and cultural self-sustenance. What is being referred to here is by no means a question of being passively looked after; it implies self-provision by taking control of one's life conditions, either alone or communally, and includes the reciprocal provision for one another's needs (Schmid 1998).

In Germany, the starting point for promoting these kinds of subsistence-oriented strategies aimed at strengthening the autonomy of the individual is not primarily a situation where material supplies are scarce; on the contrary, it is one where there is an oversupply, albeit coupled with shortages of a different nature. The provision of life's necessities by others via the market is creating a situation of increasing emotional and cultural undersupply, with various results such as the loss of subsistence capabilities and the sense of confidence and intrinsic value that goes with them, as well as tendencies towards rootlessness and social exclusion.

These 'shortages' are an extra burden on migrants. Not only is the ambivalent situation of material oversupply often completely unknown to them; as newcomers from communities where social reciprocity is both a survival strategy and the epitome of quality of life, they experience the lack of reciprocal care and concern in the host country, Germany, as particularly oppressive. They feel a strong affinity for activities which are not demanded by the market, but by life itself. Ms Abid described her life before becoming a refugee:

> In Baghdad I was always with relatives, friends and neighbours. We celebrated together, we went to the holy areas, we were always together. No one ever just stayed at home. After the evening meal we were at the neighbours' until 11, 12 o'clock. Laughing, eating, drinking and so on. We talked about everything. Lots of us could play the drums or flute, and when there is a festivity, a wedding or a birth, then everyone comes along, puts out the furniture, puts lights on everywhere, and we all celebrate. Everyone together. Until the next morning. We are not used to being alone. At home, there are always lots of us. Still today, if someone phones up and I really have a lot to do, I can't say no. We don't do that where I come from. It's simply impossible.

The migrants in the gardens are aware that the past they remember is always the reconstructed past *before* the violent break they were forced to make with it. Gabriele Rosenthal points out that flight, being a biographical turning point, can create a reinterpretation of the past, and that lived and narrated life stories mutually (re)constitute one another in a reciprocal relationship (Rosenthal 1995: 20, 143). Nevertheless, it is precisely these varied forms of reconstruction of life stories which make the International Gardens a success. Ms Ardjomandi, a fifty-one-year-old migrant from the Persian Gulf, explains that the gardens stand for continuity, because in their context social relationships enjoy a similar priority to the one they have in many of the refugees' cultures of origin:

> It is a relief to go to the garden. You work, you talk, you laugh with the others. It is the way it is at home. For example, you are at home and you're cooking. And suddenly visitors arrive. Unexpectedly. Then you just make more to eat. Here in Germany it's different. You don't feel people greet you with open hearts. Maybe they will say, yes, come in, but when you're gone, they say, oh, she just dropped in, she obviously hasn't got anything to do.

Logically enough, in the context of the International Gardens, the 'other' or the 'alien' is presented differently from the way it is in the majority society. In every case it is noticeable that, besides the shared experience of a fragmented biography, the gardeners, with their different countries of origin, cultures, ethnic groups and religions, have things in common which, in their view, make them different from Germans. For instance, they are all united in the attempt to relocate decontextualized local knowledge, e.g. by practising reciprocal exchange. For the migrants in the gardens, reciprocity is right at the top of their scale of values: social reciprocity, the collection and distribution of social capital with the aim of organizing their time together, of avoiding being isolated themselves, and seeing to it that no one else is left alone either, are elementary components of the community-forming process. It is in precisely this give-and-take that the intercultural communities in the International Gardens constitute themselves, as a direct reaction both to the loss of their native countries and to their experiences with the highly individualized German society; a society in which identity is constituted (*inter alia*) in terms of a hubristic belief that everything and anything is realizable by means of technology and social engineering or by access to commodities. Nevertheless, there is a clear recognition that social relationships among the migrants, as well as the climate in homogeneous migrant groups, do not necessarily differ 'naturally' from those in comparable German contexts. Ms Ardjomandi, who has been in Germany for thirty years, describes the special atmosphere in the gardens:

> I know a lot of people in Göttingen and also have a lot of friends, Germans and non-Germans. But in the gardens it's different. There's a special warmth there. Non-Germans also change over the years here, they become more

European. When they meet, there is also envy. They look carefully at the clothes, the cars. But I can come to the gardens as I like. With sandals, with torn trousers, with a dirty T-shirt, nobody minds. Everyone feels free here. There isn't the same competition.

Many of the gardeners are guests in Germany. In the gardens, they can be the hosts for once. If one accompanies Ms Abid on a walk through the city centre of Göttingen for instance, it may take quite a while before reaching one's destination. She meets acquaintances everywhere: Kurds, Arabs, Germans, Ethiopians, Sri Lankans and Kosovars. And if her bags are full of freshly harvested zucchinis, coriander or mint, she has usually given away half her harvest before she gets home. Ms Abid has something to give. That is not something that can simply be taken for granted by a migrant in Germany. And it visibly gives her pleasure.

Ms. Omar, sixty-five-year-old wife of a famed Kurdish resistance fighter, also likes giving away her harvested produce. In Kurdistan, she had a garden with a lot of fruit. Here, she tries to grow everything she knows from home. She manages to raise mangel-roots, radishes, two sorts of beans, two sorts of zucchini, parsley, dill, spinach, coriander, mint and sunflowers. She gets her seeds from Kurdistan, even though the plants only increase her longing for her lost home. Before she got to know about the International Gardens, she always had chocolate in the house for the neighbours' children. Now she makes presents of produce from her garden. Ms Omar makes jam, bakes date biscuits and preserves vegetables, the Kurdish way, naturally. She is proud when people taste her products. Her gifts carry the guarantee of reciprocity, the commitment to one another. They are simply friendly acts, but at the same time they uphold the connotations they had in the culture of origin: co-operation and concern as both emotional *and* economic necessities. The wish for functional social relationships is a deeply ingrained emotion, and essential to life; in exile, too, it needs to be realized.

For Migrants, Being Able to Give Something Means Being Able to Free Themselves from their Reduced Status as Refugees

Right up until the 1970s many regions in Germany still had subsistence systems which existed alongside the world market for the provision of needs (Müller 1998). Older people in particular still know the meaning of symbolic capital and remember that taking is inextricably linked to the readiness to give in return. People who don't want to enter into an exchange, therefore, reject gifts from the outset. This is an experience the activists in Göttingen have repeatedly had with German neighbours in the gardens.

Intercultural communication by no means always functions smoothly, as the following anecdote from the International Gardens demonstrates. Because the gardeners are keen to have good relationships with neighbouring gardeners, they try to include them in their activities and regularly offer them fresh garden produce. One elderly man rejected the gifts categorically month after month, until one day it was made clear to him just how rude his persistent refusals appeared to the migrants. And so the mishap took its course: a few days later, a Lebanese woman held her basket full of food freshly harvested for the weekend over the fence, intending to offer the neighbour a few carrots. Eagerly, the man lifted the whole basket over the fence, and the woman watched open-mouthed as her entire stock of weekend provisions disappeared into the well-meaning neighbour's house.

For migrants, being able to give something means being able to free themselves from their reduced status as refugees. For many of them, being cut off from active work and assigned to a life as a *recipient* of social benefit constitutes an experience of renewed exclusion. Women are frequently doubly excluded, through both social ascription and existing power relations: their radius of movement is limited; their meeting-places are no longer public places, but rather cramped flats. The gardens, however, are located outside culturally specific ideas about private and public domains. They are somewhere the women can go where they are not subject to the codes of honour of patriarchal family units. New social networks arising from female alliances develop in the gardens. Ms Abid speaks of these 'kinships' formed by choice:

> Earlier, my daughter always said to me, Mama, let's go out. And I said, where shall we go? If we go out of the flat, we're in the street. We don't know anyone whom we could visit. Now it is different. Now we have got the gardens and the people from the gardens. My daughter has lots of aunties now. She also calls the women her aunties. Aunty Hajat, Aunty Jamila, Aunty Tamdur. Ms. Omar is like a grandmother to my daughter, and she calls her that too. She wants us to spend the night at Ms. Omar's. And as for me, I can tell you my feeling, and that is that this is the right way for us. Ms. Omar is just like my own mother for me. I have the same feelings towards her.

Being able to transfer familiar feelings into a new life is an indication that migrants have arrived; that they have managed to build a bridge between the old country and the present one. Particularly after the traumatic experience of fleeing as a refugee, having a home is absolutely fundamental for survival. 'Without a home, one is worthless,' says Ms Abid, revealing the therapeutic value of grasping 'home' as a dynamic concept, one which even those who have lost theirs violently can conceive of in new ways.

When the women tell the stories of their flight, tears come quickly to their eyes. Dead relatives had to be abandoned in the mountains between Iraq and Iran; friends who had been tortured are still officially missing; they were unable to take leave of dying parents when permission to enter the country was withheld. The traumas caused by being driven out of their homes and countries, by having to flee, become daily nightmares that haunt socially isolated women in particular. They remember the heavily armed secret service men who forced their way into people's houses every day in Kurdistan–Iraq to check the number of inhabitants. They remember how family members were dragged off and never seen again; fear was ever-present and leaves its mark, even after years in exile. Ms Abid:

> If I only stay at home, I feel ill. Then my back hurts and I don't know why. Psychological, perhaps. Back home, we never had feelings like that. We just didn't know them. Now, when I come home from work and I'm tired, then I like best of all to go to the garden straight away and meet the others. There I can recover. I have to go to the garden every day. It gives me strength. When I'm tired and worn out, the garden picks me up again: the peacefulness, the greenery, the pretty landscape, the growing plants. All that wakes me up again.

The gardens give the women the opportunity to 'socialize' their para-lysing fears, their longing for what has been lost and their otherwise private suffering by carrying them into the public space, which is thus constituted anew. Ms Ardjomandi speaks about the comforting effect of the gardens: 'Sometimes I sit at home and listen to Persian music. Then I think of old times, how it was back home with my mother, my sister. Then I become very sad and cry. But then when I go to the garden, my mind quickly turns to other things. Sometimes the garden is a comfort.'

Ms Alidousti confirms this assessment:

> Many women are isolated, and sit alone at home. They cry a lot. When they become members of the gardens, this often changes. We've just got a new member. The woman said to me, I'm alone at home, what can I do with my time? Then I said, come to the International Gardens, you can put your time to use there.

'Putting your time to use' does not mean 'killing time' or letting it rush by. Instead, spending time with other people is perceived as fundamentally meaningful. 'At what moments are you happy?' I asked Ms Omar. 'When I'm amongst other people,' was her unequivocal answer.

Ms Omar has been living in Germany for more than ten years. She first learnt to read and write when she was over sixty – in the International Gardens. Here, too, the necessity of learning a foreign language arose, and a vital one at that, since the *lingua franca* used by the gardeners is German. German is the language in which comments are made on how well the seeds are growing, or experiences at the social welfare office exchanged. The German courses which the International Gardens project offers in co-operation with the Protestant Church's adult education programme are unusually successful. Here a doctor's wife from the Persian upper class sits side-by-side with an illiterate woman from Sri Lanka, after the two have finished digging the soil together. They can also try out their new language skills with the German members of the association, who often live in multicultural partnerships and want their children to have multicultural experiences. Some of them are knowledgeable about local soils and garden cultures. Exchanging information about these is a further motivation for many of the gardeners to open up to the host country, giving new impetus to the future ecological, economic and socio-cultural viability of the social reality they find here.

In the International Gardens of Göttingen, dimensions of 'foreigners' reality' emerge which cannot be located between conventional poles of either assimilation into or rejection of the host culture. The continuity represented by subsistence strategies makes new forms of integration possible; ones which do not orient themselves by 'German' norms and values, but for which migration itself is the starting point, retained and reconstructed by confronting the ruptures of expulsion and flight with continuity as a survival strategy. In this way, many migrants succeed in creating viable perspectives for a new life in exile. Yet the longing for that ever-present other aspect of themselves, the violently curtailed part of their live stories, never disappears: 'We miss our home, the neighbours, the friends, the acquaintances. We miss our sun. We miss our sky. Clear weather, our stars, we miss it all. All of that is home.'

Everyone in the garden is foreign, and close to one another at the same time. The International Gardeners are not bound together by any common origins or family traditions. What unites them is their disunity – and the wish to create a new context for their life together. There is no duality of 'self' and 'other', but only a broad palette of the 'other', united in the wish to make a home for themselves. Unexpected forms of ethnic identity-formation are being realized here. Possibly, here in the International Gardens – and not in Kreuzberg (a famously multiethnic part of Berlin) where hopes for true ethnic diversity have long since been shattered – the first tendrils of a multicultural society are sprouting; a society resting above all upon women whose first aim is to provide people with material and socio-cultural goods, and whose dynamic is rooted in their interest in and caring for one another.

(Translated by Patricia Skorge)

Notes

1. The discussion has centred particularly on the growing significance of Islam, although Klein-Hessling et al. (1999) have shown that Islamization processes by no means lead inexorably to cultural disintegration and the formation of 'parallel societies'. Islamization in this context means the rising significance of Islam within the symbolism, the communication and the social reality of western societies. The assumption that Islamization processes could possibly lead to 'parallel societies' as segregated Islamic societies within the dominant Christian culture is part of the ideological discourse led by more conservative elements in German society. These conservatives have strenuously and consistently denied that Germany is a country which routinely receives immigrants, although de facto this is quite evidently the case.

2. International Gardens is supported by the Protestant Church of Lower Saxony and the Munich-based foundation *anstiftung*, which has for the past seventeen years been active in initiating, studying the progress of and promoting practical projects featuring self-providing urban subsistence activities. As far as International Gardens is concerned, the *anstiftung* is particularly interested in the effects that the participants' work for their own subsistence have in the area of intercultural activities. In researching this aspect by means of qualitative methods such as biographical interviews and participant observation, I have been involved in the activities of the International Gardens since the summer of 1999. (Translator's note: the name *anstiftung* is an ingenious one. *Stiftung* means a charitable 'foundation', but *Anstiftung* means 'incitement' or 'instigation'.)

3. Subsistence production is use value oriented work, aimed at the immediate production and sustenance of life. One of the assumptions implicit in the popular ideas influenced by evolutionist modernization concepts is that, all over the world, subsistence production is gradually giving way to commodity production as a result of advancing social developments; that, as a 'traditional' element of 'backward' societies, it will disappear as 'productive forces' – i.e. world-wide industrialization – unfold. In contrast, the central tenet of the Bielefeld subsistence approach is that, in spite of the increasing destruction of independent regional subsistence *economies*, subsistence *production*, as the indispensable production of life as such, merely alters its character, to the extent that it is subordinated to commodity production (Mies et al. 1987).

References

Beck, U. (ed.) (1998) *Perspektiven der Weltgesellschaft*, Frankfurt: Suhrkamp.

Bennholdt-Thomsen, V. B. Holzer and C. Müller (eds) (1999) *Das Subsistenzhandbuch. Widerstandskulturen in Europa, Asien und Lateinamerika*, Vienna: Promedia.

Bielefeld, U. (ed.) (1998) *Das Eigene und das Fremde. Neuer Rassismus in der Alten Welt?*, Hamburg: Hamburger Edition.

Bronfen, E., B. Marius and T. Steffen (eds) (1997) *Hybride Kulturen. Beiträge zur anglo-amerikanischen Multikulturalitätsdebatte*, Tübingen: Stauffenburg.

Illich, I. (1982) *Vom Recht auf Gemeinheit*, Reinbek: rororo aktuell.

Klein-Hessling, R., S. Nökel and K. Werner (eds) (1999) *Der neue Islam der Frauen. Weibliche Lebenspraxis in der globalisierten Moderne*, Bielefeld: transcript.

Mies, M. and V. Shiva (1993) *Ecofeminism*, London: Zed Books.

Mies, M., V. Bennholdt-Thomsen and C. von Werlhof (1988) *Women: The Last Colony*, London: Zed Books.

Mittelsten Scheid, J. (1999) 'Mehr Eigenarbeit. Bausteine für eine menschliche Zukunft', *Das Baugerüst*, 1

Müller, C. (1998) *Von der lokalen Ökonomie zum globalisierten Dorf. Bäuerliche Überlebensstrategien zwischen Weltmarktintegration und Regionalisierung*, Frankfurt and New York: Campus.

Rosenthal, G. (1995) *Erlebte und erzählte Lebensgeschichte. Gestalt und Struktur biographischer Selbstbeschreibungen*, Frankfurt and New York: Campus.

Schmid, W. (1998) *Philosophie der Lebenskunst,* Frankfurt: Suhrkamp.

Shimeles, T. (2000) 'The International Garden', unpublished paper, Göttingen.

Wierlacher, A. (ed.) (1993) *Kulturthema Fremdheit. Leitbegriffe und Problemfelder kulturwissenschaftlicher Fremdheitsforschung*, Munich: iudicium.

15

The Practice of Subsistence: Collective Environ-
mental Action and Community Organic Farming

Elisabeth Meyer-Renschhausen

This chapter will discuss some forms of positive Utopia which developed as a correlate to Maria Mies's resistance activity to the industrial dictatorship installed in Europe after the Second World War. The process she fought against, the dictatorship of the multinational corporations, has been very efficient in West Germany; but in West Berlin, a protected enclave with special privileges, isolated in the East, far from the homogeneous western bloc, with special privileges, it was somewhat easier than elsewhere to try out creative alternatives to the mainstream consumer-oriented way of life. Berlin was the city of the famous 'Kommune 2' and a kind of centre for the rapidly growing movement of shared housing (*Wohngemeinschaften*). In the late 1970s, the former 'ufa' film studios were converted into a community for working and living that is still active. Many of the squatters of the early 1980s began restoring, renting and, in the luckiest cases, became owners of co-operatives still in existence today.

I came to Berlin in 1977 because it was the centre of the ongoing student movement – intellectual discussions took place both inside and outside the universities – and especially the women's movement. It took me some time to realize the full impact of what it meant to be in Berlin – it was the ideal place for turning criticism into practical alternatives. Contact between different branches of the social movements was stronger in Berlin; Berlin was one of the first places where it was possible to belong to the feminist movement as well as to the eco-alternatives, to live in a politically oriented women's community (*Frauen-Wohngemeinschaft*) and still be allowed to eat natural eggs, without being committed to a ready-made opinion about the Middle East conflict.

This chapter discusses the 'green' changes in the women's communities, and then presents three organic farms, each one run as a community in former East Germany. The communities are quite different from each other, yet they face similar problems in their communal organization. The

Berlin Green activists see all of them as pioneers of a necessary change in lifestyle, and as an integral part of a social change in the direction of a 'subsistence perspective' – which for me means living together in a community, without the usual consumer 'ideals', more or less without individual cars or television and with a patient respect for, even a joyful concern with, the daily necessities as well as political and social action. My research also raises the question of the world-wide meaning of organic gardening, its philosophy, and its contribution to the wider 'alternative' or counter-cultural movements in our modern, post-industrial world.

125 Peace–food Stores in the Capital of Unemployment

Berlin, the capital of the German student movement in the late 1960s, also became the centre of environmental activism in Germany. During the time of the ongoing student movement in the late 1960s and the early 70s, West Berlin became the centre for alternative culture. At the heart of the alternative movements stood the 'bio-shop movement'. 'Peace-food', the first organic food store, was founded in 1971. It aimed at social reform directed towards peace by changing people's eating habits. By the end of the 70s this had become the bio-shop phenomenon, more ecologically oriented, characteristic of the new Berlin of the mid-80s; such shops became well established after the Chernobyl reactor accident. By June 1999 Berlin had 125 organic food stores, 60 food co-ops and about 120 of the more established old reform shops in a city of 3.5 million people. As a phenomenon, more a social movement than part of a well-established economy, the whole organic food distribution and selling operation is in a state of permanent change. The shops belong to one group after another, the wholesalers are still being 'reorganized', entrepreneurs are looking for new fields of activity, small shops give up, others move or become 'bio-supermarkets'.

Organic food shops belong to a huge spectrum of citizens' initiatives in Berlin, which have yet to be studied systematically. Although these groups have met with little success of late, their numbers began to grow again in the 1990s. In the mid-90s there were 150 citizens' initiatives working in Berlin alone, and although only a quarter of these regarded their own work as successful, they were by no means ready to give up. Working with a group of like-minded people compensates for a certain amount of failure, as does the knowledge that such groups have at least managed to change public opinion significantly. My own citizens' group, Bürgerinitiative Nelly-Sachs Park, began with the aim of preventing a small park from being paved over in an area of the city, northern Schöneberg, which was already lacking in green spaces. At the same time we fought for a drastic reduction of traffic on a street that is a virtual freeway running through the middle of the city (45,000 cars daily) in order to protect the people who live there from traffic noise and the noxious smell and health dangers of exhaust fumes. We became known throughout the city when, in September 1990, following a similar initiative in Hamburg, we organized a successful occupation of the Bülowstraße, which received extensive coverage in the national news weekly *Der Stern* (24 October 1990). After that, we turned our attention to the devastation of a lushly overgrown area of unused railway tracks, the Gleisdreieck-Gelände just beyond the Potsdamer Platz. Although we were unsuccessful, we managed for a time to get almost the entire press, including the tabloid daily *Bild*, on our side.

When I arrived in Berlin there were just two organic food shops; both still exist, although in a changed form. Otherwise organic food was available only at a few of the weekly markets. Today Berlin is one of the largest markets for organic food. My immediate neighbourhood, the northern part of Schöneberg, by 1994 had at least twelve organic food shops and a number of others selling 'natural' products such as shoes, herbs and cosmetics. Schöneberg as a whole, with about 200,000 inhabitants, by 1995 had about twenty shops selling organically grown produce. Today, despite rising rents, there are still fourteen organic groceries. As far as I know, no town of the same size in Germany has as many 'bio-shops', as they are called in Berlin. The situation is similar in the neighbouring district of Kreuzberg, which in June 1999 had twenty-seven natural foods stores besides many other small alternative businesses such as bicycle shops and craft workshops. In Berlin, too, there are about six special organic markets as well as complete 'lanes' of organic farmers in the ordinary weekly markets. What is the history of this 'green revolution' in Berlin?

The first thing we changed, as the people of my women's commune did in 1978, was to give up factory-baked white flour bread (it is without vitamins, fibres or flavour, and is a major cause of digestive problems); then we decided to buy only free-range eggs from the next-door 'Reform-house'.

After some time we became more knowledgeable about organic produce and changed our eating habits more and more. We decided not to eat animals raised in crowded conditions and fed on unwholesome industrial foods such as pulverized animal by-products which, as has become apparent recently in Britain, often lead to serious illnesses. We switched to a more or less vegetarian diet of bread, dairy products, eggs, a lot of vegetables and occasionally fish. At first, in 1980, we found the vegetables in the natural food shops too small, ugly and expensive and bought our supplies at the supermarket. After reports from friends and the alternative daily paper (*Die Tageszeitung*, *Taz*) about the dangerous additives often found in industrially grown vegetables, such as those that come from hydroponic greenhouses in the Netherlands and elsewhere where they are grown without soil, we discovered that eating too many of these nitrate salads and soilless tomatoes could lead to all sorts of ailments, from headaches and allergies to cancer. We learned that 94 per cent of all conventionally produced food contains residues of pesticides and other agricultural poisons. A reason to change.

And then we discovered the difference in the taste between organic vegetables, however ugly and small, and conventionally grown produce. More and more people came to buy all of their food and other daily needs at the natural food store. I need not point out that women, including many on quite low incomes, were at the forefront both as founders of and shoppers in natural food shops. I completely changed my buying habits while working in a large alternative school. Although I earned much less money than before, these strong vegetarian young women radicalized my daily habits, and I began to purchase all my provisions in natural food stores.

'Bioland' in the Countryside: Gaia against Demeter?

West Berlin was not the only place where things were changing so rapidly; in East Berlin there were similar developments, even though it was much harder to create an alternative or green scene under the so-called German Democratic Republic (GDR). People from the Peace Library in East Berlin and the initiative against nuclear weapons came together under the protection of the Protestant Church. At a meeting at the Church Research Centre in Wittenberg, an organic gardening group was founded and people discussed growing produce without artificial fertilizers, pesticides and herbicides. Some people moved to the country and began organic farming, among them a herb farmer, an apple farmer and a number of others in areas not far from Berlin. After the fall of the Berlin Wall this group became the centre of a rapidly growing number of organic farming projects.

In May 1989, still under the GDR, these organic farmers founded an association for ecological agriculture, the GÄA. It was no coincidence that they chose a name similar to that of the Greek earth goddess Gaia. Since the change of regime and unification, the GÄA has functioned as the organic agriculture and marketing federation for the new federal states, that is, the former GDR states. Its members are 'largely self-contained farms or market gardens in the areas of landscape preservation, cultivation and animal husbandry'.[1]

In the western part of the Federal Republic such marketing associations for organic produce have existed for quite some time. In 1971, south German farmers founded the Bioland organization to distribute, advertise and control organic products (since 1987 it has been called the Bioland-Verband für organisch-biologischen Landbau). It is based on the experimental work of the Swiss agri-politician Dr Hans Müller, his wife Maria Müller, and the physician Hans-Peter Rusch in the 1920s. The Demeter association (Arbeitsgemeinschaft für biologisch-dynamischen Landbau) is even older. It goes back to the 'agriculture seminar' that Rudolf Steiner gave in 1924 at the request of farmers in Koberwitz in Silesia in today's Poland, and began as a monthly magazine, *Demeter*, edited in Marienhöhe near Bad Saarow. The members of the Demeter association committed themselves to agriculture along the biological-dynamic principles further developed by the disciples of Steiner, the anthroposophers, after his death. They have banned chemical fertilizers and chemical herbicides and fungicides, and are committed to a respect for the relationships between the microcosmos and macrocosmos, especially as regards planting, composting and fertilizing.

The city of Berlin is surrounded by Brandenburg, with 2.8 million inhabitants, one of the most sparsely settled of the federal states. Two-thirds of the population live in villages, the rest in small and middle-sized towns. These middle-sized towns often still maintain the character of pre-industrial farming settlements (*Ackerbürgerstädte*), complete with clusters of barns at their entrance. In the peripheral regions the inhabitants of these small towns still have no other source of income outside local farming. After the fall of the Wall, more than 80 per cent of these former collective farm workers lost their jobs – most of them women. The hope that tourism may become a new source of revenue has opened the minds of even conventionally thinking inhabitants to the idea of change in farming also.

Organic farms have sprung up in over 100 villages in Brandenburg, despite its poor and sandy soil, since the political changes of autumn 1989. In January 2000 there were 329 bio-farms in Brandenburg with 64,000 ha of cultivated land, corresponding to 4.8 per cent of the farmed area. One hundred of these farms, mostly in the surroundings of Berlin, sell as directly as possible to their customers and are thus open to all visitors. The list of these farms is updated and published every year to make it easy to find them.

A lot of these new organic farms were founded by young couples, but some also by communes, groups of people from the East or West German 'alternative' movement. In a few cases, entire former collective farms (LPGs or *Landwirtschaftliche Produktive Genossenschaften*) were turned into organic 'eco-villages'.[2] Most of the former LGPs became *Agrar-Genossenschaften*, the same size as before but with jobs for only a few men. The poverty of the former GDR meant that many collective farms before 1989 were already managing without artificial fertilizers or herbicides. After the demise of the GDR, many farmers were still very poor, so their willingness to turn to organic agriculture was relatively high. Crisis can offer opportunities for change.

We know that, in the early 1990s, organic farming in the United States was much less affected by the economic crisis than conventional agriculture. In Europe, poor agrarian regions, such as the Allgäu in southern Bavaria, which has often been considered 'backward' because agribusiness failed to take root, have played a leading role in environmentally oriented farming, not least because the peasants there never had much money for pesticides. In 1994 the Federal German Office of the Environment sharply criticized European Community agricultural norms, calling for a complete re-orientation of European agricultural policy; an agricultural policy that up until now has more or less supported only industrial mass production, subsidizing large farmers and marginalizing small farmers, despite the obvious effects of this policy, such as a North Sea polluted with nitrates. Organic farming does not produce the surpluses which lead to ever-sinking farm prices, and the accompanying negative consequences world-wide. Only environmentally grounded cultivation methods can preserve the richness of regional animal and plant life. In Eastern Germany, about one-quarter of the population is currently unemployed, most of them women, even if government statistics quote lower figures. Organic agriculture supports small and middle-sized farms and local processing businesses, thus creating more jobs in rural areas. On organic farms in Brandenburg there are between 200 and 300 per cent more jobs than on conventional farms.[3] At the same time, through new forms of marketing, organic production also reduces environmental pollution caused by the needless and, as we now know, dangerous transportation of agricultural goods – including living animals – across Europe.

Of course there is a problem here. Most of the converted farms in East Germany are former huge ex-LPGs, today farming co-operatives. These co-operatives, even when they are eco-farms, have areas nearly seven times bigger than a West German 'bio-farm' (in Brandenburg about 204 ha versus 30 ha on average). The West German bio-farmers feel threatened by the large-scale farming in the East. They fear a new threat to their own culture of 'peasant farming' – now being revived in the bio-farms – coming from the large-scale East German organic farms. Still, very few East Germans have ventured a new start on their own. History leaves its marks on the people, and it is a long history from the large estates (*Rittergüter*) of the nineteenth century to the collective farms of the twentieth century. So the peasants in the East prefer to work as members of a co-operative, a common practice in rural villages before the peasant wars of the sixteenth century destroyed this tradition.

The West German organic farmers argue that large farms (some more than 1000 ha) are unavoidably accompanied by industrialized methods of farming, be they 'eco' or conventional; they lack natural landscape boundaries, hedges; they keep animals in mass stables; and they produce a monoculture instead of a *Kreislaufwirtschaft*. Their protest that land erosion continues on the large bio-farms cannot be dismissed easily. The conflict is far from being resolved. The gap between East German and West German bio-farmers is still huge.

Even if it is clear that West German organic farmers fear competition from the large-scale producers in the East, and prices for organically grown grain have actually dropped, it is likely that the East German organic vegetable farms will mainly serve consumers in the former GDR including East Berlin where, until recently, organic produce was not readily available.

We will probably see an increase both in the foodstuff scandals of recent years and in the number of people buying organic products. A real change will only come, though, with a radical transformation in consumer behaviour: when people decide, for the sake of their own health and that of their families, to stop buying cheaper produce grown with the help of poisonous chemicals.

Such changes can be observed in Berlin. The number of food co-ops, at least, rose rapidly in East Berlin after reunification. These food co-ops usually consist of between ten and fifty people who share a warehouse and buy directly from particular organic farms. By avoiding middlemen, the produce is relatively cheap for them as members. To be sure, such food co-ops entail considerable work and organization, but they also put an end to 'anonymous shopping'. The members now know exactly where their cabbage comes from. Once a month they meet for tea, wine and planning at a plenary session (*Bio-Direkt* 1992).

Organic sellers are becoming more and more common at the conventional outdoor markets and have met with such success that there are now organic markets in Berlin.

This success led to the formation of further organic marketing co-operatives, such as the 1991 Märkische Wirtschaftsverbund Berlin-Brandenburg, whose members include organic farmers' societies such as Bioland, Demeter and others, as well as Berlin natural food companies such as the Weichardt and Märkisches Landbrot bakeries, or the wholesale greengrocers 'terra frisch'. They want to work together to expand the market and so they offer their products to supermarkets and large-scale food processors. The goal of the initiators, all young people, mostly from East Berlin, is to ensure 'fair prices' for producers.

In 1991 the share of natural products in the German grocery market was only 0.75 per cent or 1.5 billion DM. In Baden-Württemberg, a centre of organic agriculture, only 1 per cent of the farms were organic. While only a little more than 2 per cent of German farms are involved in organic food production today, in Brandenburg the number of hectares under organic cultivation has quadrupled over the last seven years. That means, in 2000, that about 10 per cent of the peasants in Brandenburg are organic farmers. Market researchers predict that the number of natural food markets will increase. There are still problems: although in January 2000 the Brandenburg organic farmers sold 80 per cent of their vegetables and fruit in the region, they satisfy only 10 per cent of the Berlin organic market. It 'belongs' still to the western organic farmers or wholesalers who sold their produce in West Berlin before 1989.

Today, everywhere in Europe the market for organic food is growing fast. Doubts about authenticity are the main reason people give for not buying the somewhat more expensive organic products. The taste of organically grown produce, though, is very much better. To be sure, the big supermarkets have been using the 'natural' label a lot lately without delivering what they seem to promise. After some investigation, Berlin consumer watchdog groups have been successful in forcing a number of companies to stop using the label 'natural' where it was not applicable; but doubts about 'purity' are an age-old argument against a new product, so a real transformation in thinking and behaviour, and perhaps even a small economic sacrifice, are required. In contrast, the occasional appearance of semi-natural products, such as GEHA chocolate, is not so problematic since they are sold for political reasons (Cejka 1993).

I know that my natural food shops sell fewer suspect goods than the supermarket chains if only because I can ask the people running them where they acquired their merchandise. In doubtful cases, they can ask their wholesalers for more details. When I buy produce through subscription or a food co-op, I know where it comes from.

Politicians are, of course, in a position to influence these developments if they want to: on the initiative of the Berlin Greens (or, more precisely, the party Coalition 90/ Greens/ Autonomous Women's Association), the Berlin state parliament (Abgeordnetenhaus) called upon the Berlin government (Senate) 'to encourage more strongly the use by public institutions in the state of Berlin of agricultural products grown in Brandenburg, particularly those produced by organic methods'.[4] They were referring to purchases for cafeterias and institutional kitchens in schools, town halls and hospitals. The Department of Economics and Technology (Senatsverwaltung für Wirtschaft und Technologie) thereupon sent a non-binding recommendation to the state's cafeterias and institutional kitchens suggesting they use local agricultural products from Brandenburg. The Senate denied, however, that organically grown products were healthier, retreating behind the incorrect assertion that there was no scientific proof.[5] We can assume that many institutional kitchens had never even heard of this half-hearted governmental recommendation. Nevertheless, it is now possible to eat meals prepared from organically grown produce in all university cafeterias. Besides this, every Berlin public cafeteria serves organically grown potatoes from Brandenburg, even with conventional dishes.

Three Organic Farming Communities

The three farms I will discuss below are all small ones. They work on 112 ha (Marienhöhe) or significantly less (the others). All three are collectively run with an emphasis on vegetables, surviving essentially on direct sales in Berlin. I visited them for the first time in spring 1994.

About 60 km east of Berlin, in the Eggersdorf near Müncheberg, is the commune Apfeltraum e.V. (Apple Dream Society Inc.). The group has two pieces of land and several small buildings, in part inherited and in part leased. They have a stall which formerly belonged to the local collective farm. Two couples with several children and their friends form the core of the group which includes a number of young people from East Germany, mainly Saxony. They principally process windfall fruit into juice and grow vegetables which they sell through a subscription scheme. Some members of the commune work outside, in Berlin and elsewhere, some with the intention of later devoting all their time to the farm. Like every commune they are constantly attracting new people. Part-time members come and go, interns from the Berlin universities spend from two weeks to six months and leave again, inspired or perhaps bemused. In the summer of 1994, they supplied between forty and sixty Berlin families with subscription crates (*Abokisten*) of vegetables cultivated according to organic methods. Now they have about thirty-five cows of a rare breed, draught horses, some pigs and geese.

When I visited the group for the first time with two women colleagues, at the end of an exhausting bicycle trip, we were impressed by their friendly, dreamy and radical way of welcoming their old friends and relatives from East Berlin, and by the way they made no compromise while selling their products. This attitude changed as the farm grew. What was still very uncertain in 1994 had become certain by the summer of 2000; even if they have scarcely enough room for their members and for their guests, the farm will make it, barring a major catastrophe. Apfeltraum now sells more then 140 subscription crates, mostly to rich parts of West Berlin.

On a second visit, my sister and I got an insider's view when we met a few of the Apteltraum members in the village inn where they were ordering their Sunday schnitzel. The young men looked exhausted, it was a chaotic day since people were moving in and out, but then they began to talk to us. We were invited to have a look around the farm. In the garden, next to the strawberry beds, sat Siegfried from the 'Altes Land' region near Hamburg. He had just built himself a room in one of the half-ruined buildings. His snow-white hair made him look like a seventy-year-old, but from his animated stories he seemed scarcely forty. He shared the dreams of the commune members and was interested in allotment gardening, he told us, and helped out even though he was only a guest. He enjoyed telling us about everything and cheerfully posed for a photograph.

A few kilometres down the road is a women's communal farm (Bäuer-innen GbR), in Bucholz, another small village in the gentle hill country of the Märkische Schweiz, 5 km by bicycle north-east of the Fürstenwalde railway station, and 65 km east of Berlin. In 1994 when I first visited the group, the three members of the community were West Germans. Two of them are trained in organic farming and in 1994 they seemed to me to be much more professional than the people at Apfeltraum. The two founders had already worked on organic farms in West Germany and studied organic cultivation methods, one of them in Wageningen, Holland, then the only existing teaching farm for organic agriculture. While working for an organic farmer in West Germany in 1991 they had heard that this farm was available and immediately leased it for twenty years. Every Thursday they harvest their produce and pack up their subscription crates with forty different vegetables according to the season, to be delivered to Berlin on Fridays, mainly to the 'women's scenerie' in West and East Berlin. They bring the crates to various drop-off points, such as the women's café, Begine, around the corner from my house, from where their regular customers collect them. They now work 3 ha of gardens intensively. Through the subscription system they have no surplus, and the direct contact with customers, mainly women, allows them to distribute their produce without wholesalers. They are thus already independent of subsidies and have managed to pay off most of the debts they incurred taking over the land. The subscribers also frequently visit the farm to help out. They have managed so far to make a good living, although in the summer they work from 6 a.m. to 9 p.m. and holidays are still out of the question. For this reason a number of women have come and gone, and they are looking for new women to join the farm. They have had little contact with the local village population, although they have participated in exchanges of machinery from neighbour to neighbour.

Unfortunately they cannot yet all live together in their half-ruined buildings, so they take turns eating together in their various small apartments, an arrangement that sometimes seems strange to new interns who arrive for a short stay. Corinna, a former social worker from West Berlin, whom we met transplanting seedlings, told us all about the farm with a wonderfully calm and natural friendliness. When Carola and Barbara overturned a crate of seedlings, she immediately enlisted our help in planting them in little plastic pots. Together we carried them to the plastic greenhouses, of which only two were standing after a storm at the end of the winter tore two others down. Despite their success, my colleague Carola calculated quickly, with monthly revenues of 1600 DM they had hardly any private income to speak of.

When we visited later, some things had changed. By the summer of 2000 the group had grown; sales to Berlin had also grown substantially – more than 100 subscription crates were taken every week to delivery points, mostly in East Berlin. The farm area has grown and the women even have a few animals. The exchange with the neighbouring farms for filling the crates, especially with Apfeltraum, was working well. The women were planning to double the sales of their vegetables in Berlin. There were now three trailers behind the barn, where some of the women and their helpers lived. They still could not afford to rent the house belonging to the farm. And that is a pity, said our charming host Reinhild, because that makes it difficult to spend the evenings together.

Back to spring 1994. From the women's farm we cycled against a strong wind in the direction of Bad Saarow on wooded Scharmützel Lake to Marienhöhe, the oldest Demeter farm in the Federal Republic, founded in 1928 by Dr Erhard Bartsch. The soil here is very poor, and for this reason the whole project began with the planting of hedges to stop soil erosion. These hedges have had a positive effect on the soil climate up to 30 m on either side. Thus there are many small 2 ha fields in which the crops do very well. During the Third Reich, Marienhöhe was at first protected by the prominent Nazi, Rudolf Hess. From 1941 on, with the so-called 'battle of the producers' which the Nazis instituted during the war, times were hard for organic farming. In 1942 the Demeter organization was forbidden (Bentzien 1999). After 1945 a combination of craftiness and the inter-nationalism of the organic farming movement managed to save the farm. First they sold off land in order to stay under the size limit for farms designated to be collectivized, that is, nationalized. When the owners fled the growing difficulties with which the GDR government confronted them, salvation came in the form of people from West Germany who entered the country illegally via the then still green border, armed with little suitcases and a desire to save the farm. That was the case, at least, for old Herr Hoppe whom we met during our visit as he was giving a group of un-suspecting young future health food shop clerks a tour of the premises.

After the demise of the GDR, the founders' heirs gave the farm to the Marienhöhe Non-Profit Association for Organic Farming, Cultural Work and Social Therapy in the Country. The association leases the farm to the group active here now. Next to the old and very old members, this group is composed of two groups of newcomers. The first consists of young East Germans who moved here at the time of the GDR civil rights movement in order to escape the constrictions of the system. Many of them come from Saxony, in the south-east of the former GDR. After the changes of 1989, more young people arrived from Saxony, East Berlin and also West Germany. Today, thirty-four people (including fourteen children) live here, on a tiny wage of 600 DM a month minus 200 DM for room and board. Since they are practically overrun by interested people and kindred spirits, especially from nearby Berlin, they have instituted an official tour of the farm every fourth Saturday. They cultivate several hectares of market gardens and keep twenty dairy cows, three draught horses, twenty pigs and a few sheep, which ensure a supply of manure. Today the farmed area is in all 100 ha. The vegetables and the cheese are sold directly in the new farm store which increasingly attracts local people, and in Berlin markets such as the bio-market on Chamisso Platz. They have no subscription crates, but they spend some time with the members of their Berlin food co-ops. The increase in sales has slowed down in the last two years; more bio-markets are probably needed in Berlin to reach more customers.

When we visited all three communes again in summer 2000, I was glad to find that all of them were doing very well. They now help each other to fill their orders for direct sale to different quarters in Berlin. Each has a lot of new customers in Berlin and they are all very sure that there are plenty of people in Berlin who will become their customers in the future. The two smaller groups have found new members; the women's collective has five to seven people. In the Apfeltraum community during the summer there are now about fifteen adults.

A common characteristic of all the groups mentioned here is that they are prepared to live at the subsistence level. Maria Mies, Claudia von Werlhof and Veronika Bennholdt-Thomsen describe the subsistence economy as a way of life based on everyday life and its necessities, and the willingness to limit one's own needs in the interests of other human beings and the environment. The communal organic farmers introduced above have withdrawn from the never-ending stress and panic mentality of consumer society, and to that extent have become outsiders; but they are pioneers, pointing the way for those around them. The enormous number of visitors and student interns who flock to all three farms indicates that they are seen as the forerunners of a development which many more people regard as necessary and, ultimately, essential.

Notes

For discussion and help I would like to thank Christophe Kotanyi as well as members of the three communities: Heinz-Hellmuth and Nora Hoppe and Frithjof Albert, Reinhild Benning, Kirsten Hänsel.

1. Das Giftgrüne Woche Informationsheft. Ausstellung und Veranstaltungsreihe zum Thema 'Ökolandbau um Berlin', Ökodorf e.V. January 1994, ed. by Sabine Henning-Helbig, pp. 36f.

2. Brodowin in the Uckermark, Jahnsfelde in the Märkische Schweiz.

3. Bioprodukte aus Brandenburg, Pressemappe zur Internationalen Grünen Woche 2000, see Plagge 1998.

4. Party Bündnis 90/ Grüne/ (AL)/ UFV in the Berlin Parliament, 1 April 1992, printed matter 12/ 1373. See also the press release of 11 November 1993 by Hartwig Berger.

5. Senatsverwaltung für Wirtschaft und Technologie – IV E 1, answer to small inquiry no. 4141 from 3 August 1993 by Hartwig Berger, party Bündnis 90/ Grüne (AL)/ UFV.

References

Bennholdt-Thomsen, Veronika and Maria Mies (1997) *Eine Kuh für Hillary – Die Subsistenzperspektive*, Munich: Frauenoffensive.

Bennholdt-Thomsen,Veronika, Brigitte Holzer and Christa Müller (eds) (1999) *Das Subsistenzhandbuch – Widerstandskulturen in Europa, Asien und Lateinamerika*, Vienna: Promedia.

Bentzien, Hans (1999) 'Erhard Bartsch', in Hans Bentzien (ed.), Zauberhaftes Sarow, Berlin and Bonn: Westkreuz Verlag, pp. 11–18.

Bio-Direkt (1992) Bio-Bauern in Berlin und Brandenburg, Berlin: BUND für Umwelt und Naturschutz Deutschland e.V., Landesverband Berlin, Arbeitskreis 'Ernährung und Landwirtschaft'.

Cejka, Regine (1993) 'Alles Bio, alles Öko, alles Lüge', *Ökotest*, 3.

Grosch, Peter and Gerd Schuster (1985) *Der Biokost-Report*, Munich: Biederstein.

Hoffmann, Manfred (1997) (ed.), *Vom Lebendigen in Lebensmitteln – Die bioelektronischen Zusammenhänge zwischen Lebensmittelqulität, Ernährung und Gesundheit*, Holm: Deukalion.

Kerbs, Diethart and Jürgen Reulecke (eds) (1998) *Handbuch der deutschen Reformbewegungen 1880–1993*, Wuppertal: Peter Hammer.

Krabbe, Wolfgang (1974) *Gesellschaftsveränderung durch Lebensreform*, Gottingen: Vandenhoek.

Der kritische Agrarbericht – Landwirtschaft (1999) ed. AgrarBündnis e.V./Arbeitsgemeinschaft Ländliche Entwicklung an der Universität Gesamthochschule Kassel, Kassel/Rheda-Wiedenbrück/Bramsche.

Der kritische Agrarbericht – Landwirtschaft (2000) ed. AgrarBündnis e.V./Arbeitsgemeinschaft Ländliche Entwicklung an der Universität Gesamthochschule Kassel, Kassel/Rheda-Wiedenbrück/Bramsche.

Leitzmann, Claus and Wolfgang Sichert (1987) 'Lebenssmittel – Alternative Ernährung', Ernährung heute und morgen, Beiheft der Ernährungs-Umschau, Schriftenreihe der AGEV, 5, pp. 41–5.

Meyer-Renschhausen, Elisabeth (1999a) 'Conspicious – and Thoughtless – Food Consumption. A Critical German View on Modern Eating Habits', in Uwe Kracht and Manfred Schulz (eds), *Food Security and Nutrition – The Global Challenge*, Münster: Lit, pp. 309–28.

— (1999b) 'The Porridge Debate – Grain, Nutrition and Forgotten Food Preparation Techniques', in Carola Lentz (ed.), *Changing Food Habits*, Vol. 2 of *Food in History and Culture*, Australia: Harwood Academic Publishers, pp. 181–210.

Meyer-Renschhausen, Elisabeth and Albert Wirz (1999) 'Dietetics, Health Reform and Social Order: Vegetarianism as a Moral Physiology at the Turn of the Nineteenth Century. The Example of Maximilian Bircher-Benner (1867–1939)', *Medical History*, 43, pp. 323–41.

Mies, Maria (1996) 'Frauen, Nahrung und globaler Handel – Eine ökofeministische Analyse zum Welternährungsgipfel' 13–17 November 1996, Rom, Bielefeld: Institut für Theorie und Praxis der Subsistenz.

Mies, Maria and Vandana Shiva (1993) *Ecofeminism*, London: Zed Books.

Ökohöfe in der Mark Brandenburg (2000) ed. Grüne Liga Brandenburg, D 14478 Potsdam, Waldstr.1.

Oppermann, Rainer (2000) 'Ökolandbau: Die Aussichten des Wachstums', in *Der kritische Agrarbericht – Landwirtschaft*, ed. the AgrarBündnis e.V./Arbeitsgemeinschaft Ländliche Entwicklung an der Universität Gesamthochschule Kassel, Kassel/Rheda-Wiedenbrück/Bramsche, pp. 268–73.

Piorr, Hans-Peter (1993) 'Ökologischer Landbau – auch in Großbetrieben möglich?', *bioland*, 3, pp. 31–4.

Plagge, Jan (1998) *Arbeitsgemeinschaft für biodynamischen*, Landbau: Eggersdorf.

Thomas, Frieder (1999) 'Ökologischer Landbau und sein Verhältnis zu Nachhaltigkeit, Markt und Regionalentwicklung', in *Der kritische Agrarbericht – Landwirtschaft*, ed. AgrarBündnis e.V./Arbeitsgemeinschaft Ländliche Entwicklung an der Universität Gesamthochschule Kassel, Kassel/Rheda-Wiedenbrück/Bramsche, pp. 251–6.

Weiger, Hubert (1994) 'Ökologischer Landbau heißt der Lösungsweg', in *Grünstift*, 1.

Werlhof, Claudia von (1991) *Was haben die Hühner mit dem Dollar zu tun?*, Munich: Frauenoffensive.

16

What Really Keeps Our Cities Alive, Money or Subsistence?

Veronika Bennholdt-Thomsen

No matter what question arises about the future of our cities, the first reaction from all sides is usually: Can we afford it? How much is it going to cost? One would almost think that our cities live from money. But don't they actually live far more from the activities of the people in them as they lead their daily lives, at work and play? This 'economy of daily well-being' has very little to do with money but a lot to do with human care and human contact; that is, with what we sociologists call interaction. In this case, people are not concerned with each other on some abstract level; their interaction is realized in material terms and given permanence through this. Included within this culture and economy of everyday life is child-care and caring for young and for old people and the subsistence labour of mothers and some fathers; but it also embraces the purpose behind the paid labour performed by the woman at the market stand and by the financial broker, who both earn money in order to pay for food, drink, clothes and accommodation, i.e. to pay for their subsistence.

However, on our modern scale of values, the purpose of this everyday process of human encounters, together with the social interconnection and integration which accompany them, is receding further and further into the background and being replaced by money *as a value in itself*. For us, money stands for subsistence, and the fact that it is merely a means of exchange is forgotten. These means have themselves come to epitomize the securing of the essentials of life.

The fixation with money as opposed to *people* with all their abilities, wishes and needs is closely allied to the fixation with wage-labour or, to be more exact, with the relationship between wage-labour and capital. We court capital as if wages and salaries kept us alive. Yet, today more than ever, this seems a questionable assumption. It goes without saying that in the future, as now, we will be responsible for ensuring our own and our children's survival and the smooth running of our lives together. It seems more than unlikely, however, that the majority of us will be able to do this by means of an income derived from wages or salaries, and on the level of those currently earned by skilled labour in Germany even less so.

Notwithstanding, at all levels of government, from local to national, everyone behaves as if full conventional employment for all were purely a question of the right policies. This is known in Germany as *Standortpolitik*: the term refers to policy decisions aimed at attracting investment to a particular location. The greater the financial volume of the enterprise or project thus enticed, the better it is supposed to be for all concerned, true to the principle that when the economy is thriving, everyone else is too.

This attitude is what I call 'money orientation', in the name of money orientation, subsistence orientation is systematically neglected. This is by no means an attitude that is typical only of or even mainly of the political administration; instead, it is an extremely widespread, indeed a cultural phenomenon of our society at the dawn of the third millennium. It is not things of immediate usefulness that have the highest value, but the money with which you can, supposedly, buy any useful thing, and much more besides. We no longer believe in natural growth, but in monetary growth, which is equated with economic growth. As everyone knows, the central criterion of economic growth is the gross national product, in which everything bought and sold in a country is expressed in terms of a sum of money. So a war, for example, makes an excellent contribution to economic growth.

It is only very slowly starting to dawn on us just how one-dimensional and ideologically-laden this concept of 'economy' is. What I hope to do here is shed a little more light on the general gloom, with specific reference to the economic life of the city.

Globalization, Liberalization, Privatization: The Demands of Big Capital

Since the 1980s economic and social life in our cities has been subjected to drastic changes. One visible expression of this is to be found in the large shopping centres, supermarkets and shopping malls which have sprung up everywhere, at the expense of a great many smaller and medium-sized retail outlets, even bigger shops that were not members of chains. The latter have all had to shut their doors to business.

This development did not take place all on its own, but is to a considerable extent the result of political and administrative decisions and priorities. One of the arguments trotted out most often has been that this sort of development would create jobs. This may be so, but how many jobs have been destroyed by other shops and businesses having to close? And what *kinds* of jobs have been promoted by deciding in favour of the big investor? Wage-labour jobs, exactly. But what kind of wage-labour can be seen as preferable to the independence of running a small business, as is apparently the case here? The big retailers, the Aldis and Schleckers, together with the McDonalds, Pizza Huts and Unilever-Nordsee fast-food chains have introduced insecure jobs with 'flexibilized' hours and few benefits, and established such poor working conditions as a norm, in Germany as elsewhere.

One justification sometimes heard is that decision-makers had no choice but to decide in favour of big investors and projects, since no small businesses could be found to supply the services needed in a given part of town. When I consider just how much effort it takes and has always taken in some places simply to (re)establish a weekly farm produce market in the face of stringent conditions imposed by the local administration, compared to the ease with which the infrastructure for a large supermarket is provided, I find this argument somewhat difficult to swallow. Rather, this kind of convenient mainstream attitude is an attempt to justify the almost compulsive repetition of the same kind of irresponsible behaviour. First of all the small shops and businesses were overwhelmed by supermarkets, Do It Yourself (DIY) stores and various other chains, then the gigantic shopping centres mushroomed on greenfield sites on the outskirts of town, and now the big investors are moving back into the city centres, where new, so-called shopping halls, shopping streets and centres for 'shopping experiences' are being created. A good example of this latest trend is the planning currently under way in Germany for the redesigning of downtown railway stations and the areas surrounding them as commercial centres.

Under these conditions it goes without saying that there needs to be some radical rethinking about how, for example, people can be given the chance of setting up small, independent businesses again.

When the small get elbowed out by the huge, we are often told: 'That's just the way things are.' After all, in a free market economy, competition rules, and in the so-called free-market play of one force against another, the cheaper, better and more efficient supplier is going to win the day. So the argument goes. This claim, however, is patently untrue; in view of the massive support which the large-scale projects enjoy in reality, it is simply untenable. For example, in Bielefeld, the city in northern Germany where I live, the transformation of the railway station building into a shopping centre will be financed up to 90 per cent by public funds, i.e. our taxes. The result, however, will belong to the privatized Railway Inc. (Bahn AG), which then will charge high rents to small shop-owners. That means they pay twice, while 90 per cent of the construction expenditures will be presented as a gift to the railway company. The fact is that over the last fifteen years, negotiated and backed at the political level, the course has quite deliberately been set in favour of big capital. We can inform ourselves about it every day in the newspapers and on TV, if we want to. So it is not the natural growth processes of free-market mechanisms that are ruining the smaller businesses, but deliberate political favouritism towards the big ones.

This course is being pursued at all levels. On the level of the International Monetary Fund and the World Bank, whose structural adjustment programmes force the governments of countries in the South to adopt policies that favour the big international banks, traders and manufacturers operating on the world market, as opposed to policies which would provide for the basic needs and social security of their own populations. And on the level of the General Agreement on Tariffs and Trade (GATT) talks, later part of the World Trade Organization (WTO), which since 1986 have included the agricultural sector in world-wide free trade, allowing the highly subsidized American agri-industrialist grain farmer to compete with the African peasant with a small sorghum crop in the free play of forces on the local African market for staple foods.

We find ample evidence of these same tendencies in the policies of the Organization for Economic Cooperation and Development (OECD) which designed and negotiated the Multilateral Agreement on Investment (MAI) as well as in the directives of the EU, whose agricultural policies have invariably targeted small and medium-scale farming operations for elimination. Its subsidies are for the agri-businessmen and factory farms; they only harm genuine peasants. Subsidies are paid per hectare, for instance. If you have a lot, you get a lot. Small and medium-scale farms cannot compete with the low prices that agri-industrialists are able to offer thanks to their high subsidies. And although the reasons why peasant production is dying out are more than well-known, the latest EU agricultural policies, outlined in the Agenda 2000, make no attempt whatsoever to address this crucial problem.

Between 1980 and 1993, the German government drastically lowered the tax rate paid by businesses on their profits from 33.6 to 18.3 per cent. At the same time, social welfare has been cut back, employment has been 'flexibilized' and the tax burden on employees has risen considerably (Klauss 1997: 12). It remains to be seen whether the Social Democrat–Green coalition currently in power will be willing or able to alter this course of events. And not every business is the same. Large companies, who can easily move production to less expensive venues offshore, pay only 28–30 per cent of business taxes collected by the government, whereas medium-sized businesses contribute about 66 per cent to the total revenue levied. Especially at present, despite the fact that the German export economy is booming, even the most hesitant hints that the re-distribution of wealth from the bottom to the top might be halted are greeted by big businesses with indignant threats to leave the country.

As profits continue to grow in Germany, so does unemployment. This phenomenon has been christened 'jobless growth' – a misleading phrase given the German use of the word 'job' to denote badly paid short-term contracts with poor social insurance, since 'jobs' in this sense are exactly what are on the increase, while secure and better-paid occupations and work situations are disappearing in a massive wave of rationalization.

The Urban Service Metropolis

But what has all this got to do with cities and their future?

To start with, cities are the places in whose conference halls and offices the policies I have been outlining are devised and set in motion. Or more accurately, the metropolises are where these developmental trends originate. Indeed, they have been designed specifically for this purpose, with tower blocks, motorways, airports, congress halls, shopping malls, leisure parks, hotel complexes and trade fair pavilions laid on for the international business community and political jet-set. These metropolitan trappings are now being aped by medium-sized cities and towns as well.

Cities, furthermore, repeat the pattern of globalization policies internally. The city is no longer regarded as the place where people of different ages, classes and genders make their lives together. Instead, cities are modelled on business concerns, as 'City Incorporated'.

For example, a municipality in the federal state of Hessen recently voted to build the latest shopping centre on the outskirts of town, despite the fact that permission for the project had long since been refused on economic and city planning grounds. But the big new supermarket would then have been built in the neighbouring town, and nobody wanted that, on account of the competition and the loss of revenue it would have entailed. For years, according to Wolfram Elsner, economic incentives at the municipal level have taken the form of 'prophylactic undercutting' to increase competitiveness; in the municipalities, just as at the national level, war has been waged with enticing offers to attract the big investor (Elsner 1998: 780). Presents are made of building sites, development costs are covered by the public purse, municipal building authorities devote the majority of their time to the projects of big investors, whose safety and hygiene requirements are met by public services. It is no wonder that the municipal coffers are empty.

Would it perhaps not be more appropriate if local development policies focused on those who, in terms of economic structure, offer genuine commitment to the locality instead? What about the corner shop, the small restaurant, the plumber, the joiner, all the small trade businesses and shops which do not summarily pack up and go somewhere else whenever it suits them, or suddenly decide to invest their capital in a more profitable sector. These kinds of businesses provide jobs for life and that is why those who own them or work in them have a strong attachment to the local community.

Instead of supporting small economic units, however, one has the impression that municipal and state officials are hindering them. Butcher shops in Germany are a case in point. The stringent conditions they have to fulfil may well be appropriate for a sausage factory, but in the context of a small butcher's business they smack suspiciously of ruinous chicanery. For example, butchers are charged from 200 to 300 deutschmarks for each chemical analysis of their premises by the health authorities, whose ridiculously convoluted regulations include the elimination of all right angles on work surfaces! It is common knowledge that most cases of food poisoning do not originate with small local producers or retailers. Bovine Spongiform Encephalitis (BSE or mad cow disease), the potential perils of genetically modified (GM) foodstuffs, and contamination with pesticides are the results of large-scale industrial production for world markets by chemical multinationals and food factories.

Twenty years ago, there were 168 butcher shops serving the 300,000 inhabitants of Bielefeld. Today only twenty-six are left. Those people who have lost their small businesses over the last ten to twenty years must find it a particularly bitter irony that the mushrooming 'Market Centres' (usually Americanized as 'Centers') being built by big investors are made to simulate artificially the look and feel of small businesses, albeit with the use of badly paid part-time employees or else with a new kind of pseudo-self-employment, namely by people who 'lease' the business franchise, and have to work most of the time to pay the lease. They are playing at older-style city or small-town business, without delivering the use value that this kind of business structure once really had for town dwellers. Instead, they offer articles for the yuppie consumer whose career has been made possible only by the destruction of the authentic, socially functional city.

Instead of changing course, however, the trend now is to sell off the municipal 'family silver'. For example, in a very small rural town in eastern Westphalia in the north-west of Germany, 3 ha of communal land were recently sold to reduce the municipality's debt. This example demonstrates very clearly how economic values are being rapidly and drastically reshuffled. The land sold was originally common land to which all inhabitants of the rural village had access and which provided grazing for their geese and small livestock. This meant that they were able to secure an appreciable part of their subsistence themselves. In the bigger towns and cities common land is also being sold off. To attract the big investors, common public property such as municipal land, revenues and services are handed over to big private enterprises. Related to this phenomenon are the recent campaigns to force certain population groups out of particularly chic shopping streets, sanitizing them for the use of the more well-heeled consumers. In Cologne railway station, for example, the public toilets have been taken over by an enterprise called (in German) McClean. Now one has to pay 2 deutschmarks to use the facilities, four times the amount that one used to hand over to the local toilet cleaner.

For a few years, it seemed that the strategy of giving preferential treatment to the rich and big business in order to swell the municipal coffers to such an extent that everyone benefited from the trickle-down effect was paying off; but this has not lasted long. In a recent report on city development in Frankfurt, Martin Wentz (1996), the head of the municipal planning department, wrote the following: 'For 30 years of prosperity, the fact that the economically stronger population, tradespeople and small businesses were leaving in a steady stream was accepted almost with goodwill.' Frankfurt was meant to become *the* financial centre for big banks and corporations, but obviously not a city to live in. 'Today, all the negative effects, culminating in the severely limited financial powers of the city of Frankfurt on Main, are apparent.' The same report suggests an innovative concept of city planning as a possible way out of the situation. Phrases such as '*combined use* – of flats, offices and small businesses', '*combination* – of types of buildings', 'spatial *separation* of functions' (emphasis added) dominate in this document. Summarized in one sentence, this means: 'In future, city planning as development policy *also* has to concentrate on keeping and binding together both *human* AND economic resources, if the *variety* and the functionability of the city is to be retained' (*Frankfurter Rundschau*, 2 February 1996).

In our growth-oriented culture, however, the imagination to see how this could happen seems to be lacking. As in so many other undeniably critical analyses which warn us about the urgency of adopting alternative approaches to urban planning, the recommendations for Frankfurt in the end amounted to nothing more than *Standortpolitik* once again, i.e. renewed efforts to attract big capital in order to create jobs.

Subsistence Orientation in Today's City

If our cities are to have a future shaped by urban community life and not by the profit motives of big business, then we need to shift from a money orientation to a subsistence orientation, i.e. to a system of values that looks first at the direct use of things and relationships in everyday life, and holds this to be more important than money. A subsistence orientation incorporates a world-view that seeks immediacy and satisfaction: having enough to eat, warmth, a roof over one's head and pleasure in being satisfied – in other words, one that values leisure and rejects the eternal nagging cry of 'have to' and the unremitting struggle against a contrived scarcity of resources that we believe we have to wage in order to fulfil the insatiable and imaginary needs that we have been talked into thinking that we have.

Unlike both the socialist and capitalist approaches, the subsistence orientation is not a model, or a Utopia, or a dream of a golden age, but a concept of action aimed at setting new and different processes in motion. Subsistence orientation is a plea for a re-orientation, a fresh look at relations and the setting of different priorities in decision-making. It could be applied equally well by WTO negotiators, heads of municipal building departments, city councillors and the woman and man in the street, if they based their thinking and actions on the following five principles:

1. Priority is given to the useful, to what is needed.
2. Small has priority over big.
3. Personal relationships are better than anonymous ones.
4. Decentralized solutions are better than centralized ones.
5. The local takes precedence over the international.

The word 'subsistence' means 'existing through oneself' and refers to 'the characteristic of independence', as Erika Märke has observed (1986: 138f). It also has a lot to do with providing for oneself, and self-determination.

Anyone who thinks a subsistence orientation should be banished 'to the stone age' or 'to the Middle Ages' or to the Third World, because in our developed society we have allegedly outgrown both self-provision and worries about subsistence, has failed to recognize that subsistence does not disappear, but rather changes through history and takes different forms in different contexts. At the start of the twenty-first century, subsistence looks different from the way it did twenty centuries ago or even fifty years ago. Subsistence in the city takes on forms that are different from those that it adopts in the country. Subsistence displays different characteristics in households with children than it does in childless households. But no matter when, where, or who practises it, subsistence means providing for oneself.

Subsistence refers to the manner in which people produce their own lives and reproduce them day by day, as well as to how and to what degree they hold these processes in their own hands in terms of material, substance and society. In the course of the twentieth century, though, we have relinquished our own control over these processes more and more. Absurdly enough, current political efforts to create jobs, allegedly in order to assure the subsistence of working people, are in fact the cause of ever-increasing insecurity about subsistence. This is because by 'jobs', only waged or salaried jobs are meant. No longer does anyone think in terms of small, self-employed tradespeople, independent retailers and other businesses, nor of associations of small independent businesses in the form of co-operatives, for example. Instead, everyone assumes that the only options are big companies and wage labour. Self-employment and *providing for oneself* in terms of supporting oneself, of 'earning one's living' rather than profit maximization, are dismissed as positively uneconomic; something to be prevented and destroyed. The net result is a population at the mercy of the commercial interests of big business. Everything, all the necessities of daily life – food, services, labour power, communication and even social contacts – are transformed into commodities marketed and sold to us by the big corporations.

When I speak of a 'subsistence orientation', this dismissive response often ensues: 'Oh, yes, money is bad all right, and we should get rid of it. But a complex society like ours can't function without money, so we have to bow to its mechanisms.' This is pure nonsense. First of all, we do without money and *do things* without money every day: in the care that a mother gives to her children, in relationships between friends and neighbours, in everyday acts of helpfulness and in providing for the young and the old. Honorary positions, clubs and associations and all sorts of other non-remunerated initiatives are indeed the most dynamic elements of our society.

Second, it *is* possible to organize exchange without money, even in complex societies. Maybe not in the entire global society at once, or even in an entire country, but locally and regionally. Here I am thinking of 'exchange circles' (in which people exchange services, skills and produce with a local currency which excludes interest) which are thriving in many German cities, even without the governmental support that they deserve.

However, my main point here is a different one. I contend that the heart of the problem lies in how we deal with money, rather than in money itself. In face-to-face relations and within local exchange networks reciprocity and the relationship itself are the important factors in the use of money. The bigger the enterprise, the more everything is handled in the manner of a supermarket, and the more anonymous are the relations of exchange, the greater is the power of the money per se. Therefore, one market is not the same as another. In southern Mexico, I did research in a town of 100,000 inhabitants in a region throughout which the peasants, fishers, tradeswomen and craftspeople determine their prices according to who is in front of them; their criteria are the extent of their social bonds with that person, and whether he or she owes them a favour or not. The result is not economic chaos (as many economists might predict) but a vibrant and thriving economy (see Bennholdt-Thomsen 1994).

In our cities, we do not need supermarkets and bogus marketplaces. Instead, we need small businesses, shops run by their owners and a real marketplace open to all. There are enough experts and interested individuals to transform the reality of our cities along the lines mentioned above, to put these into practice too; but the plans of prospective founders of very small businesses are frustrated by conditions imposed at the political level – conditions such as having to provide parking, separate toilet facilities for men and women and stringent hygiene rules, as well as a heavier tax burden than large-scale businesses. This is the case in Germany and the EU in any event. It is also becoming increasingly difficult to access loans, with the growing tendency of banks to reject applicants from medium-sized businesses out of preference for lending to large businesses, especially in the investment, insurance and pensions sectors instead.

The Wuppertal Institute has correctly ascertained that whereas the big corporations have rationalized away large numbers of jobs over the past decade, small and medium-sized enterprises have been creating new ones. Smaller businesses are in fact still regarded as the nation's trade school, where apprentices are ably prepared for the future. In September 2000 the institute organized a conference on small and medium-sized businesses. However, once again, genuinely small self-run enterprises were ignored since the conference was open only to businesses with more than fifty employees. Is even the Wuppertal Institute, an organization espousing the idea of sustainable economic activity, unable to free itself from the fixation on wage-labour and profit maximization? In our society, too, there is a sufficient number of people who want to exchange their money for the necessities of living on the market, and no more. These people deal with money in a different way. In market relations that follow a subsistence logic, reliability is more important to those involved than the anonymous race for profits, and more important than being able to shop as cheaply as possible (see Bennholdt-Thomsen and Mies 1999: 109–23).

Small-scale enterprises that approach the market from a subsistence perspective have an important role to play in the resolution of many of the environmental and social problems that we currently face. For a time, the market for organic products functioned according to this subsistence logic in Germany. Now, however, this sector is being appropriated by supermarket chains, and the struggle for market shares has begun in organic farming and sales of organic produce. Thus organic produce has become an important new source of profit for the factory farms, once again to the detriment of the small corner store, the small-scale farmer and the environment.

One kind of private property is not necessarily the same as another. The current wave of privatization occasioned by the policy of globalization, liberalization and privatization (GLP) views private property as the basis for profit maximization. The private property of small tradespeople and others with small businesses, small-scale farmers and home-owners, however, is the basis for their subsistence. To paraphrase the saying from Greek medicine, 'It's the size of the private property (the dose) that makes the poison'.

The belief in size, in profit maximization and wage-labour does indeed poison social relations in our cities. This is not only true in the sense that the small are being progressively expropriated by the ongoing preferential treatment of the large, but the community as such is being dispossessed and thus destroyed. Municipal land that up to now has provided space for allotments, for example, is being sold off to big investors; in other words, common land is being privatized. The same is happening to public rooms. More and more German municipalities are transforming the administration of the rooms and halls in schools, kindergartens and other public buildings into a business with a commercial cost–benefit analysis. When no lessons are taking place in them, the rooms are to be rented out. From the subsistence perspective, though, such rooms are clearly common spaces to which the whole community should have access without paying. What our cities need is not more money, but more life. Land and rooms should be deprivatized and communalized; i.e. instead of a state or a central administration decreeing what happens to them, the neighbourhood and local community should determine how they are used and administer them themselves. The dynamic element in our cities, the guarantor of social peace, is not going to be profit maximization, but social solidarity. The many-sided ways of being dependent on one another, including the market and money relations *within* the community, are the true life blood of our cities.

Those municipalities which have declared themselves MAI-free have understood this, too, at least in part. One major reason for their dissidence is the proposed regulation that any preferential conditions aimed at promoting one's own economy must, according to the draft MAI document, be made available to international corporations as well. Any conditions relating, for example, to environmental protection or rules pertaining to the creation of employment opportunities in a given city or even to aesthetic considerations, such as the height of buildings for instance, do *not* have to be fulfilled by foreign investors, in so far as they deviate from international standards. Otherwise one would be committing protectionism, *the* ultimate sin against GLP (see Mies and Werlhof 1998).

Summary

Below I would like to catalogue the elements which could give our cities a subsistence orientation in the form of ten criteria. These criteria are based on self-provision and self-determination, and will be listed starting with the smallest living unit, then going on to the neighbourhood, then to the whole city and finally to the level of the region.

1. In relation to accommodation, subsistence orientation means having the space for production for everyday needs, instead of being forcibly attached to the consumption machine: i.e. space for the storage and the tools required for home production, and also for mementos – a place with enough space for life, including life lived over the years.

2. Living also includes one's living environment. Inge Meta Hülbusch (1981) has called this relationship *Innenhaus und Außenhaus* (inside/inner-house and outside/outer-house). Here I mean that for genuine use-value and real satisfaction, more than just four walls are needed for the act of living. Also necessary is an environment in which, for example, a child experiences and becomes familiar with her or his world, or in which neighbourhood can be developed. The 'complementarity of inner–outer' is, according to a study conducted by Libor Schelhasse and Sonja Nebel (1998) in various conurbations in the South, the most important basis for securing the economy of everyday life. One of the biggest problems of our growth economy culture, however, lies in the fact that we have forgotten just how much people need social contacts in order to be happy – the family, the neighbourhood, the part of town they live in, their circle of friends and the daily culture of interaction in the city.

3. One important element of subsistence-oriented production to be found in our cities is what John F. C. Turner (1976) identified in the so-called 'popular quarters' in Mexico City. He shows how important it is particularly for people with low incomes to build for themselves, or else to be able to make decisions about how their own four walls, and above all the 'outer house', should look. Such houses can be far better adapted to the vagaries of life than the well-intentioned but dreadful designs that typify so much of state-controlled public housing. Above all, though, subsistence-oriented housing is geared to community life and economic exchange in the quarter, thus allowing the development of far more reliable social structures than those arising from paid labour (see Douthwaite and Diefenbacher 1998).

4. Subsistence-oriented production in the city is made up of many small

businesses. The International Labour Organization (ILO) in fact actually calls for official support for the smallest of the small, the so-called informal sector, also known as the shadow economy, not only in the countries of the South, but in those of the North as well (*Frankfurter Rundschau*, 29 May 1999). The ILO's argument is that without jobs, even if people are kept going with public handouts, the cities will collapse. And since formal employment in the form of waged work is nowhere in sight, the ILO urges the regulation of informal jobs instead of discrimination against them.

5. A similar recommendation is made by John F. C. Turner. With increasing deregulation and retreat of the state from any form of responsibility towards its citizens, it is particularly interesting that this recommendation comes from a man who calls himself an anarchist. He says that the poorer we are or become, the more important it is to have proscriptive rules to support and stimulate the creation of a self-regulating form (Turner 1976). Here he is appealing to the state to guarantee freedoms and spaces for the community instead of hastening ahead with privatization for the benefit of transnational corporations. Turner advocates a process I have called 'Communalization', by which I mean the protection and the re-creation of common land and spaces.

6. The elements of an urban economic structure sketched out here also fit in very well with the ideas of feminist city-planners and architects. For them a desirable city structure is one which allows a mixture of functions and uses, as opposed to 'monofunctionality' to the point where nothing is left but vast, stark residential landscapes with no infrastructure, 'which, besides the lack of opportunity for communication, also mean long, to some extent additional (e.g. driving the children around, etc.) trips for shopping and other chores' (Hünlein 1993: 118). A mixture of functions and uses is necessary too if work in the house, in paid employment and in the family are to be combined.

7. The social location we are speaking about in subsistence orientation closely resembles the female point of view *vis-à-vis* city planning. This is no coincidence, since it is women who are responsible for subsistence in our society. Conversely, though, this gender-specific separation of responsibilities as propounded in the dominating discourse is exactly what leads to an understanding of economy as resembling a permanent state of war. Because capitalist patriarchy first assigns loving and caring specifically to women as their duty within our society, and then makes the loving and caring work of women invisible with regard to the purported 'real economy', it becomes 'legitimate' to run that economy like a war, because these vital functions are being looked after 'elsewhere'.

With the concept of subsistence orientation this separation, an unfortunate division we have in our heads, can be overcome. What are labelled 'women's concerns' are in reality the subsistence concerns of the society as a whole (see Schreyögg, n.d.: 3f).

8. Subsistence orientation and community orientation, i.e. an orientation to social context and community ties instead of to economic competition, are closely linked. Community orientation cannot be created idealistically; it needs an object, some kind of base material. And just as love in the family is 'produced' by a good meal or a warm blanket, so social closeness comes about through the exchange of things, including goods, that are necessary for daily well-being.

9. Subsistence-oriented urban economic life would not mean doing without technology. Rather, the implications are that in nearly everything related to technology, 'e.g. public utilities', decentralization is to be given preference; exactly the opposite of the present trend. The resuscitation of urban subsistence technologies is an urgent task.

10. The city cannot survive without the countryside. To secure the subsistence of the city and to consolidate the urban economy, it is essential for the city to become integrated on a regional level, not tethered to international business, as is increasingly the case. The city would draw its supplies from the region and vice versa, thus strengthening the regional market; small and middle-sized farms would continue to exist, and the cultural landscape would be preserved.

(Translated from German by Patricia Skorge)

References

Bennholdt-Thomsen, Veronika (ed.) (1994) *Juchitán – Stadt der Frauen*, Reinbek: Rowohlt.

Bennholdt-Thomsen, Veronika and Maria Mies (1999) *The Subsistence Perspective: Beyond the Globalized Economy*, London: Zed Books.

Douthwaite, Richard (1996) *Short Circuit. Strengthening Local Economies for Security in an Unstable World*, Dublin, Liliput Press.

Douthwaite, Richard and Hans Diefenbacher (1998) *Jenseits der Globalisierung. Handbuch für lokales Wirtschaften*, Mainz: Grünewald (adapted German version of Douthwaite 1996).

Elsner, Wolfram (1998) 'Die Zukunft unserer Städte und Regionen. Städte und Regionen im Konkurrenzkampf und die Kehrseiten des Neuen Regionalismus', *WSI Mitteilungen*, 11, pp. 778–86.

Hülbusch, Meta Inge (1981) *Innenhaus und Außenhaus*, Schriftenreihe der Organisationseinheit Architektur–Stadtplanung–Landschaftsplanung, Schriftenreihe 01, no. 033, 2nd edn, Kassel.

Hünlein, Ute (1993) 'Regionalplanung – Frauen mischen sich ein! Ein Werkstattbericht über die Arbeit der Regionalplanungsgruppe FOPA Rhein-Main e.V.', *Frei.Räume, Streitschrift der feministischen Organisationen von Planerinnen und Architektinnen*, FOPA e.V., 6, pp. 115–20.

Klauss, Martin (1997) *Politik für mehr Reichtum. Daten und Anmerkungen zur Entwicklung von Reichtum und Armut in Deutschland*, Freiburg: CfS.

Märke, Erika (1986) *Ein Weg aus der Abhängigkeit. Die ungewisse Zukunft des informellen Sektors in Entwicklungsländern*, Heidelberg: Forschungsstätte der Ev. Studiengemeinschaft, 1986.

Mies, Maria and Vandana Shiva (1993) *Ecofeminism*, London: Zed Books.

Mies, Maria and Claudia von Werlhof (1998) *Lizenz zum Plündern. Das Multilaterale Abkommen über Investitionen (MAI). Globalisierung der Konzernherrschaft – und was wir dagegen tun können*, Hamburg: Rotbuch.

Schelhasse, Libor and Sonja Nebel (1998) *Komplementarität Innen – Aussen. Kennzeichen einfachen Wohnens in Ballungsräumen des Südens*, Munster, LIT Verlag

Schreyögg, Friedel (n.d.), 'Beteiligung von Gleichstellungsstellen an der Stadt- und Bauplanung', in *Deutscher Städtetag, Frauen verändern ihre Stadt, Beratungsergebnisse der Kommission 'Frauen in der Stadt' und der Fachkommission 'Wohnungswesen' des Deutschen Städtetages zur Wohnungspolitik*, n.p., pp. 3–6.

Turner, John F. C. (1976) *Housing by People. Towards Autonomy in Building Environments*, London: Marion Boyars.

Wentz, Martin (1996) 'Die Zukunft des Städtischen. Wohnen, Arbeiten, Verkehr und Freizeit: die Entwicklungsplanung der Stadt Frankfurt am Main für die nächsten Jahrzehnte', *Frankfurter Rundschau*, 2 February 1996.

Maria Mies – Selected Publications

Books

1980: *Indian Women and Patriarchy*, New Delhi: Concept Publishers.

1981: and Kumari Jayawardena, *Feminism in Europe – Liberal and Socialist Strategies*, The Hague: Institute of Social Studies.

1982: *The Lacemakers of Narsapur: Indian Housewives Produce for the World Market*, London: Zed Books.

1986: *Patriarchy and Accumulation on a World Scale: Women in the International Division of Labour*, London: Zed Books.

1986: *Indian Women in Subsistence and Agricultural Labour* (Series: Women, Work and Development, No. 12), Geneva: ILO.

1987: V. Bennholdt-Thomsen and C von Werlhof, *Women: The Last Colony*, London: Zed Books.

1992: *Wider die Industrialisierung des Lebens; Eine feministische Kritik der Gen- und Reproduktionstechnik*, Pfaffenweiler: Centaurus Verlag.

1993: and Vandana Shiva, *Ecofeminism*, London: Zed Books; New Delhi: Kali for Women; Melbourne: Spinifex; Halifax: Fernwood Publications.

1998: and Claudia von Werlhof, *Lizenz zum Plündern. Das Multilaterale Abkommen über Investitionen (MAI). Die Globalisierung der Konzernherrschaft und was wir dagegen tun können*, Hamburg: Rotbuch.

1999: *Patriarchy and Accumulation on a World Scale – Women in the International Division of Labour*, new edn, London: Zed Books.

1999: and Veronika Bennholdt-Thomsen, *The Subsistence Perspective: Beyond the Globalized Economy*, London: Zed Books; Melbourne: Spinifex.

Papers and Articles in Books and Journals

1973: 'Paulo Freire's Method of Education – Conscientisation in Latin America', *Economic and Political Weekly*.

1973: 'Emancipation or Class Struggle? – Women's Emancipation Movements in Europe and the USA', *Economic and Political Weekly*, 15 December 1973.

1976: 'The Shahada Movement – A Peasants' Movement in Maharashtra', *Journal of Contemporary Asia*, 6, 2; also, *Journal of Peasant Studies*, 3, 4.

1981: 'Utopian Socialism and Women's Emancipation', in M. Mies and K. Jayawardena, *Feminism in Europe – Liberal and Socialist Strategies*, The Hague: Institute of Social Studies.

1981: 'Scientific Socialism and Women's Emancipation', in M Mies and K. Jayawardena, *Feminism in Europe – Liberal and Socialist Strategies*, The Hague: Institute of Social Studies.

1982: 'The Dynamics of the Sexual Division of Labour and Integration of Women into the World Market', in Lourdes Beneria (ed.), *Women and Development: The Sexual Division of Labour in Rural Societies*, New York: Praeger.

1983: 'Towards a Methodology for Feminist Research', in Gloria Bowles and Renate Duelli-Klein (eds), *Theories of Women's Studies*, London, Boston, Melbourne and Henley: Routledge. Reprinted in Martin Hammersley (ed.), *Social Research, Philosophy, Politics and Practice*, London: Sage Publications, 1993.

1988: 'Woman, Nature and the International Division of Labour – Maria Mies interviewed by Ariel Salleh', in *Thesis Eleven*, 21, ed. Sybylla Co-operative Press, Melbourne.

1990: 'Science, Violence and Responsibility', *Women's Studies International Forum*, 13, 5.

1991: 'Women's Research or Feminist Research? The Debate Surrounding Feminist Science and Methodology', in Mary M. Fonow and Judith A. Cook (eds), *Beyond Methodology; Feminist Scholarship as Lived Research*, Bloomington and Indianapolis: Indiana University Press.

1993: 'Consumption Patterns of the North – The Cause of Environmental Destruction and Poverty in the South', in F. C. Steacly (ed.), *Women and Children First: Environment, Poverty and Sustainable Development*, Rochester, VT: Schenkmann Books.

1996: 'Global Restructuring', in *Encyclopedia of Women's Studies*, London: Routledge.

1996: *Women, Food and Global Trade: An Ecofeminist Analysis, Contributions to the Discussion on Subsistence*, 1, Bielefeld: Institut für Theorie und Praxis der Subsistenz (ITPS).

1996: 'Liberating Women, Liberating Knowledge. Reflections on Two Decades of Feminist Action Research', *ATLANTIS A Women's Studies Journal*, Special Issue: *Connecting Practices, Doing Theory*, 21, 1.

1997: 'Do we Need a New "Moral Economy"?', *Canadian Women Studies*, 17, 2, University of York.

1997: 'Women, Work and a Sustainable Society', *Cross Currents, The Journal of the Association for Religion and Intellectual Life*, Winter.

1997: 'Europe in the Global Economy, or: The Need to de-Colonize Europe', paper presented at ESA-Conference University of Essex, 27–30 August 1997. Reprinted in P. Hermann (ed.), *Challenges for a Global Welfare System*, New York: Nova Science Publishers.

1998: 'Globalization of the Economy and Women's Work in a Sustainable Society', *Gender, Technology and Development*, 2, 1, Asian Institute of Technology, Bangkok.

1999: 'New Ethnic States and Population Policy', *Canadian Women Studies*, 18, 4, Special Issue: *In Honor of Mary O'Brien*, York University.

1999: 'Women in the World Economy', in Molly Scott Cato and Miriam Kennet (eds), *Green Economies Beyond Supply and Demand. To Meeting People's Needs*, Aberystwyth: Green Audit Books.

1999: 'Neoliberale Globalisierung: Das Multilaterale Abkommen über Investitionen (MAI) und internationaler Widerstand', in Olaf Kaltmeier and Michal Ramminger (eds), *Links von Nord und Süd. Chilenisch-deutsche Ortsbestimmungen im Neoliberalismus.* (Kontroversen 11.) Munster: LIT-Verlag.

2000: 'Globalisierung von unten, Seattle, 30. Nov.–4. Dez. 1999', *Infobrief 2 des Netzwerks gegen Konzernherrschaft und neoliberale Politik*, Cologne.

Index